FORMGIVING

FORMGIVING

FORMGIVING

TASCHEN

THE FUTURE
IS ALREADY
HERE—
IT'S JUST
NOT VERY
EVENLY
DISTRIBUTED !

WILLIAM GIBSON

WAS FUN TO CHAT IN THE RED SAUNA!

PAST

MAKING

8

SENSING

12

SUSTAINING

16

THINKING

20

HEALING

24

MOVING

28

PRESENT

THE OXYMORON

THE X-RAY

THE RESPONSE

REINCARNATION

THE Z-AXIS

THE SYMBIOTE

FUTURE

MOON

MARS

EARTH

ANNEXES

PLAY

FROM FACT TO FICTION

FORMGIVING AT DAC

BIG OVERVIEW

2020

FROM TAKING SHAPE TO GIVING FORM...

The Danish word for "design" is "formgivning", which literally means: to give form to that which has not yet taken shape. In other words: to give form to the future. And more specifically: to give form to the world that we would all like to one day find ourselves living in the future. To feel that we have license to imagine a future different from today, all we have to do is look back ten years, a hundred years, a thousand years, to realize how radically different things were then than they are today. The same will be true if we can look ahead with the same clarity of vision.

Since we know from our past that our future is bound to be different from our present, rather than waiting for it to take shape on its own we have the power to give it form. To create the sense of how the world around us has taken shape from by our ancestors from the past to the present, we have organized the first pages of this book into a decelerating logarithmic timeline counting down from the Big Bang, the oldest known point in time, to the present. The timeline is organized around six evolutionary threads: the history and future of how making, sensing, thinking, moving, sustaining, and healing have evolved and will continue to evolve.

1. The evolution of making starts at the genesis of matter, and its manipulation through craft and industry, and extends to robotic construction.
2. The evolution of sensing takes us from our ability to perceive reality to our ability to create virtual reality and augmented reality.
3. The evolution of thinking spans from the dawn of intelligence to the emergence of artificial intelligence and collective intelligence.
4. The evolution of moving evolves from the movement of life forms across the planet to a future of interplanetary migration, adding new geologies to our human habitat.
5. The evolution of sustaining is the escalation in the ability of living beings to harvest energy from our surroundings—from heat, sunlight, chemicals, biomass, gravity, and nuclear radiation.
6. The evolution of healing has taken us from reactive to proactive medicine.

The trajectories we start to see may allow us to plot a course from the past through the present and into the future. As we tackle the complexities of everyday life these trajectories allow us to place a firm gaze on the horizon of time to prevent us from being derailed by the random distractions of today. In a way, the six evolutionary trajectories become our map to the future—to navigate time rather than just space.

Rather than continuing the timeline into an unknown future, we let it arrive in the present with a selection of projects that currently populate our studios in Copenhagen, London, Barcelona, and New York. In the words of William Gibson: "The future is already here, it's just not very evenly distributed." When you look at the desks, in the model shop, and on the screens of our design studio, what you find are in fact specific fragments of the future in the making, five or 50 years from now. We know that we don't have the powers of prediction, but we do have the power of proposition. However limited our impact may be, if everybody attempts to make a difference within their own capacity there is almost no limit to the collective impact of 8 billion people, all of them being the change they wish to see in the world.

MAKING

The evolution of making starts at the genesis of matter, and its manipulation through craft and industry, and extends to robotic construction.

Architecture is the art and science of turning fiction into fact. What has changed are the tools at hand to make our ideas into reality. We architects are not only bound by the limits of our imagination, technical skills, and ingenuity, but also by our ability to instruct and empower others to construct what we have conceived. The world of design has acquired incredible tools for computer-aided design and building information management. But the sophistication ends when the building is built, and medieval technologies of ink-on-paper and hammer-in-hand take over.

When we designed the 2010 Danish Pavilion for the World Expo in Shanghai, we delivered the project as a fully digital building information model, designed for CAD CAM cutting steel with 2mm tolerances. In the end, the contractor who won with the lowest bid, decided to print two-dimensional drawings, cut them into templates with scissors and transfer the drawings onto the steel with chalk. The hand-drawn chalk lines were 3 times thicker than our tolerances. And finally, the steel was cut with handheld blowtorches.

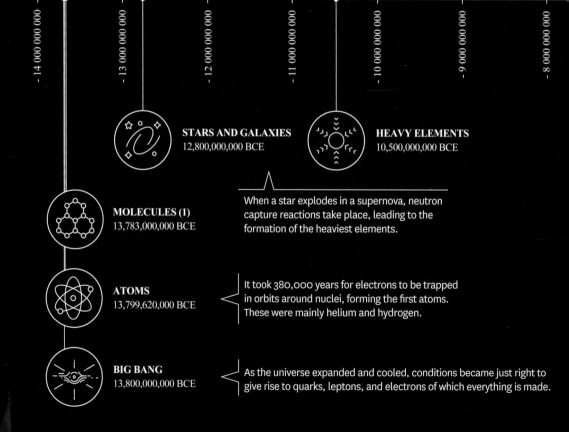

– 14 000 000 000 – 13 000 000 000 – 12 000 000 000 – 11 000 000 000 – 10 000 000 000 – 9 000 000 000 – 8 000 000 000

STARS AND GALAXIES
12,800,000,000 BCE

HEAVY ELEMENTS
10,500,000,000 BCE

MOLECULES (1)
13,783,000,000 BCE

When a star explodes in a supernova, neutron capture reactions take place, leading to the formation of the heaviest elements.

ATOMS
13,799,620,000 BCE

It took 380,000 years for electrons to be trapped in orbits around nuclei, forming the first atoms. These were mainly helium and hydrogen.

BIG BANG
13,800,000,000 BCE

As the universe expanded and cooled, conditions became just right to give rise to quarks, leptons, and electrons of which everything is made.

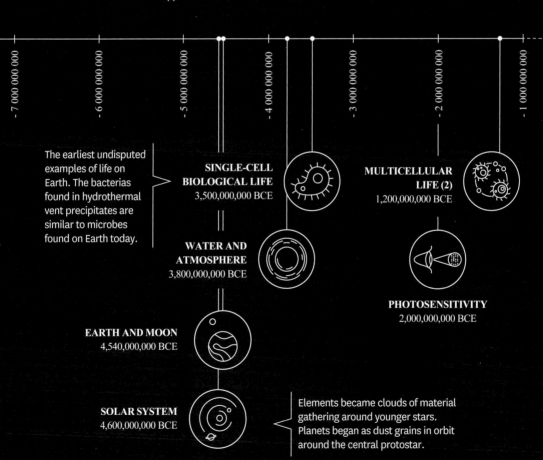

(1) Chemical structure of a vitamin B12 molecule.

The earliest undisputed examples of life on Earth. The bacterias found in hydrothermal vent precipitates are similar to microbes found on Earth today.

SINGLE-CELL BIOLOGICAL LIFE
3,500,000,000 BCE

MULTICELLULAR LIFE (2)
1,200,000,000 BCE

WATER AND ATMOSPHERE
3,800,000,000 BCE

PHOTOSENSITIVITY
2,000,000,000 BCE

EARTH AND MOON
4,540,000,000 BCE

SOLAR SYSTEM
4,600,000,000 BCE

Elements became clouds of material gathering around younger stars. Planets began as dust grains in orbit around the central protostar.

- 7 000 000 000
- 6 000 000 000
- 5 000 000 000
- 4 000 000 000
- 3 000 000 000
- 2 000 000 000
- 1 000 000 000

The inevitable inaccuracies were solved with a very large hammer. Our design efforts were half lost in translation from data to matter.

Robotic manufacturing will empower us to deliver anything that we are able to imagine. Robotic manufacturing is the direct materialization of virtual reality into physical reality. It won't mean the end of craft. It will be a new way to preserve it. Take Japanese joinery: A craft that lives and dies with the craftsmen that keep it alive. Once Japanese joinery is codified and taught to a robot, it will have been preserved for good. And once design AI starts playing with it, it will not only be preserved, but rather resurrected and ready to evolve. Architects are at the convergence of all things real and conceptual. Wielding massive amounts of data from the dawn of time, and in real time, we can preserve these elements of history, combining new technologies with ancient craft. The future of making will bring about a complete confluence of data and matter. Intention and execution as one and the same.

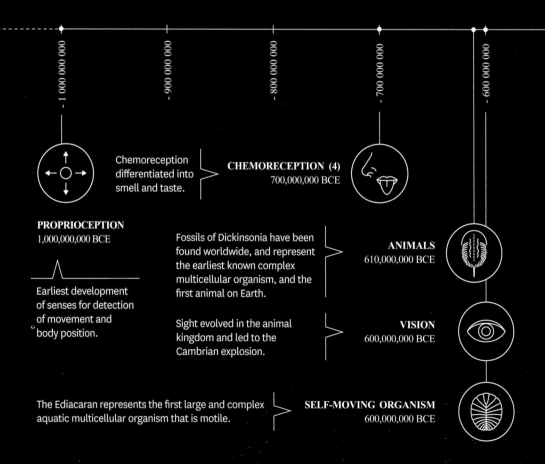

- 1 000 000 000   - 900 000 000   - 800 000 000   - 700 000 000   - 600 000 000

Chemoreception differentiated into smell and taste.

CHEMORECEPTION (4)
700,000,000 BCE

PROPRIOCEPTION
1,000,000,000 BCE

Earliest development of senses for detection of movement and body position.

Fossils of Dickinsonia have been found worldwide, and represent the earliest known complex multicellular organism, and the first animal on Earth.

ANIMALS
610,000,000 BCE

Sight evolved in the animal kingdom and led to the Cambrian explosion.

VISION
600,000,000 BCE

The Ediacaran represents the first large and complex aquatic multicellular organism that is motile.

SELF-MOVING ORGANISM
600,000,000 BCE

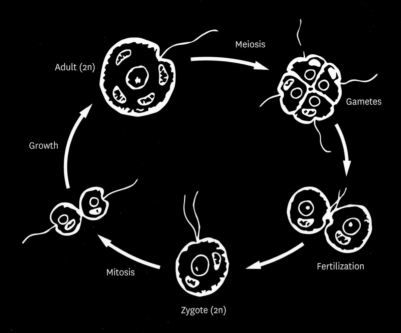

(2) Illustration of a gametic meiosis.

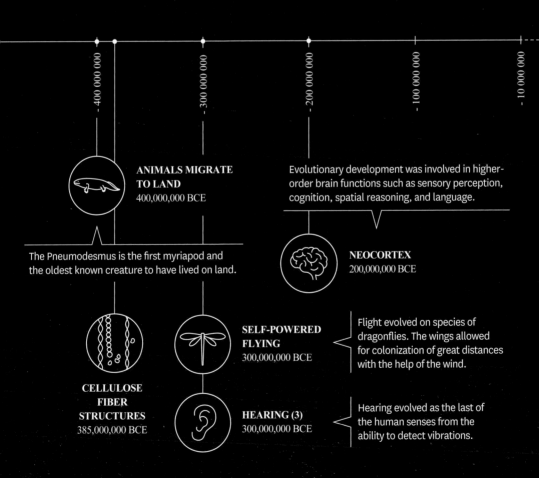

– 400 000 000 – 300 000 000 – 200 000 000 – 100 000 000 – 10 000 000

ANIMALS MIGRATE TO LAND
400,000,000 BCE

Evolutionary development was involved in higher-order brain functions such as sensory perception, cognition, spatial reasoning, and language.

The Pneumodesmus is the first myriapod and the oldest known creature to have lived on land.

NEOCORTEX
200,000,000 BCE

CELLULOSE FIBER STRUCTURES
385,000,000 BCE

SELF-POWERED FLYING
300,000,000 BCE

Flight evolved on species of dragonflies. The wings allowed for colonization of great distances with the help of the wind.

HEARING (3)
300,000,000 BCE

Hearing evolved as the last of the human senses from the ability to detect vibrations.

SENSING

Sensing takes us from physical reality to augmented reality.

According to Kevin Kelly, the Web was the first big platform that collected all information and subjected it to the power of algorithms. The second platform was social media, collecting human relationships and making them subject to the power of algorithms. The third platform is when every single physical object becomes connected and subject to the power of algorithms, sensing and responding to each other. For every physical object there will be a digital twin. For every physical space, a virtual space. This platform, the Mirrorworld, is the return of the relevance of architecture.

- 10 000 000   - 9 000 000   - 8 000 000   - 7 000 000   - 6 000 000

Walking on two legs offers a species several advantages. It raises the head, allows a greater field of vision, and frees up two hands for other purposes.

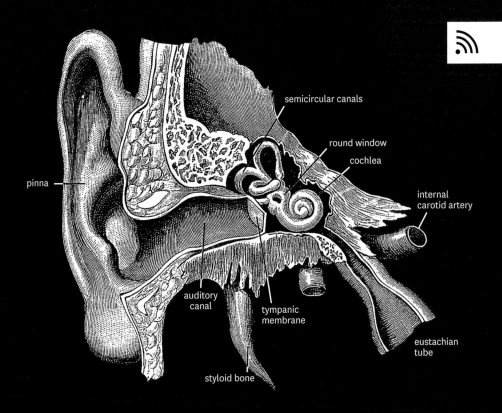

semicircular canals

round window

cochlea

pinna

internal carotid artery

auditory canal

tympanic membrane

eustachian tube

styloid bone

(3) Schematic diagram of the human external and internal ear.

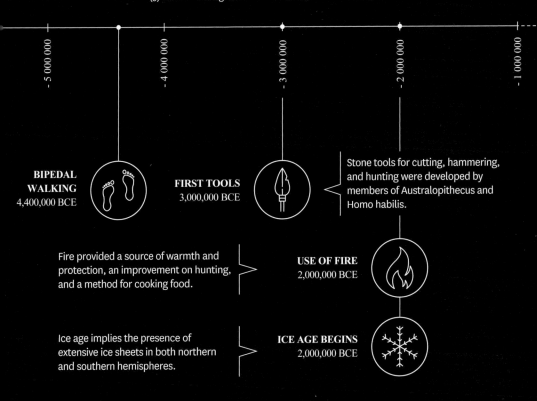

BIPEDAL WALKING
4,400,000 BCE

FIRST TOOLS
3,000,000 BCE

Stone tools for cutting, hammering, and hunting were developed by members of Australopithecus and Homo habilis.

Fire provided a source of warmth and protection, an improvement on hunting, and a method for cooking food.

USE OF FIRE
2,000,000 BCE

Ice age implies the presence of extensive ice sheets in both northern and southern hemispheres.

ICE AGE BEGINS
2,000,000 BCE

- 5 000 000

- 4 000 000

- 3 000 000

- 2 000 000

- 1 000 000

Animism is the ancestral origin of all religions. It is the belief system that all the animals and objects around us are alive, animated by spirits—the deer, the tree, the river, and the rock. We will initiate animism 2.0 when widespread IOT technology turns belief into prophecy as all objects around us become alive and aware, sentient and sensory. This time it will be technology and creativity, rather than faith and superstition, that make our surroundings come alive. After four decades of investment and innovation almost exclusively devoted to the immaterial and the digital, Silicon Valley is finally about to step through this new portal from the virtual into the actual world. These portals or spaces of confluence will be the future frontier of formgiving, where architects may finally have an expertise in the digictal revolution: physical space long forgotten augmented to renewed relevance.

| -1 000 000 | -900 000 | -800 000 | -700 000 | -600 000 |

Homo erectus emigrated from Africa into Asia and Europe. The population in Africa evolved into Neanderthals, and Homo sapiens.

DIVERGENCE OF HUMAN FROM NEANDERTHAL
600,000 BCE

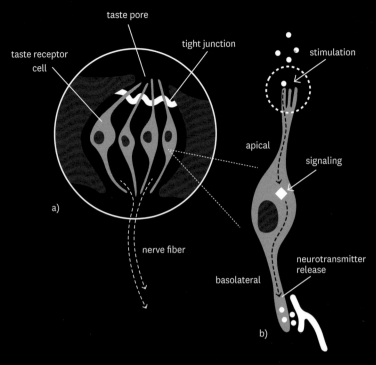

(4) Taste bud (a) and taste receptor cell (b) illustrations.

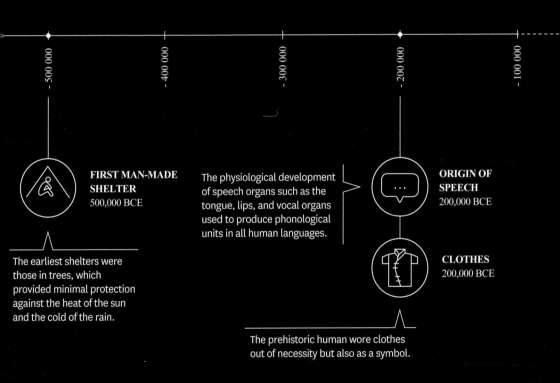

- 500 000   - 400 000   - 300 000   - 200 000   - 100 000

FIRST MAN-MADE SHELTER
500,000 BCE

The physiological development of speech organs such as the tongue, lips, and vocal organs used to produce phonological units in all human languages.

ORIGIN OF SPEECH
200,000 BCE

CLOTHES
200,000 BCE

The earliest shelters were those in trees, which provided minimal protection against the heat of the sun and the cold of the rain.

The prehistoric human wore clothes out of necessity but also as a symbol.

SUSTAINING

The evolution of sustaining is the escalation in the ability of living beings to harvest energy from our surroundings—from heat, sunlight, chemicals, biomass, gravity, and nuclear radiation.

Life is the universe's (only) invention to resist entropy. Our first efforts to impose order on a chaotic world came as a basic form of survival. From foraging and roaming, we learned ways to tame nature, domesticate plants and animals, harness energy in the waterflows and the winds, and release the stored energy in biomass and fossils through fire. Architecture and urbanism may simply be the byproducts of our accelerating efforts to feed ourselves and power our man-made environments.

The Anthropocene is believed to have been triggered by the advent of agriculture and the sedentary lifestyle 12,000 years ago, making this the year 12020 of the Anthropocene calendar. Our intentional ability to dam rivers, water deserts, and turn forests into fields has begun to spin out of control in the form of global warming, melting glaciers, thawing tundra, rising waters, and accelerating windspeeds.

- 100 000   - 90 000   - 80 000   - 70 000   - 60 000

50 CM

50 CM

30 CM

50 CM

(a)

(b)

(5) Section (a) and plan (b) of a horizontal Persian windmill.

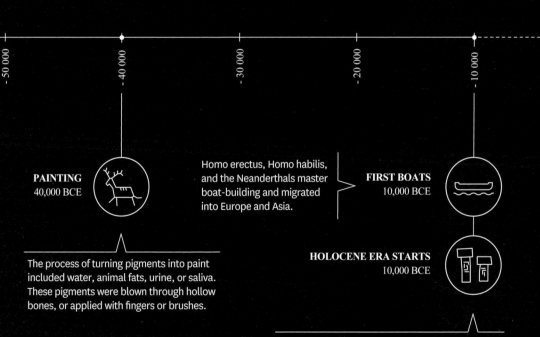

- 50 000

- 40 000

- 30 000

- 20 000

- 10 000

PAINTING
40,000 BCE

Homo erectus, Homo habilis, and the Neanderthals master boat-building and migrated into Europe and Asia.

FIRST BOATS
10,000 BCE

The process of turning pigments into paint included water, animal fats, urine, or saliva. These pigments were blown through hollow bones, or applied with fingers or brushes.

HOLOCENE ERA STARTS
10,000 BCE

The Holocene calendar is a year numbering system that adds exactly 10,000 years to our current numbering scheme, placing its first year when humans transitioned from a hunter-gatherer lifestyle to agriculture and fixed settlements.

Our local lifestyles have turned out to have global consequences. And our old ways of thinking about the world are detrimentally outdated. The world viewed as an infinitely large place where our local actions dissipate into thin air must be replaced by an understanding of the world as a closed loop. Emissions turn up in the outer atmosphere as greenhouse gasses; plastic bottles become a Pacific archipelago twice the size of Texas. Preservation becomes futile without a global perspective, as the Galapagos are choked by plastics from Asian rivers thousands of miles away. To preserve nature we must manage it on a global scale. The city can no longer be conceived without the countryside. The urban and the rural, development and preservation, infrastructure and recreation must become multiple facets of the same prismatic form. Just as we can apply the power of formgiving to an object, a building, a neighborhood, a city, or a country, we can and must apply it to the scale and scope of our entire planet.

Our search for sustenance has led us to the necessity of sustainability. Resource extraction must become renewable resources. Linear processes shall fold into circular loops. Earth 2.0 will replace the inevitable entropy of a culture that is running out with a new world powered by perpetual motion.

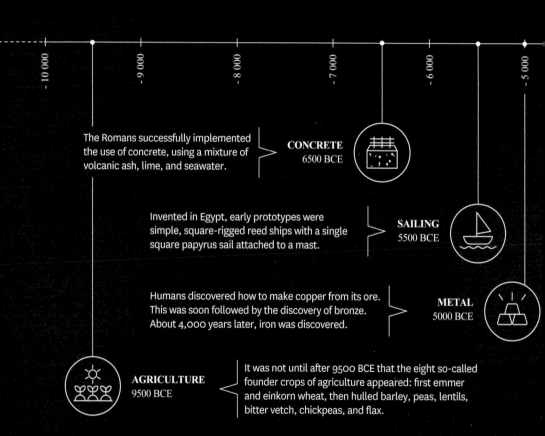

| - 10 000 | - 9 000 | - 8 000 | - 7 000 | - 6 000 | - 5 000 |

The Romans successfully implemented the use of concrete, using a mixture of volcanic ash, lime, and seawater.

CONCRETE
6500 BCE

Invented in Egypt, early prototypes were simple, square-rigged reed ships with a single square papyrus sail attached to a mast.

SAILING
5500 BCE

Humans discovered how to make copper from its ore. This was soon followed by the discovery of bronze. About 4,000 years later, iron was discovered.

METAL
5000 BCE

AGRICULTURE
9500 BCE

It was not until after 9500 BCE that the eight so-called founder crops of agriculture appeared: first emmer and einkorn wheat, then hulled barley, peas, lentils, bitter vetch, chickpeas, and flax.

(6) An engraving depicting Thomas Savery's steam engine.

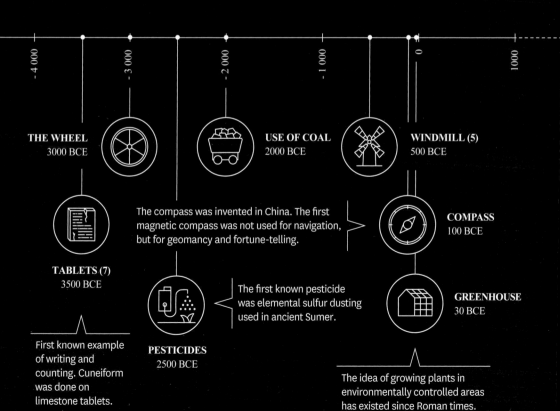

-4 000 -3 000 -2 000 -1 000 0 1000

THE WHEEL
3000 BCE

USE OF COAL
2000 BCE

WINDMILL (5)
500 BCE

The compass was invented in China. The first magnetic compass was not used for navigation, but for geomancy and fortune-telling.

COMPASS
100 BCE

TABLETS (7)
3500 BCE

The first known pesticide was elemental sulfur dusting used in ancient Sumer.

GREENHOUSE
30 BCE

PESTICIDES
2500 BCE

First known example of writing and counting. Cuneiform was done on limestone tablets.

The idea of growing plants in environmentally controlled areas has existed since Roman times.

THINKING

The evolution of thinking is a journey from the dawn of biological intelligence to artificial intelligence. We believe artificial intelligence will inevitably be deployed in the creative process, making the human element incrementally more important.

Today, the most powerful chess computer can beat the world's greatest grandmaster. But together with a powerful chess computer a grand master can beat any machine. The man-machine symbiosis is the most powerful. The architect—like the grandmaster—enabled by AI will have unprecedented powers to give form. And we are neither talking about incremental increases in efficiency nor speed, but rather the capacity to generate forms and ideas that would be unimaginable by a human designer alone. The tireless processing power, the patient execution of countless experiments, and the instant access to all the knowledge of the world, make AI a powerful ally for analytical experimentation. It may eventually be able to intuit possibilities that are simply too many moves ahead for the human designer to fathom. If we want to go beyond the limits of our own imagination, we will have to ally ourselves with artificially intelligent designers.

1100   1150   1200   1250

Historians believe that the first eyeglasses were produced in Italy. Glasses for nearsightedness likely arose in the 15th century.

LENS
SPECTACLE
1285

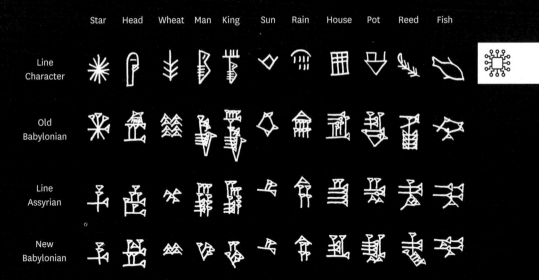

	Star	Head	Wheat	Man	King	Sun	Rain	House	Pot	Reed	Fish
Line Character											
Old Babylonian											
Line Assyrian											
New Babylonian											

(7) Table illustrating the simplification of cuneiform signs.

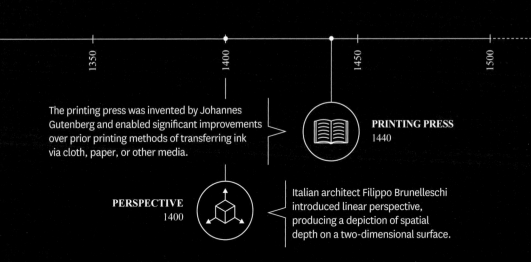

1350 — 1400 — 1450 — 1500

The printing press was invented by Johannes Gutenberg and enabled significant improvements over prior printing methods of transferring ink via cloth, paper, or other media.

PRINTING PRESS
1440

PERSPECTIVE
1400

Italian architect Filippo Brunelleschi introduced linear perspective, producing a depiction of spatial depth on a two-dimensional surface.

(8) Woodcut engraving depicting Robert Hooke's microscope

1500   1550   1600   1650

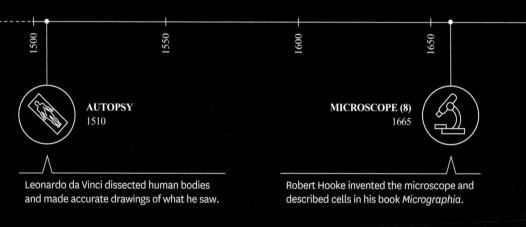

AUTOPSY
1510

MICROSCOPE (8)
1665

Leonardo da Vinci dissected human bodies
and made accurate drawings of what he saw.

Robert Hooke invented the microscope and
described cells in his book *Micrographia*.

Thomas Savery, an engineer and inventor,
patented a machine that could effectively draw
water from flooded mines using steam pressure.

STEAM ENGINE (6)
1698

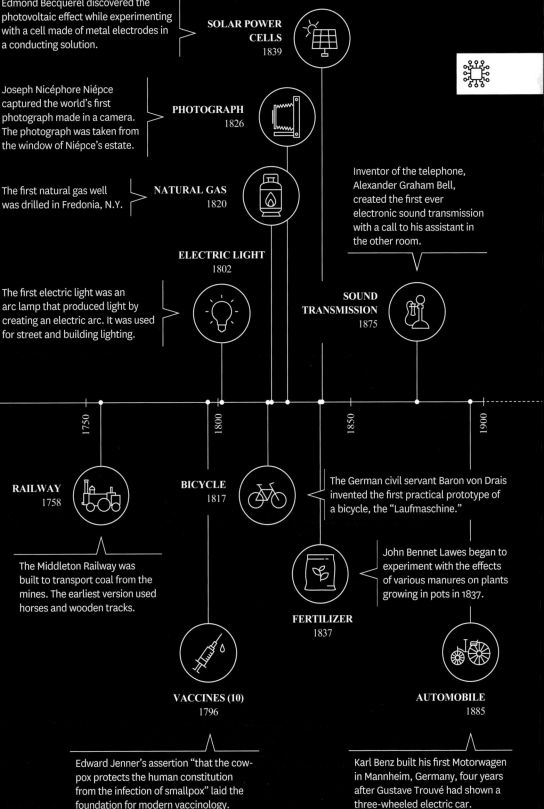

Edmond Becquerel discovered the photovoltaic effect while experimenting with a cell made of metal electrodes in a conducting solution.

SOLAR POWER CELLS
1839

Joseph Nicéphore Niépce captured the world's first photograph made in a camera. The photograph was taken from the window of Niépce's estate.

PHOTOGRAPH
1826

The first natural gas well was drilled in Fredonia, N.Y.

NATURAL GAS
1820

Inventor of the telephone, Alexander Graham Bell, created the first ever electronic sound transmission with a call to his assistant in the other room.

ELECTRIC LIGHT
1802

The first electric light was an arc lamp that produced light by creating an electric arc. It was used for street and building lighting.

SOUND TRANSMISSION
1875

1750

1800

1850

1900

RAILWAY
1758

BICYCLE
1817

The German civil servant Baron von Drais invented the first practical prototype of a bicycle, the "Laufmaschine."

The Middleton Railway was built to transport coal from the mines. The earliest version used horses and wooden tracks.

John Bennet Lawes began to experiment with the effects of various manures on plants growing in pots in 1837.

FERTILIZER
1837

VACCINES (10)
1796

AUTOMOBILE
1885

Edward Jenner's assertion "that the cow-pox protects the human constitution from the infection of smallpox" laid the foundation for modern vaccinology.

Karl Benz built his first Motorwagen in Mannheim, Germany, four years after Gustave Trouvé had shown a three-wheeled electric car.

HEALING

The evolution of healing has taken us from reactive to proactive medicine. Life has evolved on Earth by gradually adapting to its surroundings, each eco-niche offering a new habitat that has in turn shaped its inhabitants, until we discovered the power of formgiving and created tools, technology, and architecture. Then we acquired the power to adapt our surroundings to us. We didn't have to climb a tree—we could design our own tree. We didn't have to explore a cave—we could design our own cave. And with that power came the question, what kind of tree and what kind of a cave would we like to live in? We started to give form to the world we wanted to live in—a world shaped by our lives.

Now our journey is about to come full circle, as the power of healing has gone from repairing or replacing broken abilities to inventing new abilities. From bringing back lost senses to inventing new ones—the sixth, seventh, and beyond. From delaying the inevitable decay of senescence to bioengineering an eternally renewable subscription to life.

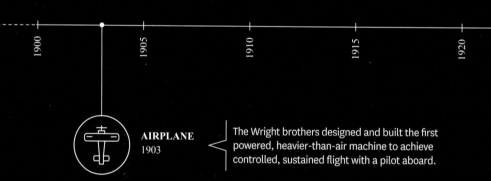

1900 | 1905 | 1910 | 1915 | 1920

AIRPLANE
1903

The Wright brothers designed and built the first powered, heavier-than-air machine to achieve controlled, sustained flight with a pilot aboard.

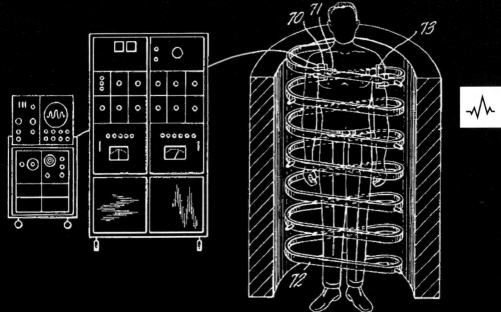

(9) Patent drawings of the first MRI scanner.

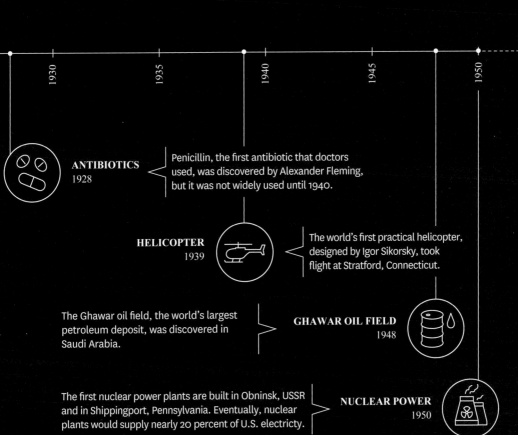

1930   1935   1940   1945   1950

ANTIBIOTICS
1928

Penicillin, the first antibiotic that doctors used, was discovered by Alexander Fleming, but it was not widely used until 1940.

HELICOPTER
1939

The world's first practical helicopter, designed by Igor Sikorsky, took flight at Stratford, Connecticut.

The Ghawar oil field, the world's largest petroleum deposit, was discovered in Saudi Arabia.

GHAWAR OIL FIELD
1948

The first nuclear power plants are built in Obninsk, USSR and in Shippingport, Pennsylvania. Eventually, nuclear plants would supply nearly 20 percent of U.S. electricty.

NUCLEAR POWER
1950

If escape velocity is the minimum speed needed for an object to escape from the gravitational influence of a massive body, then longevity escape velocity can be attained when life expectancy extends faster than the passing of time. Life expectancy has been gaining incrementally as treatments and technologies improve, but more than one year of research is required for each additional year of expected life. Longevity escape velocity occurs when this ratio reverses, so that life expectancy accelerates faster than one year per year. The speed of lifespan extension is slowly but surely gaining on the speed of time.

Finally, if we shape our surroundings and, in return, they shape us, when we ask ourselves how we want to live, in extension we are also asking who we want to be. As we migrate to other planets, the first generations of trueborn Lunarians and Martians will inevitably grow taller and skinnier than their Terran ancestors, unencumbered by the heavy gravity of Earth. As we start to struggle with the Herculean task of terraforming Mars or the Moon, we may find that it may be simpler to change ourselves than to change our worlds. It is time to apply the power of formgiving to ourselves, by asking not just who we are, but who and what we want to become. From Human Beings to Human Becomings.

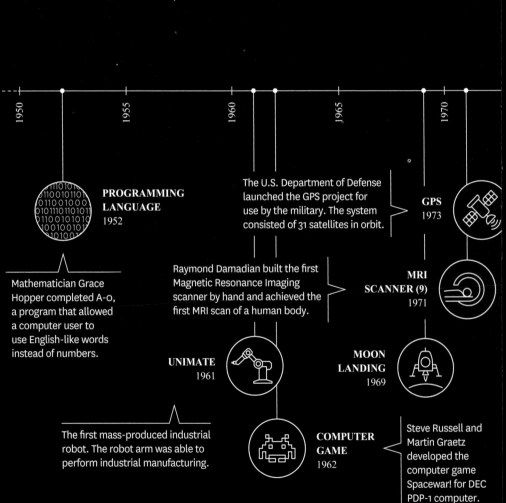

1950   1955   1960   1965   1970

PROGRAMMING LANGUAGE
1952

The U.S. Department of Defense launched the GPS project for use by the military. The system consisted of 31 satellites in orbit.

GPS
1973

Mathematician Grace Hopper completed A-0, a program that allowed a computer user to use English-like words instead of numbers.

Raymond Damadian built the first Magnetic Resonance Imaging scanner by hand and achieved the first MRI scan of a human body.

MRI SCANNER (9)
1971

UNIMATE
1961

MOON LANDING
1969

The first mass-produced industrial robot. The robot arm was able to perform industrial manufacturing.

COMPUTER GAME
1962

Steve Russell and Martin Graetz developed the computer game Spacewar! for DEC PDP-1 computer.

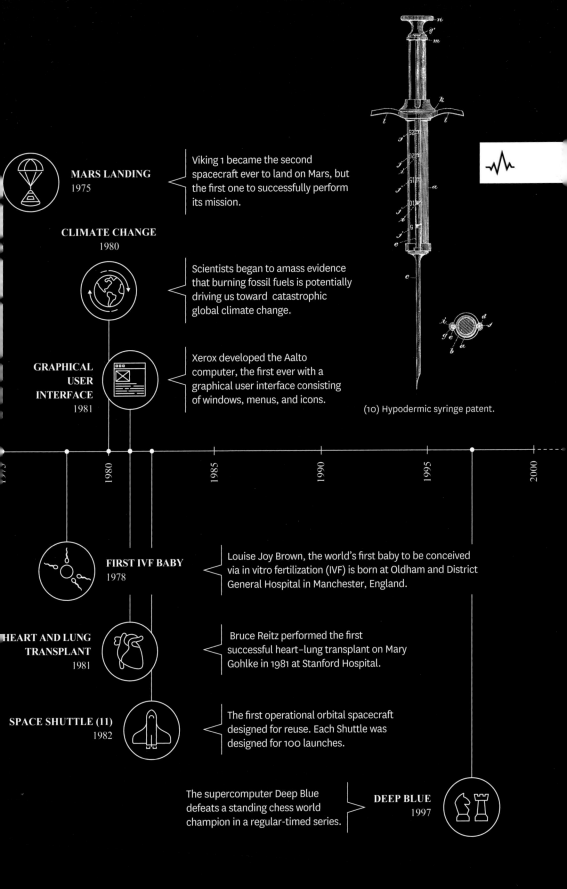

MARS LANDING
1975

Viking 1 became the second spacecraft ever to land on Mars, but the first one to successfully perform its mission.

CLIMATE CHANGE
1980

Scientists began to amass evidence that burning fossil fuels is potentially driving us toward catastrophic global climate change.

GRAPHICAL USER INTERFACE
1981

Xerox developed the Aalto computer, the first ever with a graphical user interface consisting of windows, menus, and icons.

(10) Hypodermic syringe patent.

1980 | 1985 | 1990 | 1995 | 2000

FIRST IVF BABY
1978

Louise Joy Brown, the world's first baby to be conceived via in vitro fertilization (IVF) is born at Oldham and District General Hospital in Manchester, England.

HEART AND LUNG TRANSPLANT
1981

Bruce Reitz performed the first successful heart–lung transplant on Mary Gohlke in 1981 at Stanford Hospital.

SPACE SHUTTLE (11)
1982

The first operational orbital spacecraft designed for reuse. Each Shuttle was designed for 100 launches.

The supercomputer Deep Blue defeats a standing chess world champion in a regular-timed series.

DEEP BLUE
1997

MOVING

Moving has taken us across the entire Earth to the Moon and Mars, entering the dawn of interplanetary migration. Life, in its very essence, is about space exploration. Originating in water, life has migrated to land.

Humans have constantly gone beyond our comfort zone. It is deeply rooted in our nature to go where it is difficult, and to invent the necessary technologies to survive. Humans would never have made it to Scandinavia without sophisticated technologies such as fire, fur, tools, and shelter. For the next step in our exploration—the human migration to Mars—we will merely have to navigate an ocean of space rather than water. They say there's no evidence we get less creative with age, but we do get less creative the longer that we're doing the same thing. We can't imagine anything more revitalizing for the architectural profession than tackling the challenges of building on a different planet. It may take hundreds of years and many generations to terraform Mars to have a biosphere. But the cathedrals took hundreds of years and many generations to build. And we built them anyway.

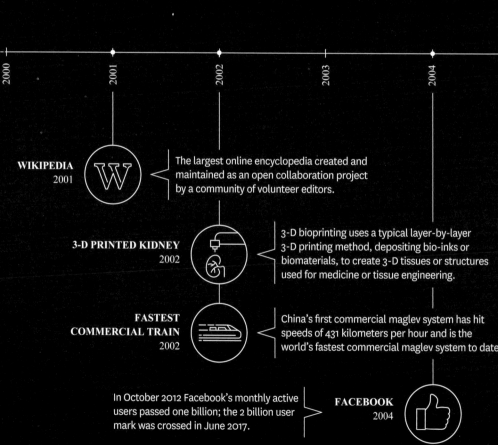

2000   2001   2002   2003   2004

WIKIPEDIA
2001

The largest online encyclopedia created and maintained as an open collaboration project by a community of volunteer editors.

3-D PRINTED KIDNEY
2002

3-D bioprinting uses a typical layer-by-layer 3-D printing method, depositing bio-inks or biomaterials, to create 3-D tissues or structures used for medicine or tissue engineering.

FASTEST COMMERCIAL TRAIN
2002

China's first commercial maglev system has hit speeds of 431 kilometers per hour and is the world's fastest commercial maglev system to date

In October 2012 Facebook's monthly active users passed one billion; the 2 billion user mark was crossed in June 2017.

FACEBOOK
2004

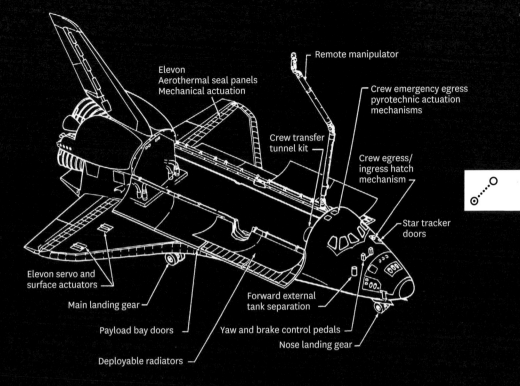

Remote manipulator

Elevon
Aerothermal seal panels
Mechanical actuation

Crew emergency egress
pyrotechnic actuation
mechanisms

Crew transfer
tunnel kit

Crew egress/
ingress hatch
mechanism

Star tracker
doors

Elevon servo and
surface actuators

Main landing gear

Payload bay doors

Deployable radiators

Forward external
tank separation

Yaw and brake control pedals

Nose landing gear

(11) Axonometric drawing of Space Shuttle Columbia.

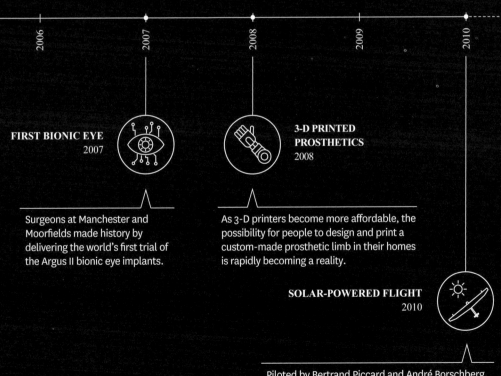

2006   2007   2008   2009   2010

FIRST BIONIC EYE
2007

**3-D PRINTED
PROSTHETICS**
2008

Surgeons at Manchester and
Moorfields made history by
delivering the world's first trial of
the Argus II bionic eye implants.

As 3-D printers become more affordable, the
possibility for people to design and print a
custom-made prosthetic limb in their homes
is rapidly becoming a reality.

SOLAR-POWERED FLIGHT
2010

Piloted by Bertrand Piccard and André Borschberg,
the Solar Impulse 2 completed the first round-the-
world flight powered by renewable energy.

If the overview effect is the cognitive shift reported by astronauts when they see the Earth from outer space, then imagine what sense of universal citizenry our children or grandchildren will feel staring at the night sky of the planet they now call home—pointing toward this tiny blue dot that reminds them of our earthly origins and our galactic destiny.

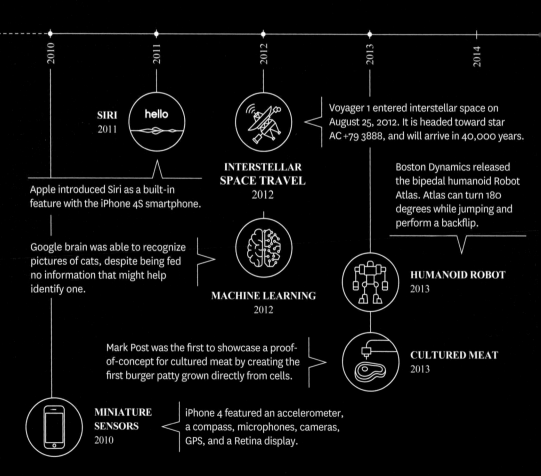

2010   2011   2012   2013   2014

SIRI hello
2011

Voyager 1 entered interstellar space on August 25, 2012. It is headed toward star AC +79 3888, and will arrive in 40,000 years.

Apple introduced Siri as a built-in feature with the iPhone 4S smartphone.

INTERSTELLAR SPACE TRAVEL
2012

Boston Dynamics released the bipedal humanoid Robot Atlas. Atlas can turn 180 degrees while jumping and perform a backflip.

Google brain was able to recognize pictures of cats, despite being fed no information that might help identify one.

MACHINE LEARNING
2012

HUMANOID ROBOT
2013

Mark Post was the first to showcase a proof-of-concept for cultured meat by creating the first burger patty grown directly from cells.

CULTURED MEAT
2013

MINIATURE SENSORS
2010

iPhone 4 featured an accelerometer, a compass, microphones, cameras, GPS, and a Retina display.

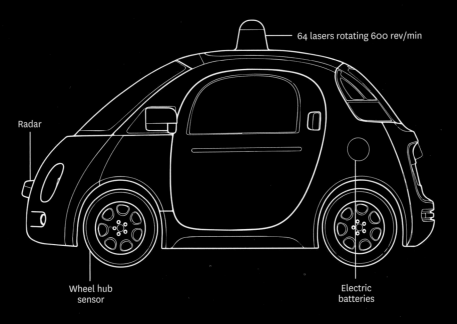

64 lasers rotating 600 rev/min

Radar

Wheel hub
sensor

Electric
batteries

(12) Waymo self-driving car.

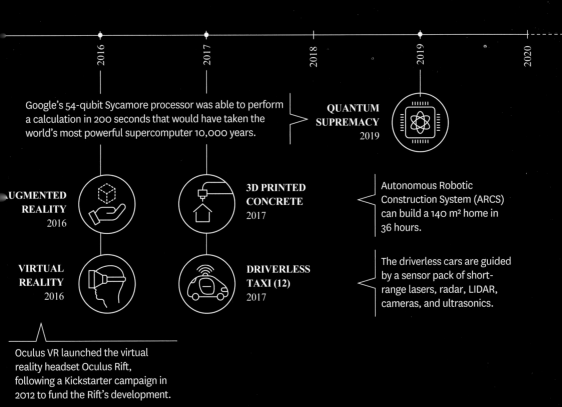

2016

2017

2018

2019

2020

Google's 54-qubit Sycamore processor was able to perform a calculation in 200 seconds that would have taken the world's most powerful supercomputer 10,000 years.

QUANTUM SUPREMACY
2019

UGMENTED REALITY
2016

3D PRINTED CONCRETE
2017

Autonomous Robotic Construction System (ARCS) can build a 140 m² home in 36 hours.

VIRTUAL REALITY
2016

DRIVERLESS TAXI (12)
2017

The driverless cars are guided by a sensor pack of short-range lasers, radar, LIDAR, cameras, and ultrasonics.

Oculus VR launched the virtual reality headset Oculus Rift, following a Kickstarter campaign in 2012 to fund the Rift's development.

THE 10 GIFTS

As architects we don't have political power because we don't write the rules. Neither do we have financial power, because we don't write the checks. But we do have the power of giving form, to go above and beyond what we have been asked to do and give the world a gift that makes the world more of how we wish it to be. The gift is not a question of philanthropy. It is a gift because no one asked for it—but now that it has been offered—the world would be a lesser place without it, and future generations will be better off because of it. The gift is the world-changing power of architecture. It is our capacity to design spaces and places that make a difference, that are the change we want to see in the world.

We just opened a waste-to-energy power plant here in Copenhagen that is so clean that we have been able to turn its façade into a climbing wall, and its roof into an alpine park for hiking and skiing. We've married disparate concepts: a public utility becomes a public park, a power plant becomes a mountain. I have a one-year old son. He and his friends are going to grow up in a world not knowing there was a time when you couldn't ski on power plants. This will be the new baseline for him and his generation, so imagine how far they will be able to mentally leap while standing on top of a human-made mountain—what wild ideas they will have for their collective future.

To explore the notion of the gift as the proactive power of architecture, we have organized our work according to the gifts that they give. To their users. To their neighborhood. To the city. To the landscape. To the environment. To the world. And to the future. Life is lived forwards but understood backwards. Since our practice is a constant work in progress, and our ideas and agenda mature and evolve over time, the clarity of our vision rarely matches the skewed perspective of our realized reality. The gifts are neither mutually exclusive nor collectively exhaustive, they are merely examples of the power we hold to give the world something more than form.

THE OXYMORON

An oxymoron is a figure of speech in which apparently contradictory terms appear in conjunction: hedonistic sustainability, pragmatic utopia, social infrastructure. The architectural equivalent is a structure that combines seemingly incompatible activities or building types into a single structure.

Our cities and buildings are built on a paradigm of front of house and back of house. City infrastructure projects are utilitarian machines, isolated from the urban inhabitants they serve. You can find them on Google like cancerous tissue on a city map. The more specialized a utility becomes, the more reasons to separate it from the public to improve its performance and efficiency. We all know that a piece of infrastructure can have negative side effects, like the underside of an overpass, the shadow cast by a chimney, the noise of a highway, or the gaping wound of a parking lot. But we also know that once a piece of infrastructure shuts down, it can be reborn with positive programs. Train tracks become a park. A power plant becomes a museum. What if we could start by combining the utilitarian and the social? What if our urban infrastructures opened on day one with positive social and environmental side effects?

In the future, as technologies evolve to become clean, noiseless, and emission-free, the practical reasons for isolating utilities will evaporate, opening up countless new unions between served and servant spaces. Public utilities with programs for the people. Imagine the necessary flood protection for Manhattan designed so that a seawall doesn't segregate city life from the water around it. Rather, it makes the waterfront more accessible and enjoyable. A waste-to-energy power plant so clean that we can turn its roof into an alpine park for hiking, climbing, and skiing. Novel transportation technologies eliminating the traditional infrastructure of stations and waiting halls. Parking structures doubling as markets or co-working environments. An entire city remapped and the street reborn as a woven linear park or a promenade. The underside of a bridge turning into an upside-down gallery—street art's equivalent of the Sistine Chapel. Or in reverse, a museum that doubles as a bridge?

Taking the profane and the elevated, we can create a city of higher complexity and greater resiliency. If one use dissipates, the other consolidates. One is nocturnal, the other diurnal. In fact, the more different two activities are, the more likely they are to produce the unprecedented. In architecture, as in love, opposites attract.

COPENHILL

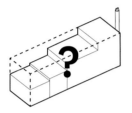 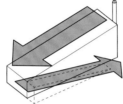 

Built to replace a 50-year-old waste-to-energy plant in Copenhagen, CopenHill is the cleanest waste-to-energy power plant in the world. In fact, it is so clean that no toxins are emitted from the chimney, merely some steam and a reduced amount of CO_2. In asking ourselves how we could express this marvel of modern engineering that would otherwise be invisible to the human eye, we considered how Denmark has snow, but no mountains. We have to travel six hours by car to reach the nearest alpine ski park in Sweden. So what if we could turn the giant roof of the power plant into a ski slope? The internal volumes of the power plant are determined by the precise organization of its machinery in height order. Ventilation shafts and air-intakes create a variation of topography. It's year-round skiing on natural turf reinforced with a low-friction mat. It has the same grip as a freshly groomed slope. There will only be powder when the gods deliver. Inside the power plant, the machinery is kept in shades of raw metal, silver, or gray making it look like the interior of a spaceship. The façade is made from folded aluminum mega bricks that double as planters. On the tallest corner the aluminum bricks bulge out, forming the tallest climbing wall in the world. As you ride the elevator to the roof you look to the insides of the mountain, or out through a view filtered by mountain climbers gripping onto the windows. Finally, the fifth façade, the roof, is populated with hundreds of indigenous trees, bushes, grasses, and flowers form a hikeable mountain meadow. Hikers, runners, and mountain bikers are welcome to enjoy the roofscape without a lift card. The alpine park is a literal extension of the Copenhagen topography. CopenHill is our most blatant manifestation of social infrastructure: a piece of public utility with premeditated positive social and environmental side effects.

Copenhagen, DENMARK
41,000 M² | Culture
2019

ALDO AMORETTI

LAURIAN GHINITOIU

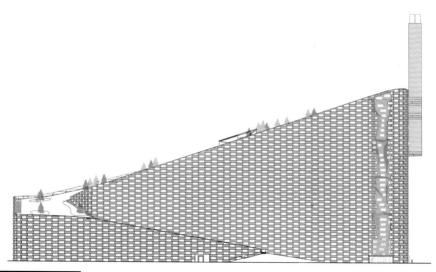

north elevation

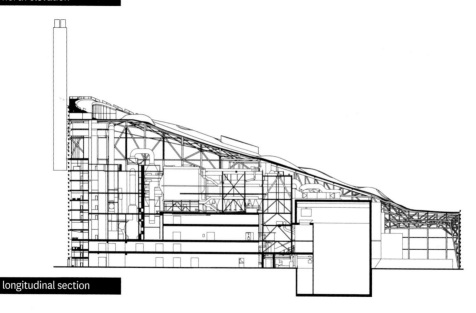

longitudinal section

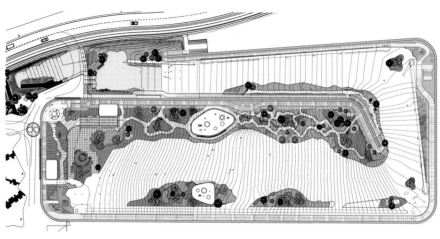

roof plan

0 5 10   25   50M

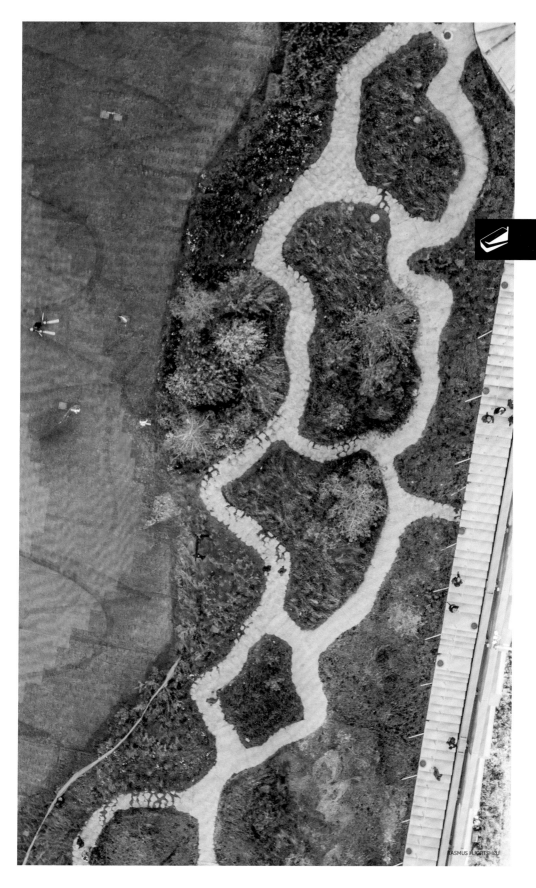

RASMUS HJORTSHØJ

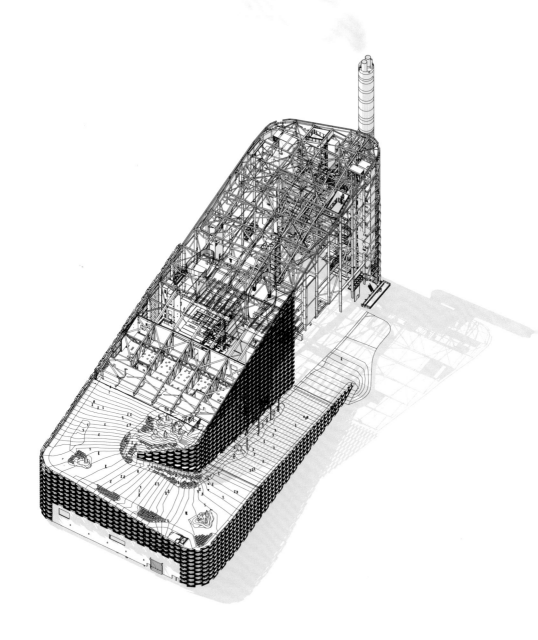

axonometric view

SØREN AAGAARD

JAKOB LANGE

LAURIAN GHINITOIU

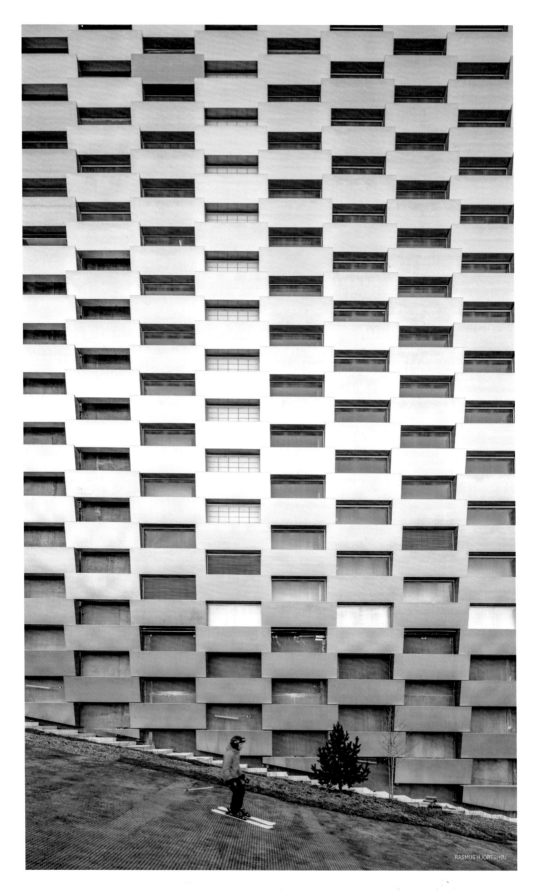

RASMUS HJORTSHØJ

EHRHORN HUMMERSTON

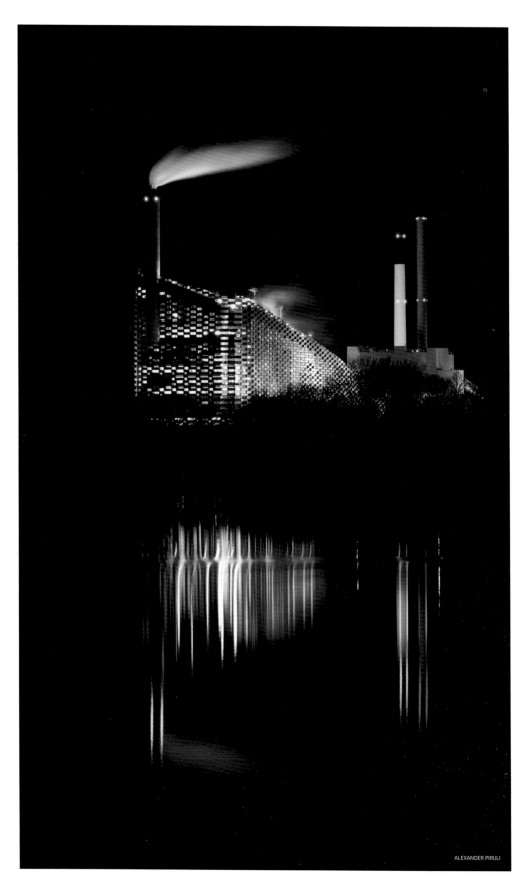

ALEXANDER PIRULI

RASMUS HJORTSHØJ

ALDO AMORETTI

THE TWIST

Located in Jevnaker outside of Oslo, The Twist is a hybrid spanning several traditional categories: It's a museum, it's a bridge, and it's a sculpture. As a bridge, it reconfigures the sculpture park, turning the journey through the park into a continuous loop. As a museum, it connects two distinct spaces— an introverted vertical gallery, and an extroverted horizontal gallery with panoramic views across the river. A third space is created through the blatant translation between these two galleries creating the namesake twist. From either direction, visitors experience the twisted gallery as though walking through a camera shutter. The Twist constitutes a tectonic enigma. As the bridge connects the two riverbanks, it rotates 90 degrees forming a warped, ruled surface. Two pure functional forms united by complex curvature. Appearing as arches and curves, the form is created from purely straight lines with standard sheets of aluminum and simple wooden sticks. An expressive organic sculpture composed of rational repetitive elements.

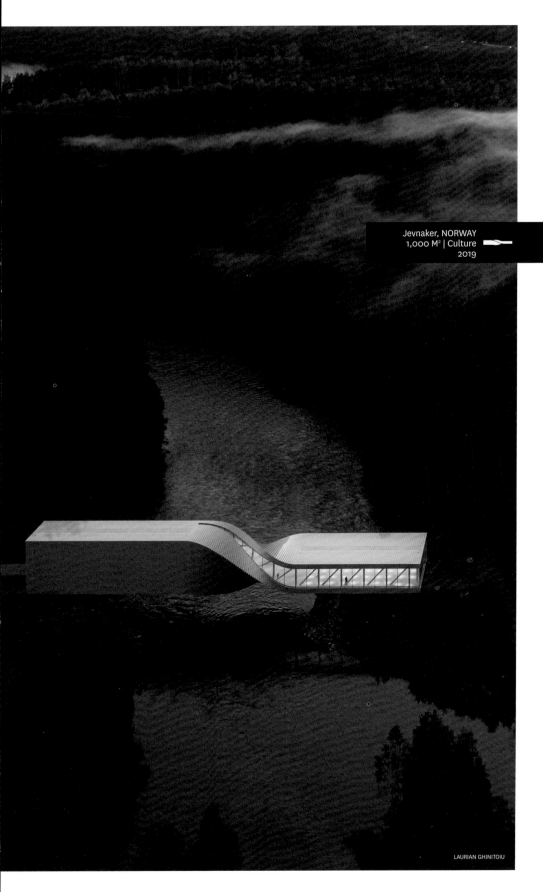

Jevnaker, NORWAY
1,000 M² | Culture
2019

LAURIAN GHINITOIU

ANDREAS NUNTUN

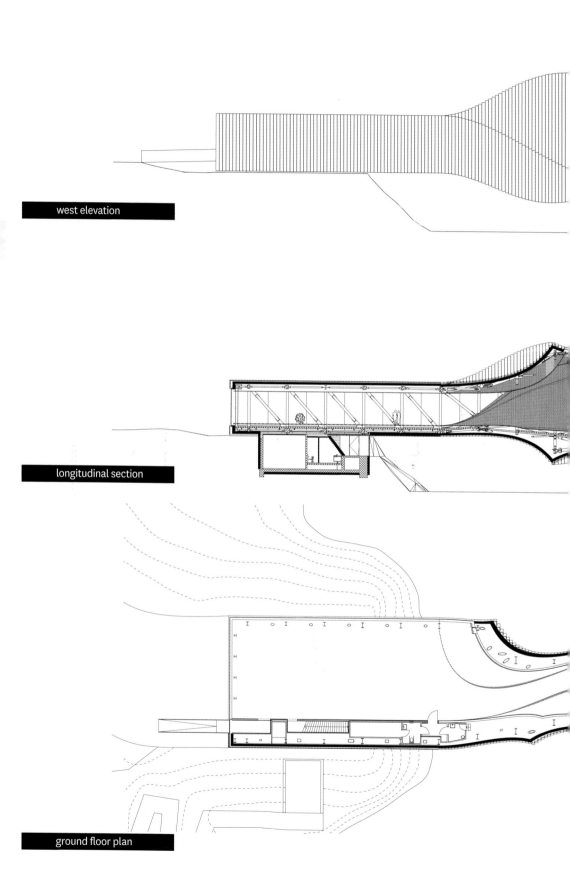

west elevation

longitudinal section

ground floor plan

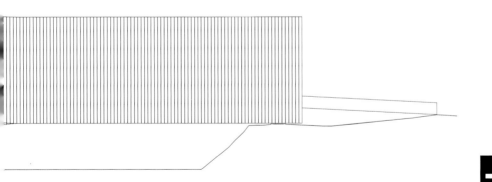

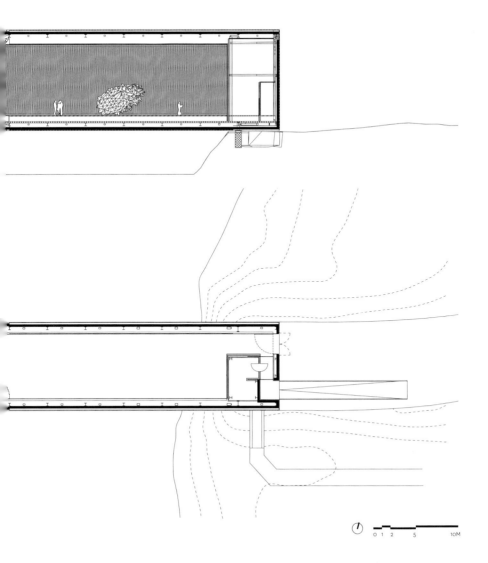

0 1 2   5   10M

LAURIAN GHINITOIU

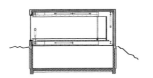

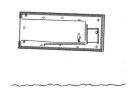

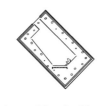

0 1 2   5   10M

LAURIAN GHINITOIU

LAURIAN GHINITOIU

EVA SEO-ANDERSEN

TOMASZ MAJEWSKI

SIGNE DON

KIM ERLANDSEN

BENJAMIN WARD

TONY OURSLER

EVA SEO-ANDERSEN

LAURIAN GHINITOIU

THE HYPERLOOP

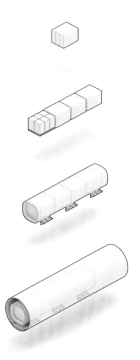

With Virgin Hyperloop One we have given form to a mobility ecosystem
of pods and portals, where the waiting hall has vanished along with waiting
itself. Hyperloop One combines collective commuting with individual freedom
at near supersonic speed. All elements of the travel experience are designed
to increase convenience and reduce interruptions. Hence, the stations are
called portals. All departure gates are immediately visible upon entering
the portal. Passengers will travel in pods that have room for six people. The
pods are contained within a transporter, a pressure vessel attached to a
chassis for levitation and propulsion that can accelerate the transporter to
1,100km/h. Passengers board the next pod that is available, which moves onto
a transporter to their final destination. The relatively small unit-size of the
pods, paired with a high arrival- and departure-rate, allows for on-demand
travel. The pods operate autonomously from the transporter, which means
they are not limited to the portal area and can move on regular roads and pick
up passengers at any point. At portals, pods are loaded onto the transporter
and hyperjump to another portal, where they merge onto the street and drop
passengers off at their final destination. Low energy, supersonic, on-demand
and direct to destination.

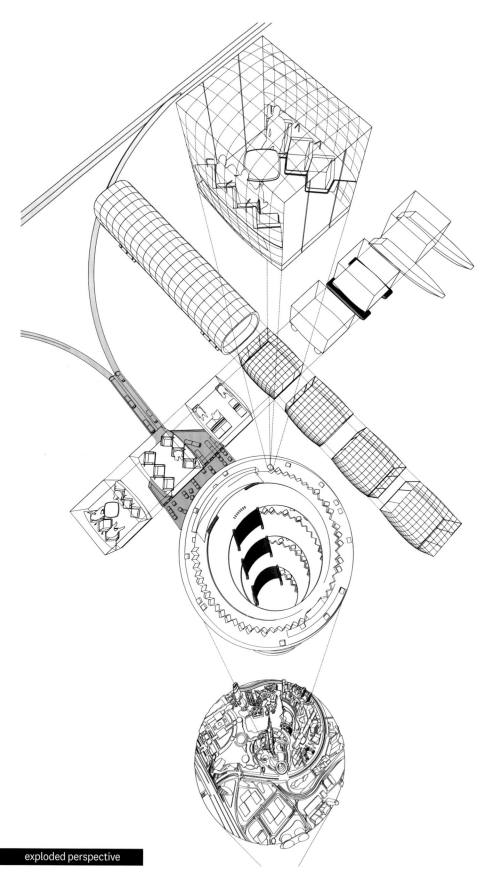

exploded perspective

∞

THE ARTERY

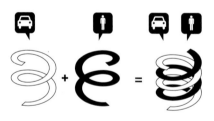

The Artery is a parking garage designed to double as a cultural hub. The Artery is a double helix: One helix is dedicated to maker spaces and marketplaces, and the other helix is dedicated to cars. The car ramp is enclosed and compressed; the market ramp is open and generous. The two ramps wrap around a central void, forming an informal performance space visible from all levels. As the market ramp reaches the top, it is transformed into a public roof garden. Part infrastructure, part social space, The Artery is like the fairground or the marketplace folded up into the third dimension.

Abu Dhabi, UAE
29,000 M²
Culture

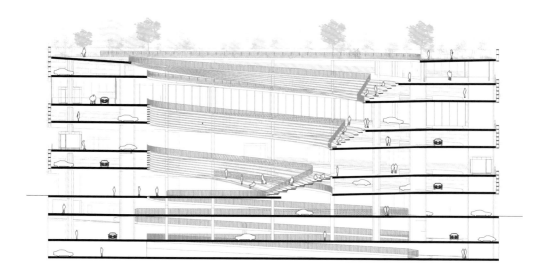

longitudinal section

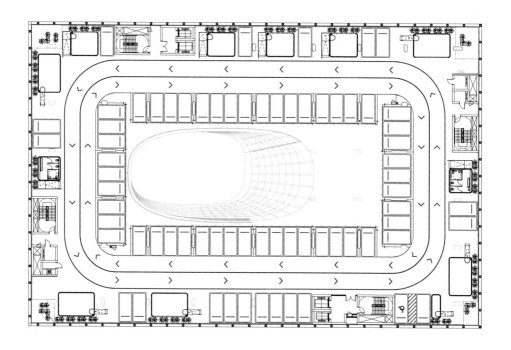

plan level 1

0 1 2   5   10   15M

THE BIG U

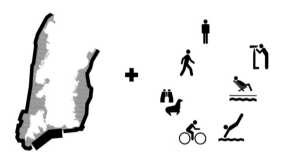

The BIG U marries physical resiliency with social resiliency to create 10 miles of continuous flood protection for Lower Manhattan. The site stretches from West 57th street south to The Battery, and up to East 42nd street, and comprises low-lying geography with the incredibly dense, vibrant, yet vulnerable urban area. The BIG U proposes to rethink infrastructure as a social amenity—what we call social infrastructure. Infrastructure in the United States as it's traditionally conceived has not been civic, accessible, or designed for interaction with the public in mind. Rather, it has been imposed upon our cities without engagement with community needs at a large scale, at times with terrible consequences for the urban experience. The BIG U combines the mandate to create large-scale protective infrastructure with a commitment to meaningful community engagement. It fuses "Robert Moses" hard infrastructure with "Jane Jacobs" locally based, community-driven sensitivity. The BIG U's flood protection won't look like a wall, and it won't separate the community from the waterfront. Instead, the very structures that protect us from the elements will become attractive centers of social and recreational activity that enhance the city and lay a positive groundwork for its future public realm.

SANDY SURGE LEVELS
2050 100-YR STORM
2050 500-YR STORM

CLINTON

CHELSEA

HOSPITAL ROW

SOBECA

GANSEVOORT ST

L.E.S. NORTH-EAST RIVER PARK
COMPARTMENT 1 C1

TWO BRIDGES / CHINATOWN
COMPARTMENT 2 C2

DFD

BATTERY / FINANCIAL DISTRICT
COMPARTMENT 3 C3

BATTERY PARK BERM

HARBOR MUSEUM

BMB PLAZA

ECO-PIER

ANHATTAN 2050

 contains the symbol U with an up arrow in the upper right.

TOYOTA WOVEN CITY

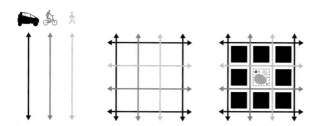

Toyota has become the largest automaker in the world through constant reinvention. Starting as a loom company in the 1890s, Toyota applied its ingenuity in mechanical engineering by pivoting to engines and then automobiles, going on to pioneer the path toward electric, hydrogen, and autonomous vehicles. In 2018, Mr. Akio Toyoda, CEO of Toyota Motor Company, announced that Toyota would transform yet again from a car company to a mobility company. This has challenged the company to look beyond vehicles to examine how people move in all aspects of their everyday lives. Toyota Woven City is envisioned as a living laboratory to test and advance personal mobility, autonomy, and mobility as a service, connectivity, hydrogen-powered infrastructure and industry collaboration. The typical road is split into three: a street optimized for vehicular traffic with logistical traffic underneath; a promenade for micro-mobility such as bikes, scooters, and personal mobility; and a linear park for pedestrians, flora, and fauna. These three strands form the DNA of the city, which are woven together to create a 3x3 city block module. Eight buildings comprise the block, which frames a central courtyard accessible by the promenade and linear park. This framework is extended and replicated to form neighborhoods, and by distorting the grid, two courtyards are enlarged to create a large plaza or park, becoming an amenity at the city scale. Even if tailored for Mt. Fuji, the principles of the Woven City are so universal that they can easily be postapplied to existing city fabrics as diverse as New York, Barcelona, or Tokyo.

Susono, Shizuoka, JAPAN
708,200 M²
Urbanism

SQUINT OPERA

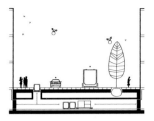

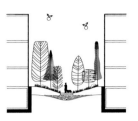

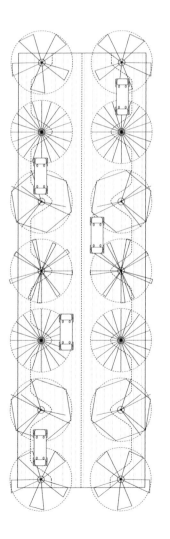
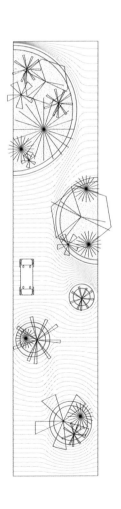

0 1 2   5   10M

vehicular road   **recreational promenade**   **linear park**

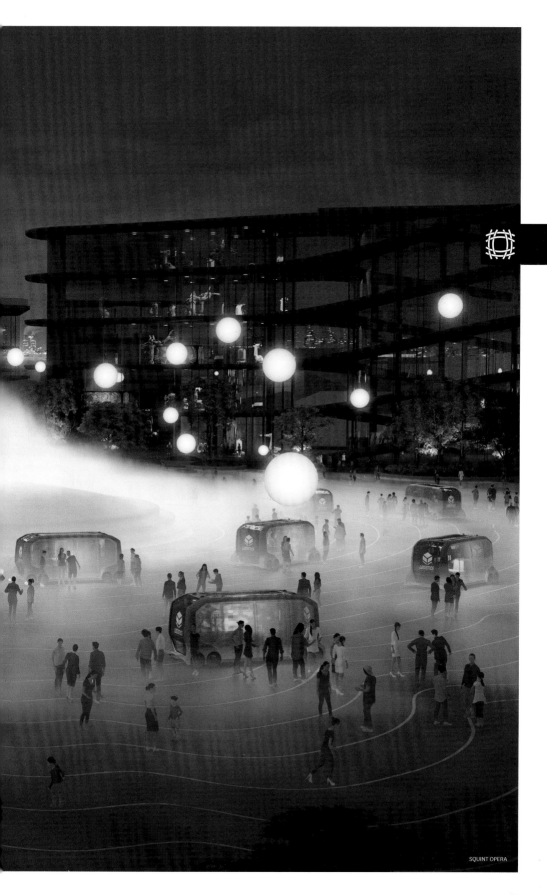

SQUINT OPERA

THE X-RAY

"I love the everyday," wrote Dan Turèll. Not Sunday nor the holidays—but the everyday. The world is already incredibly interesting as it is, and the everyday aspects of our built environment are the most exhilarating things we'll ever find. We don't have to come up with arbitrary artistic expressions to make architecture exciting. All we have to do is look, listen, and learn about what is going on—and let it show.

Architecture is like portraiture. The success of a portrait lies not only in the artist's capacity for self-expression, but also in the artist's ability to express the subject. Portraiture is more than its mere appearance, it captures the character and soul of the subject, the site, or the program. Architecture as portraiture bares the bones of the structure, and celebrates the marvel of human flows to reveal the hidden spectacle and future potential.

The world has become so used to the segregation of form and content, of hardware vs. software. Architecture has become like the iPhone—an empty container, a boring box—that comes to life only once you insert a program. We have all experienced a construction site that looks more exciting than the final work, like the cookie dough tasting better than the cookie—the concrete skeleton, the filigree of studs, the X-ray through the unfinished structure revealing proximities and relationships—that only disappear after the final finishes are applied and the paint is dry.

By exposing what happens inside—like revealing the inner mechanisms of a clock—performance becomes form, and surface reveals underlying depth. We want to give the gift of exposing the life, energy, and movement inside a building on its outside. Let's show the personality of the inhabitants by rearranging their homes around their lifestyles. Let's turn the content of the building into its form. Let's express where working becomes living. Let's reveal that all high-rises are like Matryoshkas of towers nested within each other, the concrete core hidden within a glass container. Let's celebrate the vertigo of vertical movement in the middle of a city.

The world is one giant urban laboratory. Eight billion people experimenting everyday how to best live their lives. Let's resist fitting that life into a universal mold—a one-size-fits-all solution by perpetuating preconceived notions of what the world should look like, like the angry infant hammering a round peg into a square hole. We have the vision to see life as it is and as it evolves, and to show it in the most blatant way possible. To turn practicalities into poetry. To create the extraordinary out of the ordinary.

MUSÉE ATELIER AUDEMARS PIGUET

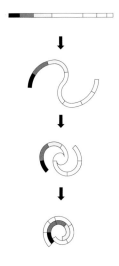

Like architecture, watchmaking is the art and science of giving inanimate matter intelligence and performance. The museum for the watchmaker Audemars Piguet on the site of the company's historic manufacturer is inspired by the convergence of form and content in clockwork. It is conceived like the coils of a watch, ticking and advancing in perpetuity like the gallery visitors and watchmakers moving cyclically within the structure. Every element is governed by the functional requirements of the exhibition, while appearing as a striking sculpture conceived in a single gesture. We turned the galleries into a chronological journey, creating a double spiral with the largest galleries in the middle that then unwind. With the materials, we've done more with less, taking tips from the art of watchmaking: miniaturization, making the elements as small as possible; skeletonization, excavating or subtracting all the unused material, so the object becomes like a wireframe; and complication, loading as many functions as possible in the smallest amount of space. We eliminated all of the columns so that the roof is carried by glass, like a spring hovering overhead. The resultant architecture is a land-based spiral jetty, a coil of grass on the meadows of the valley. An architecture in which the form is inseparable from its content, exposed like the gears and springs in a skeletonized open work.

Le Brassus, SWITZERLAND
3,000 M² | Culture
2020

IWAN BAAN

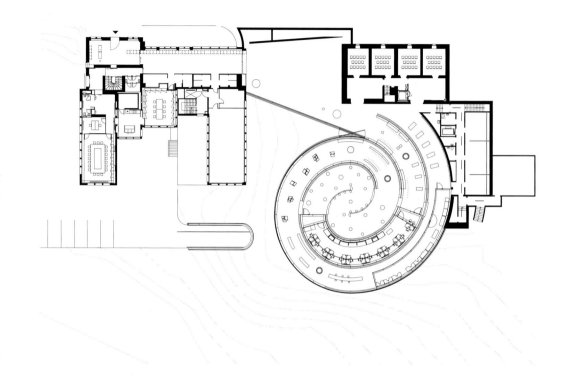

ground floor plan

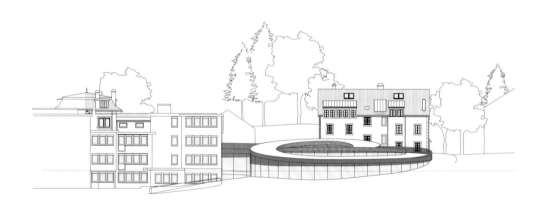

north elevation

0   5   10   25M

IWAN BAAN

OLAF ROHL

OLAF ROHL

OLAF ROHL

IWAN BAAN

IWAN BAAN

ALEX FILZ

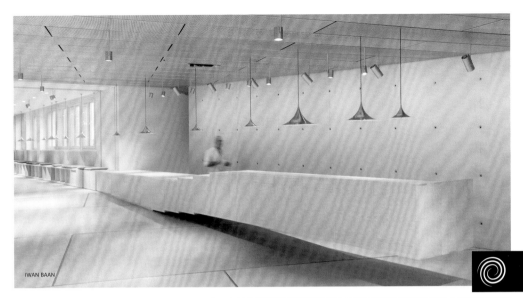

IWAN BAAN

IWAN BAAN

ALEX FILZ

IWAN BAAN

IWAN BAAN

HÔTEL DES HORLOGERS

As the design of the museum advanced, it became evident that we had to redesign the hotel for the visitors of Audemars Piguet. The site of the hotel is located along the longest cross-country ski route of the Jura Mountains in Switzerland. We thought the hotel, like the museum, could become part of the valley. Rather than standing out as a five-story structure, we opened all of the amenities and rooms to the landscape, creating a human-made extension of the natural ski path. The hotel is comprised of five zigzagging slabs that expand into a gently sloping exterior path. A continuous sloping corridor continues on the interior, allowing the staff to reach every room on a single descent. The amenities are tucked under the inclined slabs and oriented toward the light and views of the environment. From the main access road, the stepping slabs frame views of the serene landscape, retaining the connection between the village and the pastoral landscape.

Le Brassus, SWITZERLAND
7,000 M² | Commercial
2021

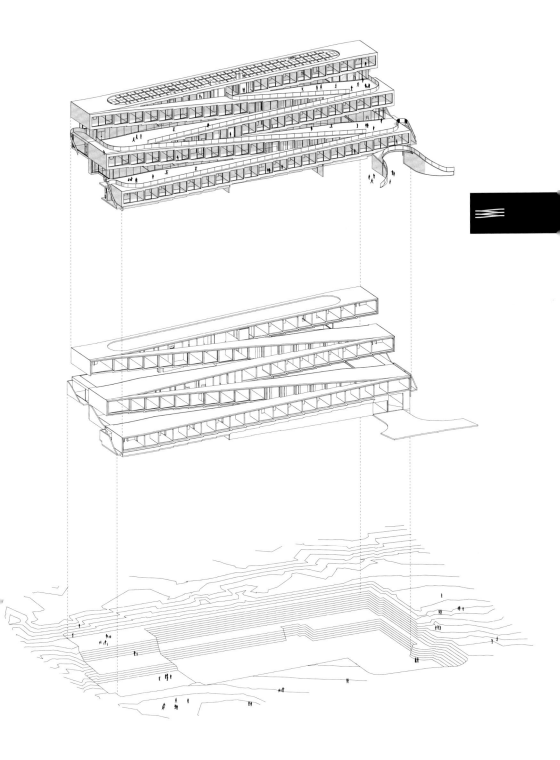

exploded axonometric

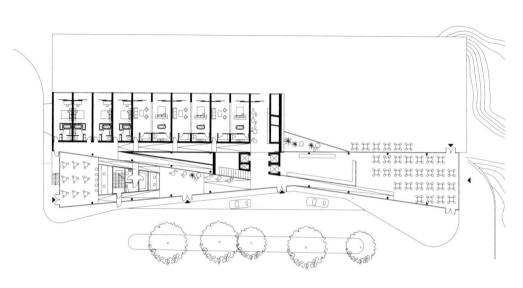

ground floor plan

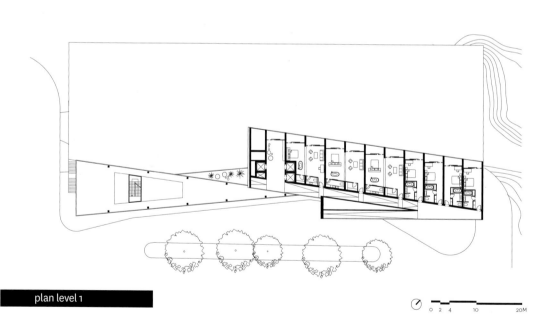

plan level 1

0 2 4   10   20M

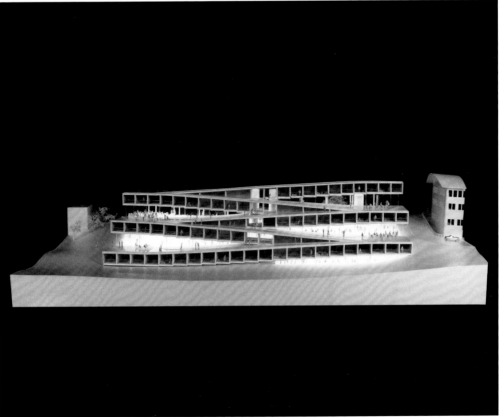

TELUS SKY

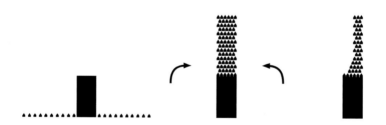

Downtown Calgary has developed as a typical North American city center with a cluster of corporate towers surrounded by low-density suburban homes. The best of two building types, Telus Sky is designed to seamlessly accommodate the transition from working to living as the tower takes off from the ground to reach the sky. The base and lower floors of the mixed-use tower are clean and rectangular, resulting in large efficient layouts for workspace. As the building rises, the floor plates gradually reduce in size, stepping back to provide slender residential floor plates with nested balconies. In a similar fashion, the texture of the façade evolves from smooth glass at the base of the building to a three-dimensional composition of protrusions and recesses. The resultant form expresses the unification of the two programs in a single gesture—rational straight lines composed to form a feminine silhouette. Surrounded by blocky skyscrapers occupied by petroleum companies, Telus stands like a lady in a cluster of cowboys.

Calgary, CANADA
70,725 M² | Commercial
2020

EMA PETER

EMA PETER

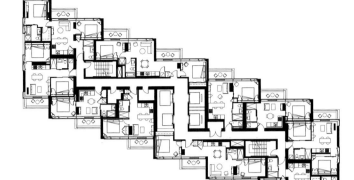

plan level 45

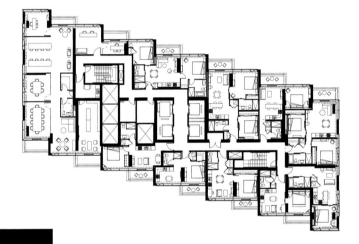

plan level 31

plan level 22

0   5   10   20M

EMA PETER

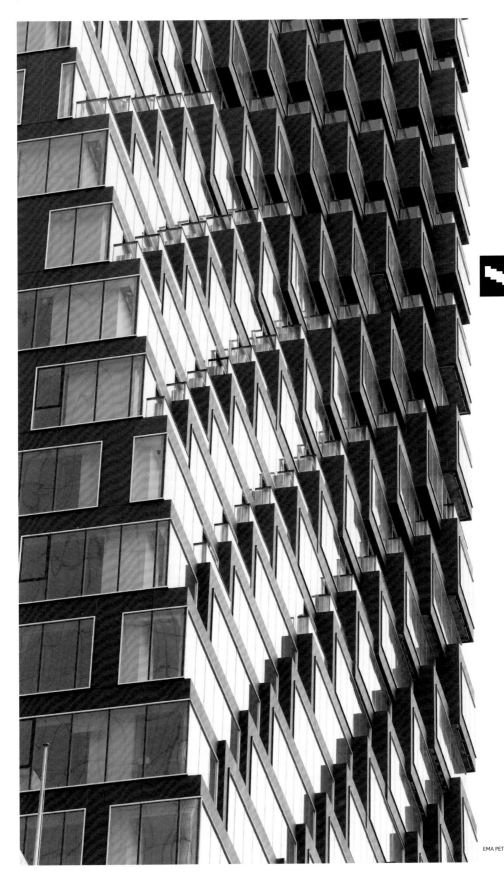

EMA PETER

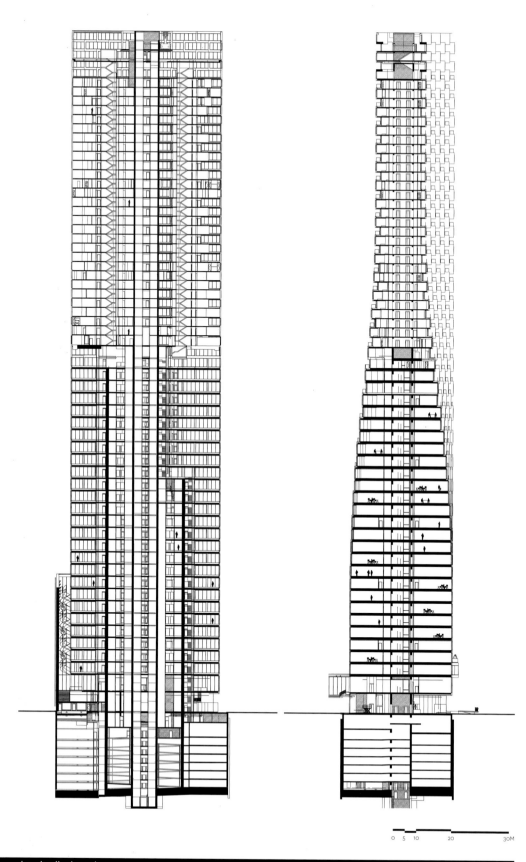

0 5 10   20   30M

longitudinal section   cross section

EMA PETER

EMA PETER

EMA PETER

OMNITURM

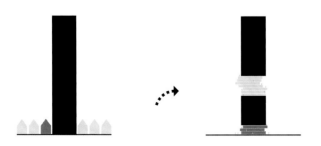

Frankfurt is the financial engine of Germany and one of the few European Cities to boast a Central Business District of high-rises ascending above the typical European perimeter blocks. People live in the low-rises and work in the high-rises. Omniturm attempts to bring mixed-use to the vertical dimension. Located at the first intersection in mainland Europe with a tower in each corner, it contains three types of tenants. The lower half is a large floor plate for creative workspaces; the upper half is a boutique floor plate for corporate clients. Sandwiched between the two is a stack of homes, shifting and sliding under the weight of the building above. The overhangs and indentations create outdoor terraces extending the life of the residents into the urban canyon of downtown Frankfurt. The result is a seemingly classic corporate silhouette of a tower that seems to wiggle to life at its waistline. A kick of the hip indicating mixed-use has come to town.

Frankfurt, GERMANY
70,000 M² | Commercial
2020

HABIB KARIMOV

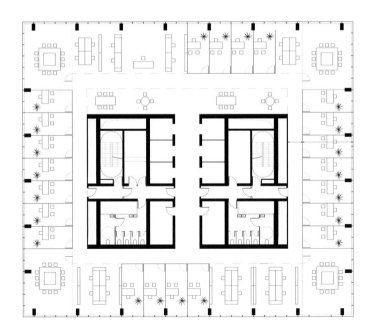

office plan

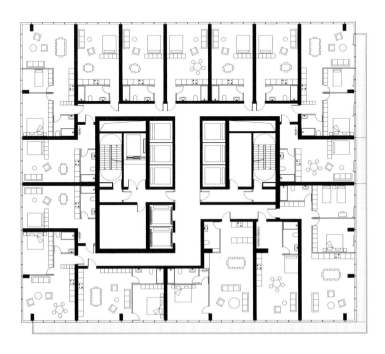

residential plan with shifted terrace

0 1 2   5   10   15M

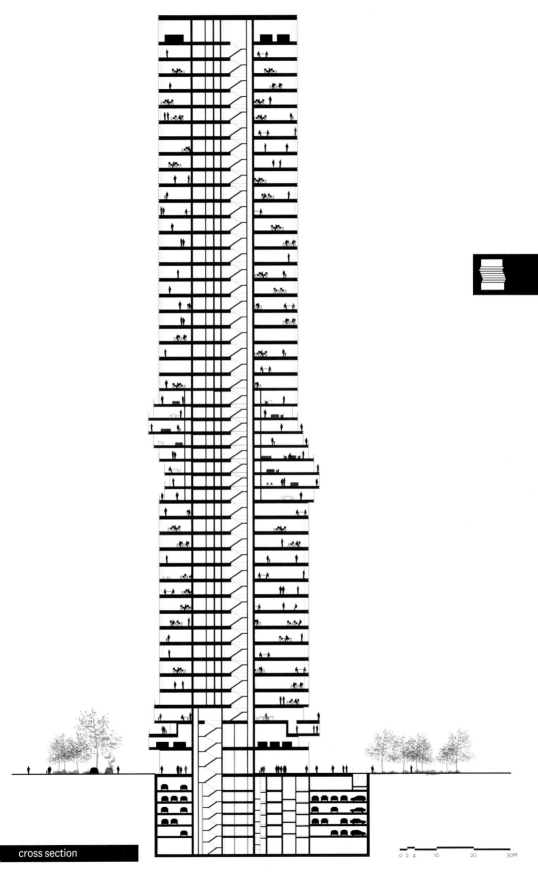

cross section

0 2 4   10   20   30M

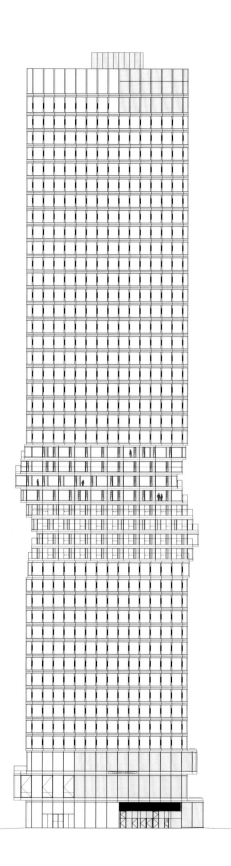

south elevation

0 2 4   10   20   30M

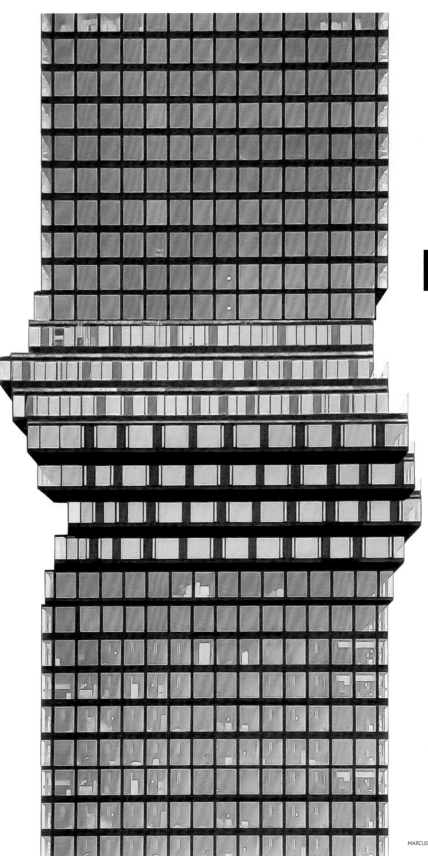

MARCUS WAGNER

NILS KOENNING

NILS KOENNING

NILS KOENNING

NILS KOENNING

NILS KOENNING

MARBLE COLLEGIATE CHURCH TOWER

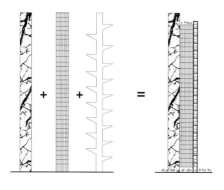

The dense mid-block site in Manhattan's NoMad neighborhood tormented by holdouts resulted in an irregular footprint precluding the conventional rectangular extrusion. We decided to split the typical tower into the three basic programmatic requirements: one tower for circulation, one for work, and one for nature. Each tower is tailored to its unique program. The work tower is a crystal volume with four meter floor-to-ceiling glass, column-free corners, and an open plan maximizing freedom and flexibility, daylight and views. To one side, a single egress stair constitutes a kind of stem from which petals of terraces cantilever to form a staggered pillar of hanging gardens. The circulation core condenses stairs and elevators, mechanical rooms and bathrooms into a freestanding marble monolith. Giant polished precast panels of 3x8.5M in white concrete are rippled in irregular patterns to compose the texture of a gargantuan block of marble. Like a 305M-tall Oldenburg among the skyscrapers of midtown Manhattan. Rather than forcing all the towers and all of their programs within into a single form, the bundle of towers allows each of them to express its true nature in the most blatant and powerful way. A dynamic and diverse trio rather than a sedated solo.

New York, USA
6,500 M²
Residential

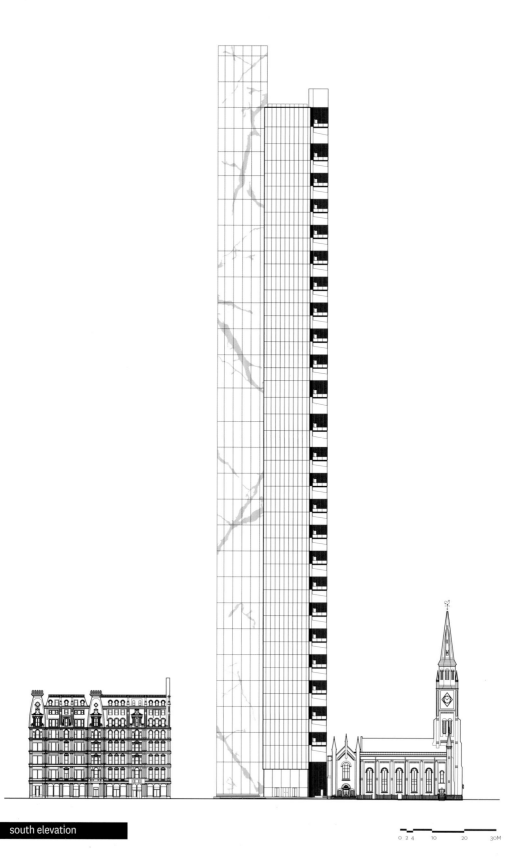

south elevation

0 2 4   10   20   30M

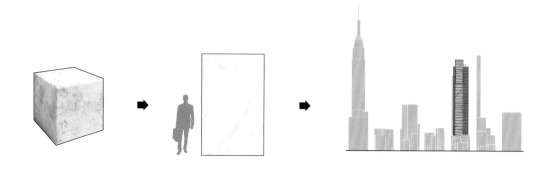

material concept	façade stone panel	marble pattern city scale

marble	pattern extraction	pattern applied to precast concret

UNION CENTER

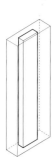  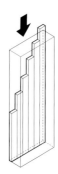

Union Center is a tower without a site. It rises above Station Street, straddling across the right-of-way to allow the steady flow of people and vehicles to pass unobstructed underneath. As a consequence, the banks of elevators that traditionally constitute the central core have been evicted to the perimeter of the building, freeing up the floor plates for maximum internal connectivity and openness. Since the elevator banks are now the actual façade, both elevators and shafts are clad in glass forming a kind of double glass façade for the vertical flow of people from the street to the roof. Sitting at your desk you might see a bird or a plane or a cab full of people pass by. The typical cascading elevator diagram where each bank of elevators reaches a certain group of floors, is now expressed openly on the façade like a giant glass stair of vertical circulation. At night the lit elevator cabins become a vertical pulse riding up and down the curtainwall. Suspended above Station Street, a major concert venue takes advantage of the open floor plate. Above, a pixelated park of tiered terraces forms the city's largest roof garden on the top of town.

Toronto, CANADA
118,707 M²
Mixed-Use

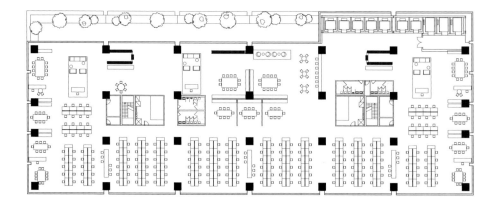

high-rise plan

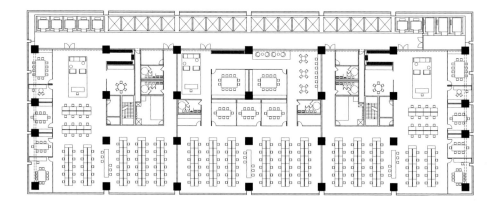

low-rise plan

0 1 2   5   10   15M

THE RESPONSE

Modernism was obsessed with the tabula rasa as the point of departure. The clean slate. Starting from scratch. As its opposite we have contextualism, driven by the firm belief that the context dictates what and how we build. Essentially that the future should be dictated by the past. The former involves an almost catastrophic erasure of history; the latter confines the future to a straitjacket of the past. Architecture must always respond to existing conditions—the culture, the climate, the landscape, the city. Responsive architecture responds to its surroundings like an answer to a question in a conversation. Rather than mimicking what is already there, but responding to it, we can elevate the context while inheriting forms that would be difficult and unnecessary for us to explore on a blank canvas.

Responsive architecture twists and turns in answer to the complexity of a three-dimensional urban context. It captures the transient sand formations in natural dunes. It turns balconies into human aquariums mirroring the Bahamian waterscape. It melts into rock formations. It reacts to the prevailing winds and the arc of the sun. By responding to climatic conditions, the otherwise invisible context of sunrays and thermal flows, responsive architecture can turn performance into form. Rippled façades minimize thermal exposure and glare. Parametric patterns of organic striations bend and turn to counter the incoming sunrays. By ignoring our context and climate, we miss the opportunity for architectural dialogue. By responding to it we turn nature into culture by making the natural forces visible to the human eye. The future is not found in an abstract laboratory, but right here in the concrete conditions of the actual conditions. The city of tomorrow is already here—all we have to do is respond responsibly in order to continue the architectural conversation toward the future.

SHENZHEN ENERGY HQ

The skyscraper has evolved as an economically efficient way to provide flexible, functional floorspace for dense populations. Originally powered by abundant energy for AC and ventilation, today the skyscraper must evolve into a new sustainable species. The Shenzhen Energy HQ is our first realized example of "engineering without engines"—the idea that we can engineer the dependence on machinery out of our buildings and let the architecture perform in its place. The zoning dictates the volume as two connected towers of 110 and 220M, leaving the façade as the only element left to design. For a 100,000M² workplace in a humid subtropical climate, the main challenge for the envelope is to resolve the dilemma of how to maximize daylight and views while minimizing thermal exposure and glare. A rippled façade undulates like an Issey Miyake fabric. The zigzag pattern alternates between open and closed. The orientation that gets the most sunlight is opaque; the one that gets the least is transparent. Without any active technology, purely based on the geometry of the façade, this reduces the overall energy consumption of cooling by 30 percent. Sustainability with positive aesthetic side effects.

Shenzhen, CHINA
96,000 M² | Commercial
2018

CHAO ZHANG

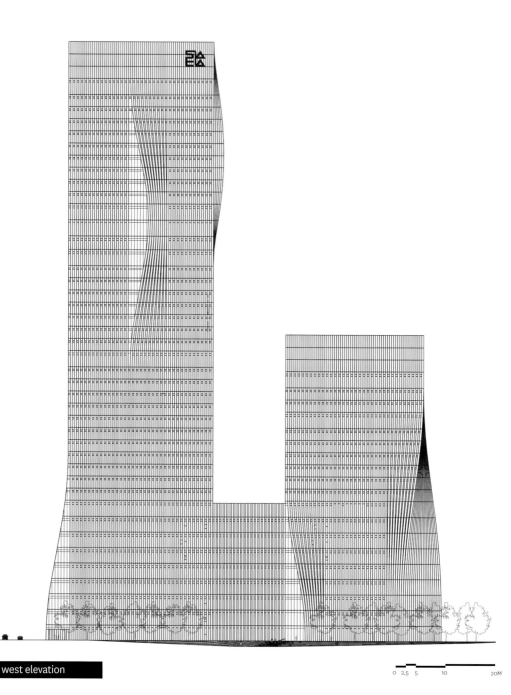

west elevation

0 2,5 5   10   20M

CHAO ZHANG

159

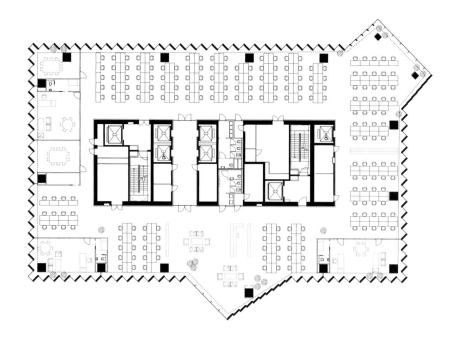

plan level 35

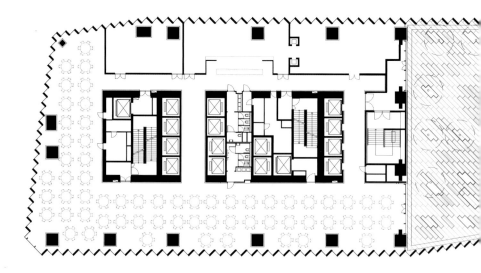

plan level 7

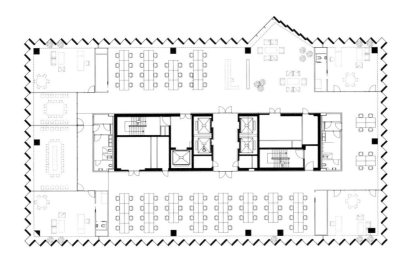

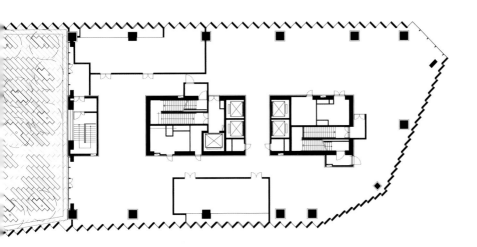

0   2.5   5   10   20M

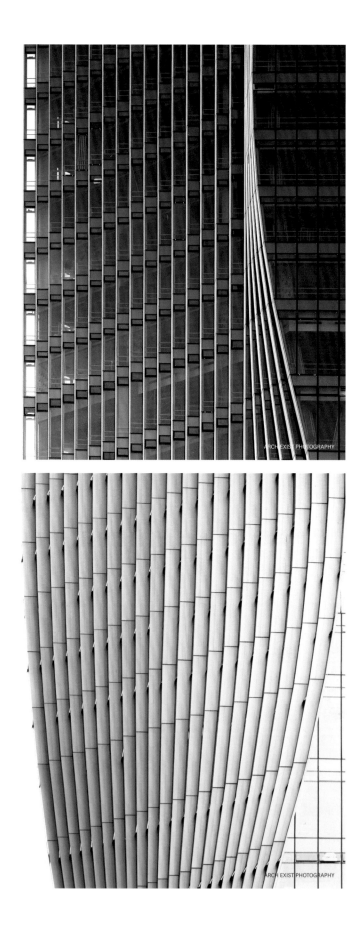

CHAO ZHANG

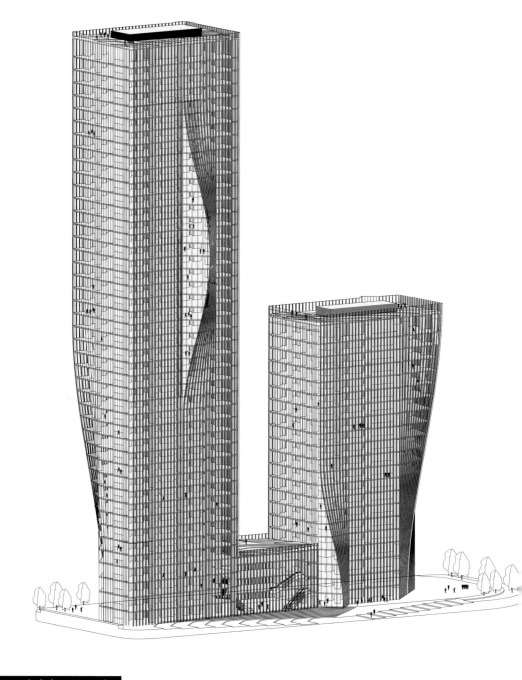

exploded axonometric

CHAO ZHANG

LAURIAN GHINITOIU

THE XI

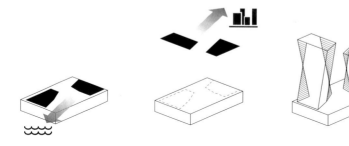

The Eleventh is located along the High Line neighboring a cluster of buildings by Frank Gehry, Jean Nouvel, and Shigeru Ban, among others. Two towers rise from the dense urban context to find unobstructed views in all directions. The responding design is two different configurations merged from top to bottom: One at the base proportioned to open views toward the river— the other at the top reoriented to give views across the High Line. The two configurations are connected as they rise from the ground to the sky, morphing from one layout to the other. The sloping façades on each tower open up and allow light and air to descend into the pocket park of the courtyard. The elevations are a blatant expression of the structural grid, stepping to follow the movement of the towers' geometry. The sculptural form is a direct response to the site's historic industrial heritage and contemporary architecture. It is the means, not the end. The resulting architecture merges the past and present of Chelsea into a new hybrid identity.

New York City, USA
83,000 M² | Mixed-Use
2020

DBOX

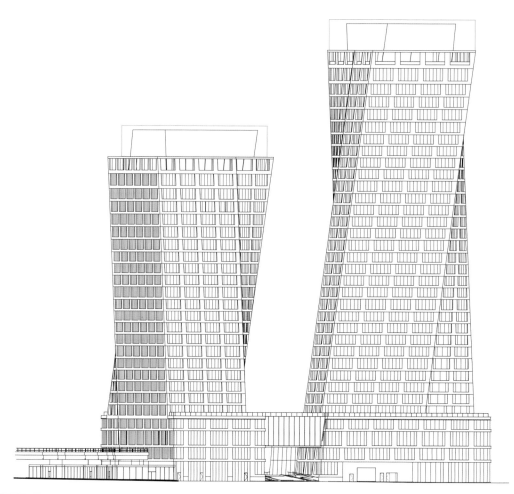

north elevation

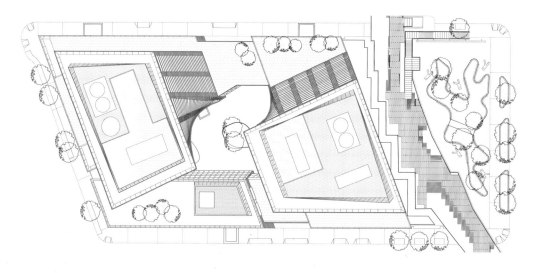

rooftop plan

0 2 4   10   20   30M

CHRIS COE

DBOX

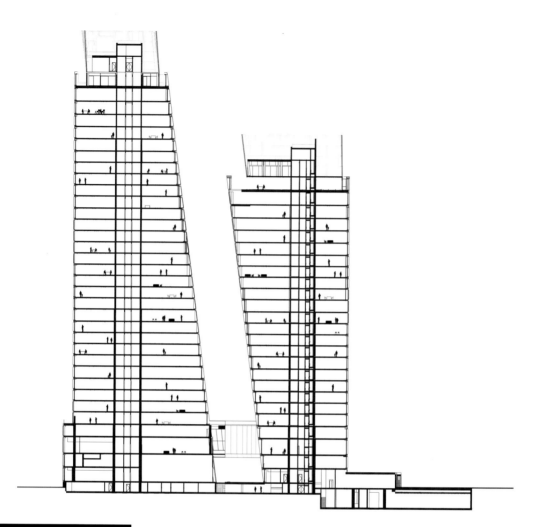

east-west section

plan level 5

0 2 4   10   20   30M

DBOX

THE HONEYCOMB
& THE SANCTUARY

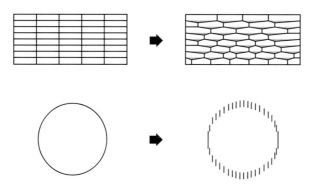

The Honeycomb is designed in response to the Bahamian lifestyle. Each home has a giant balcony forming an outdoor living room with a summer kitchen and a pool sunken into the floor. The floor slab dips down to accommodate the body of water. The weight of the water is carried by the four meter high partition wall between the homes below serving as a room-high concrete beam. The fourth wall of the pools is made from acrylic aquarium glass. Swimmers become fully immersed in the view of the marina like a human aquarium. The resultant façade, composed of interlocking hexagonal pools, appears like a giant beehive. At its base the Sanctuary is a recording studio designed in response to the requirements of light and sound. The striated volume appears like a rippled seashell made from parallel walls facing east and west to block the low incoming sunrays, while opening up toward the Marina and the private garden. The undulating roof is made from tilted slabs ensuring that there are no parallel surfaces between floor and ceiling. The resultant elevation appears like parallel columns of light like the digital display of an equalizer.

Nassau, THE BAHAMAS
21,000 M² | Mixed-Use
2020

JAKOB LANGE

plan level 4

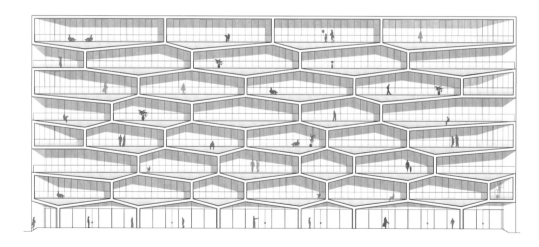

south elevation

0 1 2   5   10   15M

GOLDEN DUSK PHOTOGRAPHY

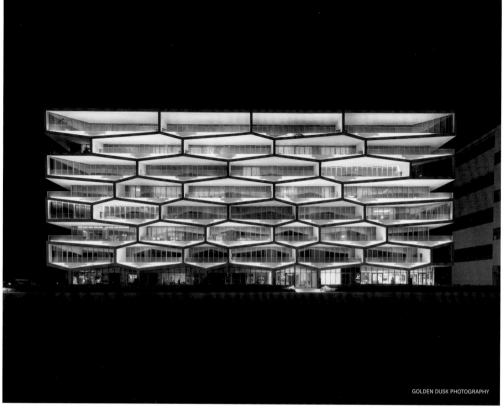

GOLDEN DUSK PHOTOGRAPHY

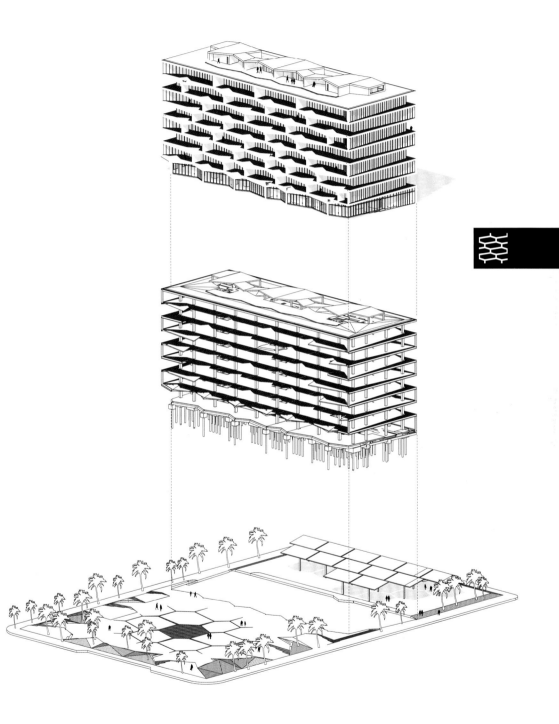

exploded axonometric

HUFTON – CROW

HUFTON + CROW

CHERYL FLEMMING | JAMES LANE

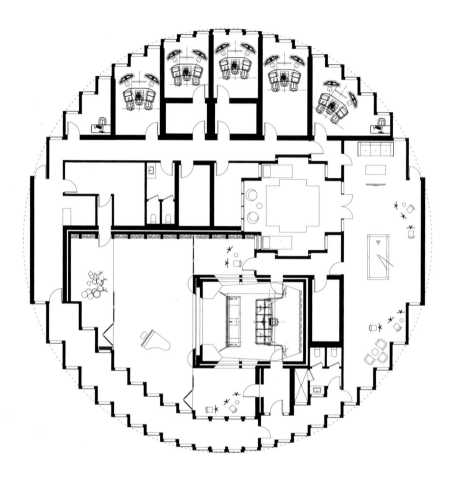

recording studio plan

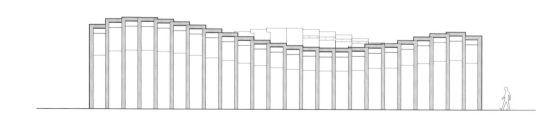

recording studio elevation

0 1 2   5   10M

CHERYL FLEMMING | JAMES LANE

CHERYL FLEMMING | JAMES LANE

CHERYL FLEMMING | JAMES LANE

CHERYL FLEMMING | JAMES LANE

VANCOUVER HOUSE

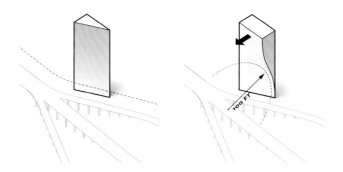

Vancouver House is located at the main entrance to Vancouver right where Granville bridge *triforks when it reaches downtown. The resulting triangular slices of land had remained undeveloped until now. We started by mapping the constraints: setbacks from the streets and the bridges, including a 30M setback from the bridge, to ensure that no one lives right next to traffic. A neighboring park should be protected from shadows. After all the constraints, we were finally left with a tiny triangle nearly too small to build. But if the 30M separation is a minimum distance, then once we get 30M up in the air the building can grow back out and we can double the floor plate. And so we did. The expanding silhouette appears as if someone is drawing a curtain aside, welcoming visitors to Vancouver. Underneath the bridge, we have worked with Vancouver artist Rodney Graham to create what we have nicknamed the Sistine Chapel of street art: an art gallery turned upside down, including his gigantic Spinning Chandelier suspended above the street. This inverse art gallery turns the negative impact of the bridge into a positive. As you see the Vancouver House emerging from the ground, expanding as it rises, it appears like a Genie let out of the bottle. What seems like a surreal gesture is in fact a highly responsive architecture—shaped by its environment.*

Vancouver, CANADA
60,600 M² | Housing
2020

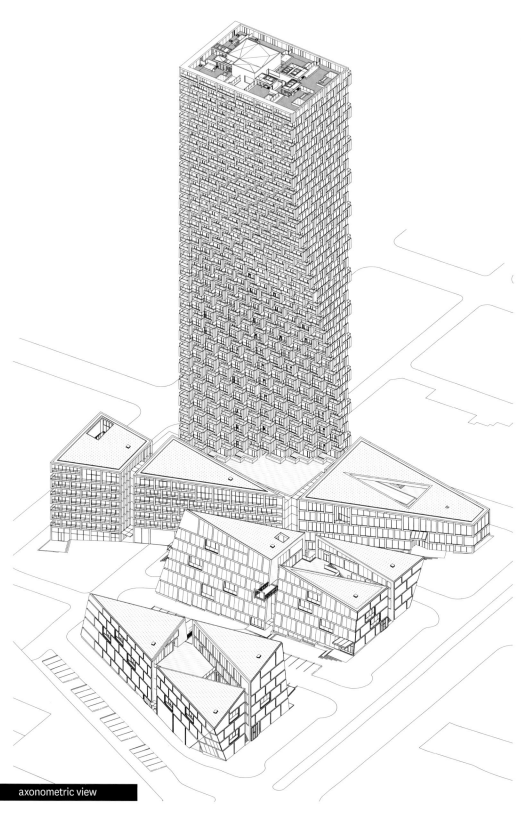

axonometric view

EMA PETER

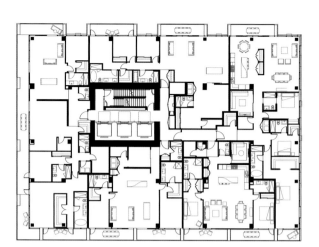

plan level 29

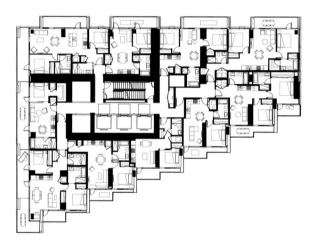

plan level 13

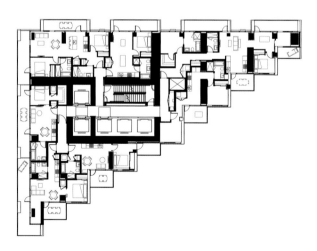

plan level 5

0 1 2   5   10   15M

EMA PETER

EMA PETER

EMA PETER

EMA PETER

RON FRIESEN

GLENN SANTIAGO

LYCIUM

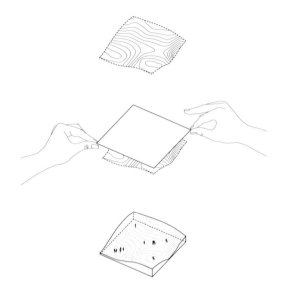

Fanø is a sandy island in the Wadden Sea off the coast of southwestern Denmark. It is known for its infinite sandy beaches and strong westerly winds. The site of Lycium, a small local museum, sits between old villas and a late 1960s prefabricated hotel on a naturally formed, waving sand dune covered with patches of lime grass. The design of the museum is conceived as a literal cast of the dune—a human-made imprint from the natural geological sand formations. The existing terrain is used to form the shell by casting concrete directly on the sand with all its layers including grasses, mosses, and seashells, like an amber sand dune frozen in time. Once the concrete is dry the space is excavated underneath, leaving the thin sheet of frozen beach hovering above. Like a new sand dune vernacular for Fanø, Lycium will appear as if it was always there, shaped by the winds and the water moving sand across centuries.

Fanø Bad, DENMARK
1,100 M²
Culture

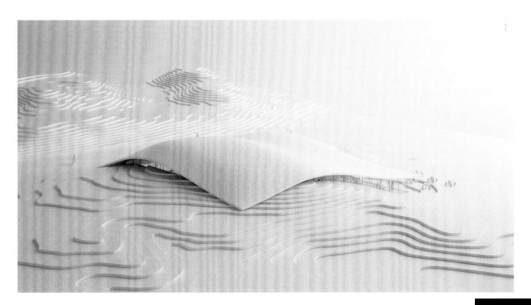

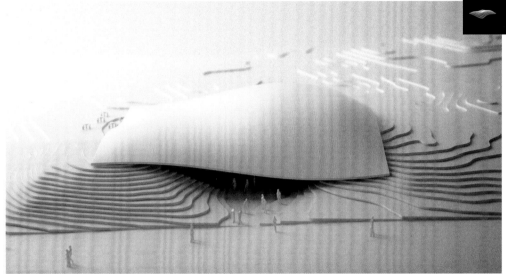

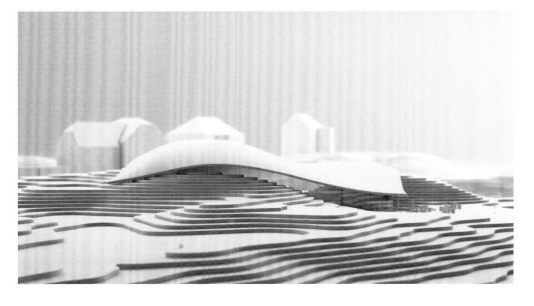

NATIONAL STADIUM OF GREENLAND

Located on a precipice on the rocky shore of Nuuk, the design of the National Stadium is a blatant response to the harsh conditions of the arctic climate. A giant domed roof structure spans the football field to protect the stadium from the elements. The perfect circle of the dome is cropped to a square, leaving only four points to touch the ground. The four corners efficiently and elegantly shed snow, and the shallow aerodynamic form minimizes wind loads. The 4 touchpoints frame massive glass walls with panoramic views of the fjords and mountains, while providing ample covered outdoor space to protect fans on the way to and from the games. Massive cross-laminated timber beams form a coffered ceiling providing a warm welcoming texture to contrast the cool arctic surroundings. Consolidating the 5,000 spectators on the land side allows for an entire side to open up to the fjord. As a visitor to the National Stadium, you will have no doubt you are in Greenland when distracted by the view of an iceberg floating by.

Nuuk, GREENLAND
34,600 M²
Culture

213

REINCARNATION

The only constant in life is change. And as life evolves so must the framework that accommodates it. It is the inescapable destiny of every building to be used for another purpose eventually or simply to be torn down. There is only one way for a building to last forever. It is not by the durability of its materials, although the German bunkers from WW2 along Europe's West Coast come close. But they too will perish. Even the pyramids fall into ruin once the Pharaohs are gone. The only way for a structure to last forever is to remain relevant to its inhabitants. There is a wooden building on the Faroe Islands that has persisted for a thousand years—longer than any of the materials it is made from. By being continually inhabited, loved, and cared for, it prevails. And if the use is discontinued, the love for the structure will inspire the inhabitants to invent new uses for the old frames.

Reincarnation is the gift of breathing new life into old bodies: architecture as radical reinterpretation. No matter how careful an architect designs a building to its brief, it must be open to change to remain in use after the inevitable end of its original purpose. By extending spaces, adding new structures, or reincarnating the original building, we can enable existing structures to evolve with life.

New structures can be tailored for indetermination, to accommodate the maximum number of possible programs. They can be built as a physical framework that inhabitants can download their desired programs onto, just as we do apps on our iPhones. As a gift to the future, the adaptive structure allows transient elements to transform the building, increasing its odds for survival through adaptation—a building that constantly adapts so that the building tomorrow is gently different from the building yesterday. Architecture as the physical platform for human life.

TIRPITZ
MUSEUM

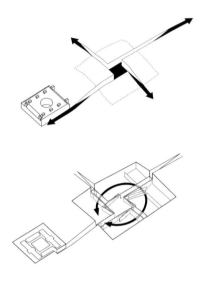

The Tirpitz Museum transforms one of the world's largest Nazi bunkers into an exhibition landscape carved out of the dunes. Working within a nature preserve, the invisible museum nests into the sand like a bas-relief around the bunker. With four precise incisions into the topography, it's the antithesis of the concrete block, and a dramatic counterpoint to the war history of the site. At first, visitors only see the German bunker until they walk along heath-lined paths and descend into a sunken plaza at the heart of the complex. A point of connection is developed between the four institutions housed in the museum, as well as the beginning of an underground umbilical cord leading to the restored bunker. Where the original artillery fortress is an immense structure rejecting its surroundings, the new museum is inviting and open like a bunker in reverse. It becomes an architecture that contrasts new with old, openness with protection, landscape with object, and light with darkness.

Blåvand, DENMARK
2,850 M² | Culture
2017

RASMUS HJORTSHØJ

site plan

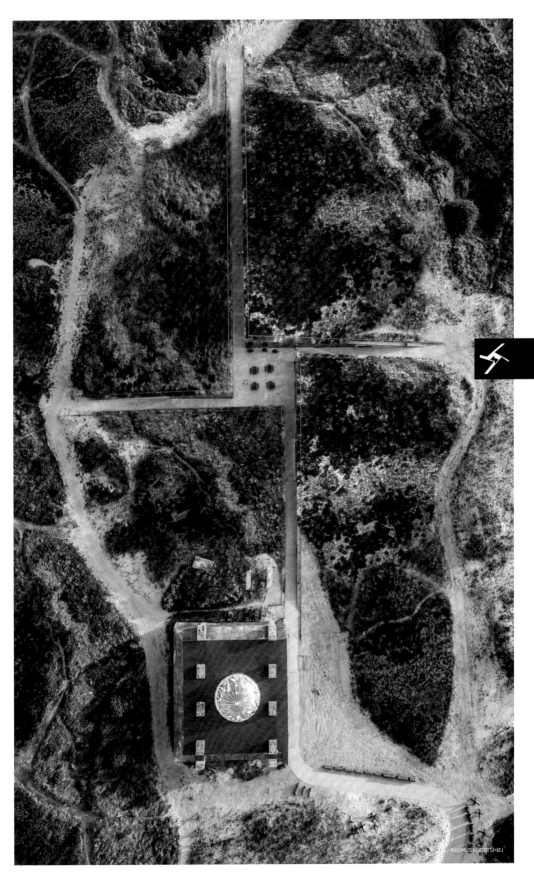

© RASMUS HJORTSHØJ

RASMUS HJORTSHØJ

RASMUS HJORTSHØJ

RASMUS HJORTSHØJ

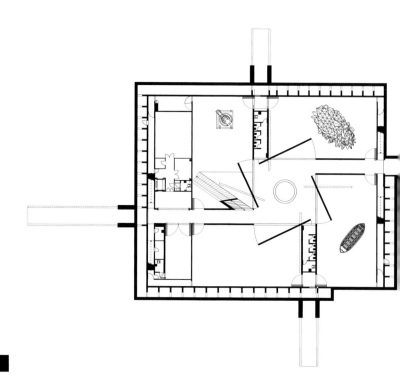

ground floor plan

longitudinal section

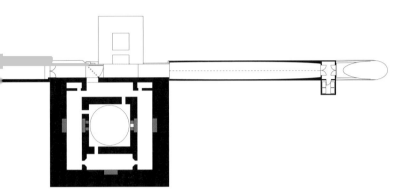

0   5   10   25   50M

RASMUS HJORTSHØJ

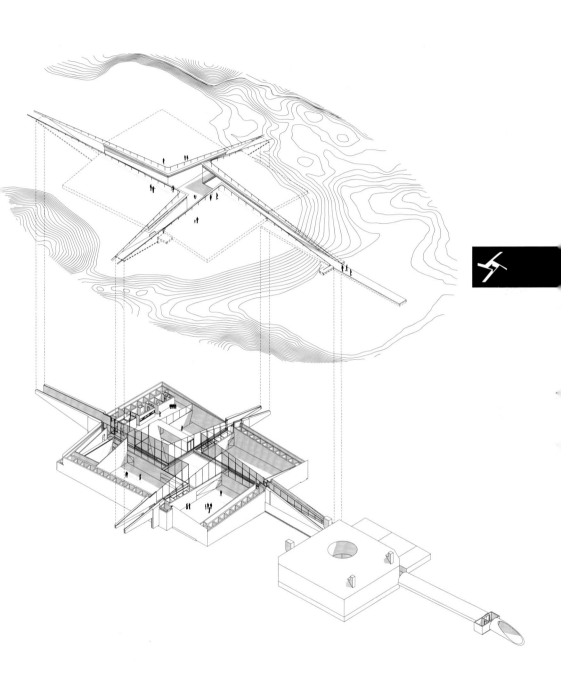

exploded axonometric

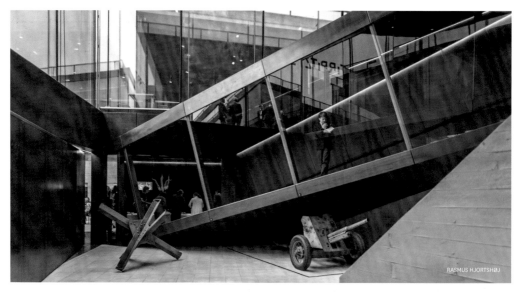
RASMUS HJORTSHØJ

RASMUS HJORTSHØJ

LAURIAN GHINIȚOIU

RASMUS HJORTSHØJ

RASMUS HJORTSHØJ

RASMUS HJORTSHØJ

ISENBERG SCHOOL OF MANAGEMENT

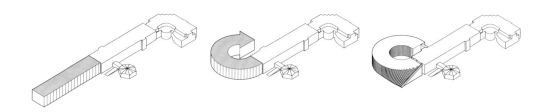

Our addition to the Isenberg School of Management at the University of Massachusetts Amherst extends the school's existing 1964 building from the north and east sides in a wide circular loop. By combining old with new, the addition renews the relevance of the existing building, accommodating the expanding school program with a minimal footprint and a façade that blends with the all-brick campus. The upper floors of the addition and the existing building are connected, consolidating faculty under one roof. The triangular glass entrance creates a singular point of arrival shaped by a domino effect of cascading copper beams. Its distinct appearance is shaped without any curved elements; rather it's wrapped in straight vertical pillars that gradually fall. Daylight enters between the accordion-like pillars to illuminate the multistory interior public space for student gatherings and study, special events and award ceremonies. The courtyard, at its heart, provides a green oasis between the classrooms and faculty space, as well as a new outdoor space for picnics and parties.

Massachusetts, USA
6,500 M² | Education
2019

MAX TOUHEY

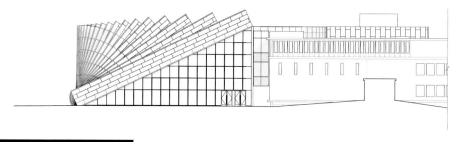

west elevation

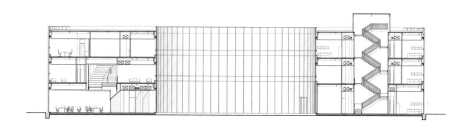

north-south section

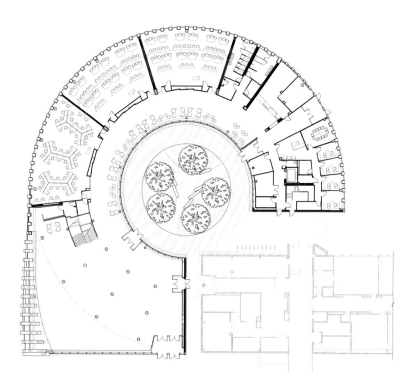

ground floor plan

0 2 4   10   20M

LAURIAN GHINITOIU

MAX TOUHEY

LAURIAN GHINITOIU

MAX TOUHEY

MAX TOUHEY

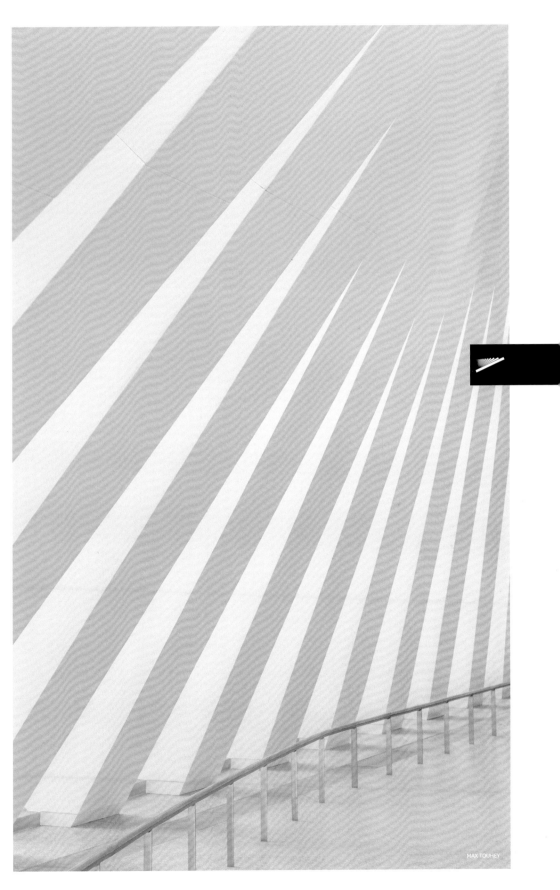

MAX TOUHEY

LAURIAN GHINITOIU

GALERIES LAFAYETTE CHAMPS-ÉLYSÉES

Rather than messing with the old bones and original grandeur of the 1932 Art Deco bank building, the Galleries Lafayette on the Champs-Élysées adapts to the 21st century by operating at the scale of furniture. When we inherited the space, most of the original Art Deco elements were covered with black-painted drywall. The cupola was hidden behind sheetrock and there were no connections to the Avenue des Champs-Élysées. Today shoppers enter a glowing bridge into the heart of the building: a circular atrium covered by a monumental glass cupola. The entire store unfolds on the ground floor and creates an illuminated urban living room for cultural events and fashion shows. A continuous golden ring of perforated metal wraps around the columns to create a series of rooms and alcoves situated toward the central atrium. A grand staircase, which doubles as an auditorium, takes visitors to spaces shaped by a family of flexible pavilions that can transform over time. As online retail undermines the monopoly of physical space for transaction, the renewed relevance of retail becomes its quality as a public space for people to enjoy and to meet. To be a good retailer, you have to become a great urbanist.

Paris, FRANCE
6,800 M² | Commercial
2019

FLORENT MICHEL

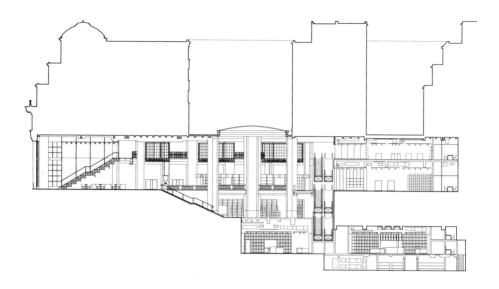

longitudinal section

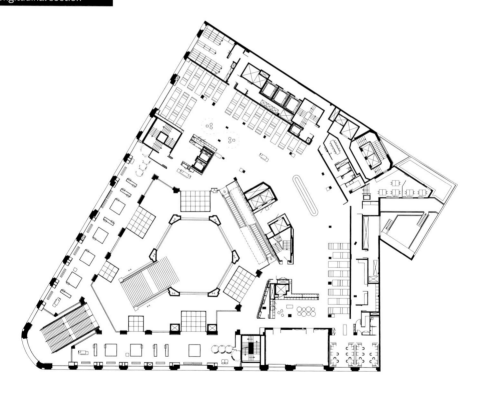

plan level 1

0 2 4   10   20M

FLORENT MICHEL

DSL STUDIO

FLORENT MICHEL

FLORENT MICHEL

FLORENT MICHEL

FLORENT MICHEL

FLORENT MICHEL

FLORENT MICHEL

FLORENT MICHEL

GALERIES LAFAYETTE CHAMPS ELYSEES

DIOR

SALEM MOSTEFAOUI

SALEM MOSTEFAOUI

TRANSITLAGER

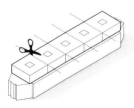

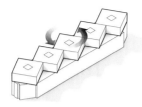

Situated next to the Herzog de Meuron Foundation and the Academy of Art and Design FHNW, Transitlager is part of a larger redevelopment of a new arts district in Basel, Dreispitz. The neighborhood is characterized by weaving geometries of infrastructure: intersecting railways, loading docks, and a puzzle of linear buildings with sharp edges and staggered façade lines. The former concrete warehouse is reborn as the pedestal for an elevated structure of steel and fiberglass. Like opposite twins, both the old and the new are the same size, born out of the same structural grid, but they assume different massing, geometry, and scales of use. One is straight, the other zigzagged; one is singular, the other is serial; one is open and flexible, the other bespoke; public contrasts private; and vibrant urban spaces complement private gardens.

TRANSIT
LAGER

LAURIAN GHINITOIU

LAURIAN GHINITOIU

LAURIAN GHINITOIU

LAURIAN GHINITOIU

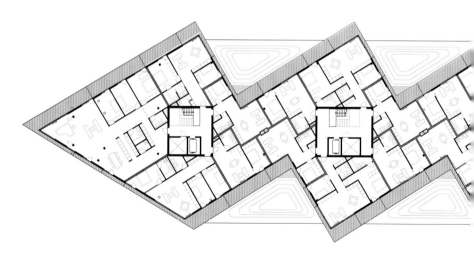

plan level 5

MARIS MEZULIS

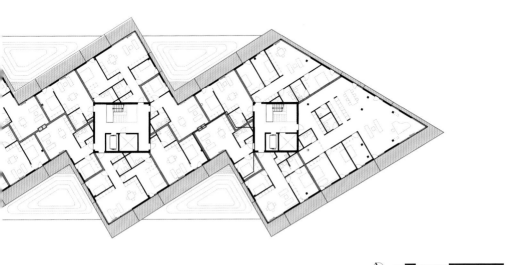

0 2 4   10   20M

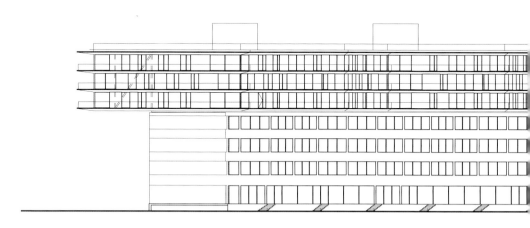

longitudinal section

LAURIAN GHINITOIU

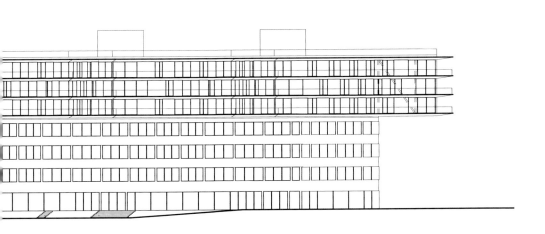

0 2 4   10   20M

THE SMILE

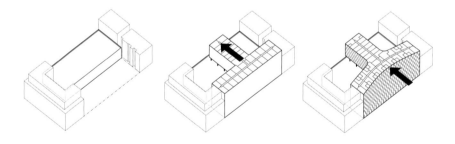

The Smile breathes new life into an area in dire need of housing by wrapping a layer of homes around an existing commercial structure. Conceived like an infill and overlay, between and on top of the existing neighbors, the architecture is shaped by the character, rules, and regulations of the neighborhood. Toward 126th street the street wall requirements dictate a phantom façade with a dormer defined as a certain percentage of the overall volume. By turning the rules inside out we ended up with a drape, that seems to sag inwards as it spans from neighbor to neighbor. The catenary inclination creates a crescent smile in silhouette against the Harlem sky. As the homes rise above and beyond the commercial neighbor building they jump the fence toward 125th street to capture the views and sunlight from the south. The interlocking façade elements of glass and steel works like the bracelet of a wristwatch, allowing a chain of identical elements to describe a soft organic geometry. Within, a raw industrial palette of materials is contrasted by explosions of Caribbean colors.

New York City, USA
25,600 M² | Housing
2020

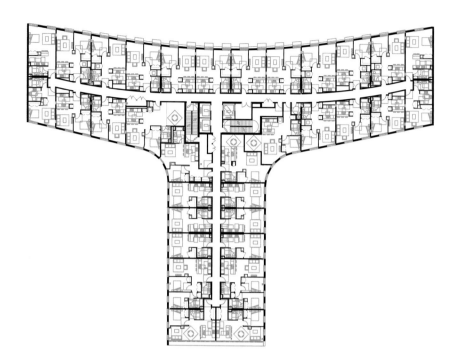

plan level 7

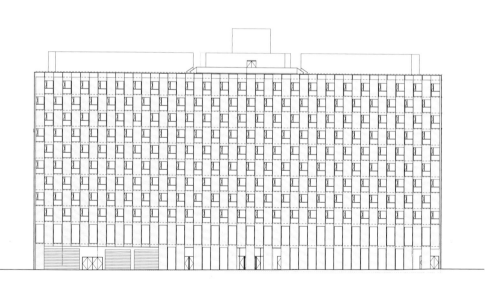

north elevation

3 XEMENEIES

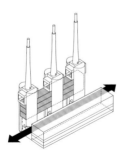 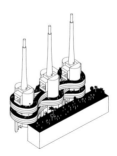

3 Xemeneies is a former steam power plant that was constructed 50 years ago in Barcelona, and stands as a monument to its outdated technology. Once the plant was retired, the remaining three chimneys and turbine hall became a local cultural landmark. The three chimneys still standing remain the tallest structures in the region and are undeniable icons in search of new symbolism and significance. Our proposal preserves the sculptural beauty of the three chimneys by wrapping the new programs around them like vines around tree trunks. Lifted above the ground, they allow a new pedestrian promenade to pass through and under the majestic structure—replacing the flow of steam with the footfall of people.

Barcelona, SPAIN
60,000 M²
Mixed-Use

670 MESQUIT

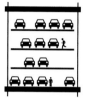

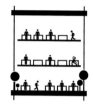
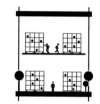

The Arts District in Los Angeles is experiencing a rapid renaissance, drawing creatives from fine arts to engineering. We asked ourselves if we could renew the Arts District by embracing rather than replacing the qualities that have spawned this unique urban culture. 670 Mesquit is one step toward a future when we will design buildings that are made to adapt and evolve with life from day one. Located along the Los Angeles River, the complex consists of two connected 30-story buildings organized on a grid of concrete cubes measuring 14M on each side. Like a flexible framework, the project operates on two scales: the big bare bones of the buildings and the human-scale completion for its individual inhabitants. The freedom of the warehouse loft meets the individual customization of the stick-built case-study house. The large size of the modules allows interior spaces to be subdivided based on program types and tenant needs. The structure is filled with secondary, lighter volumes of two to four levels, occasionally spilling out to inhabit roofs and sundecks. The coexistence of the two scales—the industrial and the human—the warehouse and the case-study house—turns the ancient dilemma between the generic and the specific inside out. The flexibility and freedom of the framework becomes the unique character of the structure. By turning the interior fit-outs into the exterior finishes, the diversity and indeterminacy of the structure becomes its signature identity.

Los Angeles, USA
240,000 M²
Mixed-Use

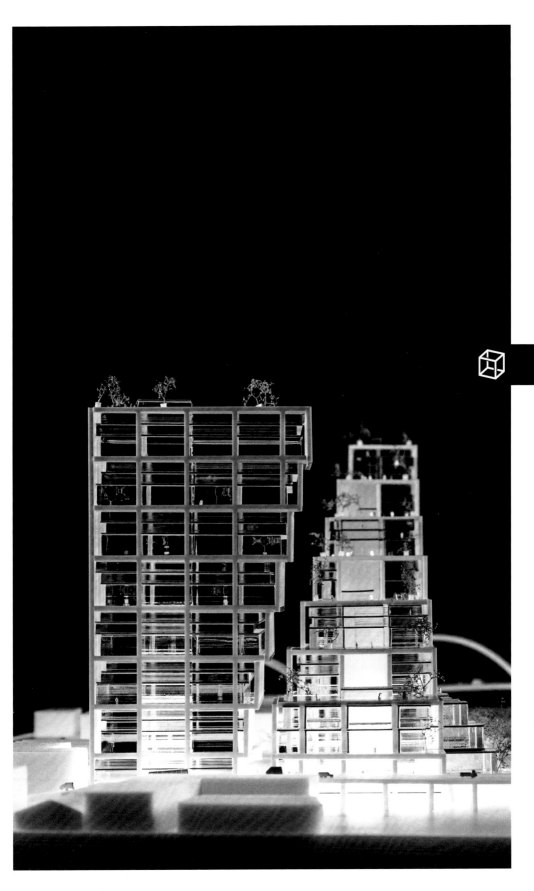

S. PELLEGRINO FLAGSHIP FACTORY

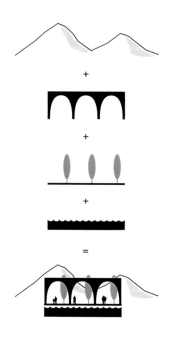

The new San Pellegrino Factory in the heart of Bergamo is an authentic extension of the rational and functional architecture of the existing factory where the natural mineral water has been bottled since 1899. We've imagined the extension as the aquatic equivalent of a wine cellar: light, transparent, fresh, natural. Like the mineral water itself, the Factory will appear to spring from its natural source, rather than imposing a new identity on the existing complex. This creates a seamless continuity between the environment of production and consumption, preparation and enjoyment. Visitors and employees will walk through vaults and covered tunnels that frame the history and heritage of San Pellegrino. Combining the modular architecture of the factory with the repetitive elements of Italian Classicism and Rationalism, the architecture sculpts space by expanding and contracting the span of the arches that constitute its framework. The seriality of the arches sets up views to the surrounding landscape from the snowcapped summit to the running river at its base, recounting the 30-year journey of the mineral water as it descends from the glaciers to the source.

San Pellegrino Terme, ITALY
16,300 M² | Commercial
2021

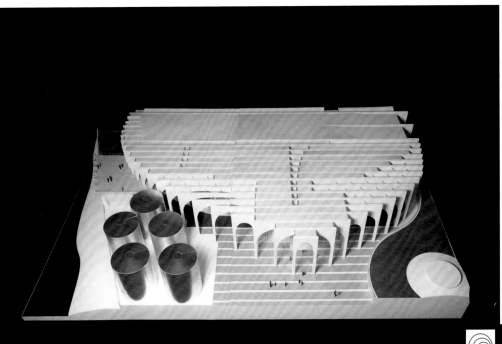

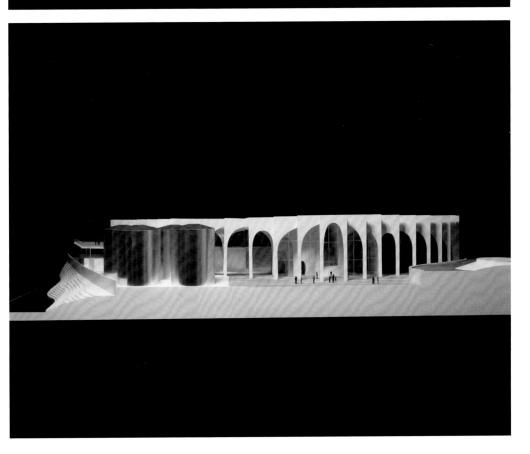

THE Z-AXIS

Planning is a two-dimensional exercise for designing public space. Its etymological roots come from the notion of leveling a plane. But the city is inherently three-dimensional. The Nolli Map is a legendary depiction of Rome that didn't make the traditional distinction between inside and outside, but rather between public and private. Church halls, market halls, and city halls were shown as public, creating an awareness that the public realm extended under roofs and behind façades. By extending the Nolli Map into the third dimension, we can expand our thinking from planning to spacing, transporting shared spaces from the ground floor to destinations up and down the Z-axis.

The traditional planning tools of axis, diagonals, sight lines, portals, porticos, and passages are extended to include ramps and rooftops, spirals and springs, topographies and platforms, ledges and outlooks. By adding the third dimension, architecture ceases to be a zero-sum game of limited ground, and becomes the art of printing real estate in the upper strata. Virgin islands in the sky.

The Z-axis extends in both directions from the horizon. Imagine three schools wrapped around a central cascading piece of stylized Faroese fell. A Parisian Metro bringing the sky to the tunnel in an homage to the retrofuturism of Charles De Gaulle's legendary Terminal 1. A school stacking and fanning single-story buildings to expand education to the outdoors on all levels. A skyscraper that continues the High Line into the skyline. A stack of cascading oases suspended midair between tower and guy ropes. As the ultimate example of urban elevation, imagine a neighborhood of warehouses, where a forest of columns carries a series of buildings, forming layers of perimeter blocks hovering above. In between, under, and above the buildings, a three-dimensional public realm is interspersed and interconnected, creating a new equality between X, Y, and Z. By lifting our buildings and landscapes, private and public spaces, streets and squares, we are extruding the Nolli Map to become a Nolli Model, in anticipation of a future when we will move effortlessly in all three dimensions.

THE HEIGHTS

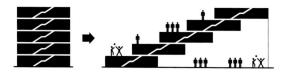

The Heights opens as a cascade of green terraces fanning from a central axis, addressing the academic needs of Arlington's two countywide school programs while forming a vertical community within its dense urban context. Situated within a compact urban site bounded by roads on three sides as well as the Rosslyn Highlands Park, The Heights is conceived as a stack of five rectangular floor plates that rotate around a fixed pivot point, maintaining the community feeling and spatial efficiencies of a one-story school. Green terraces above each floor become an extension of the classroom, creating an indoor-outdoor learning landscape for both students and teachers—an educational oasis rather than a traditional school setting. A cascading staircase cuts through the interior of the building to connect the five-tiered terraces, allowing students to circulate outside as well as inside forging a stronger bond between the neighborhood and the school. The Heights' exterior is materialized in white-glazed brick to unify the five volumes and highlight the oblique angles of the fanning classroom bars, allowing the sculptural form, the energy, and the activity of the inside to take center stage.

Virginia, USA
16,700 M² | Education
2019

LAURIAN GHINIȚOIU

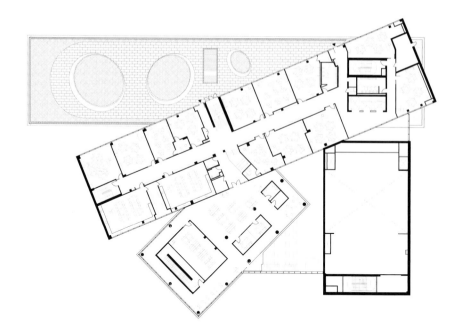

plan level 2

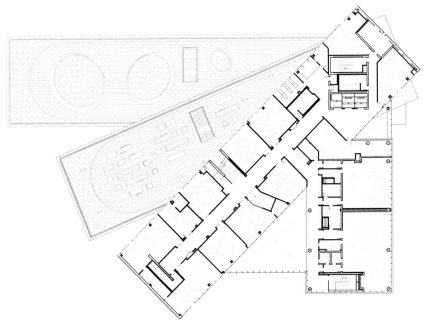

0 2 4   10   20M

LAURIAN GHINIȚOIU

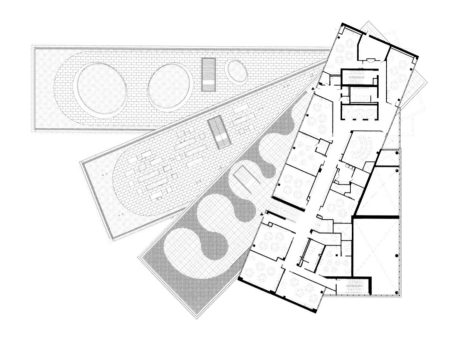

plan level 4

LAURIAN GHINITOIU

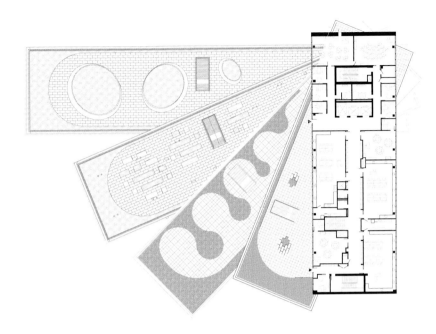

0 2 4 10 20M

LAURIAN GHINITOIU

LAURIAN GHINITOIU

LAURIAN GHINITOIU

LAURIAN GHINITOIU

LAURIAN GHINITOIU

LAURIAN GHINITOIU

AARHUS Ø

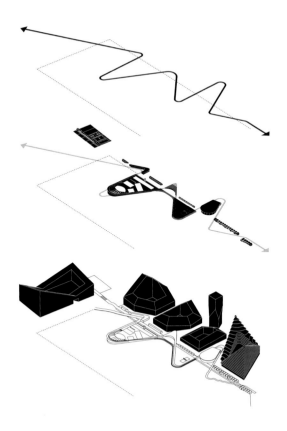

Denmark's second largest city is in the process of rediscovering its old port. Asked to master-plan an entire island on a decommissioned pier, we found that city life had already arrived ahead of us. A beach bar made with a few containers and a pile of sand was proof that life doesn't need the buildings—it is the other way around. We decided to reverse the process and design the public space of the master plan before the surrounding buildings, so the buildings are shaped by the life that preceded them. A new public promenade connects the city to the sea. Rather than politely following the quayside, we propose a pulsating trajectory defining a series of new public spaces on land and water: a harbor bath, a floating beach, a theater, and a series of bathhouses built as pavilions in the public realm. Life between the buildings, ahead of the buildings themselves. We designed three structures, along the waterfront. Two peaks of homes with terraces marking the entrance to the port. A ziggurat hotel extending the promenade from the water into the sky. And a campanile—a residential form of Big Ben—designed as a freestanding slender clock tower, allowing its residents to live inside the clockface. We often find ourselves unable to create the quirky charm that we love in old neighborhoods. By allowing life to come first, we have created an urban island in Aarhus infected by some of the imperfections that are the natural side effects of real life.

Aarhus, DENMARK
26,500 M² | Mixed-Use
2019

JAKOB LANGE

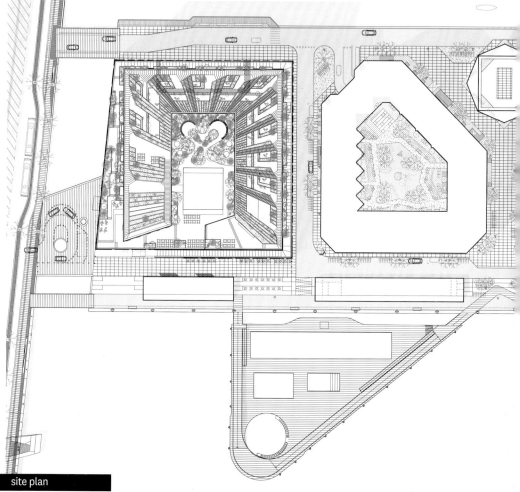

site plan

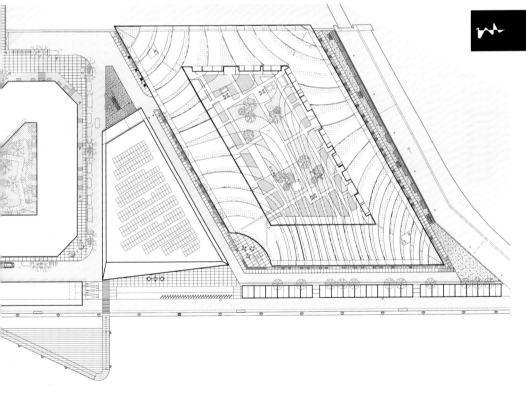

0 3 6   15   30   45M

RASMUS HJORTSHØJ

RASMUS HJORTSHØJ

RASMUS HJORTSHØJ

RASMUS DANIEL TAUN

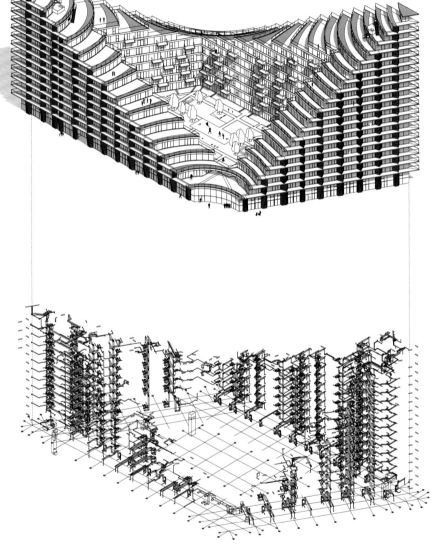

exploded axonometric

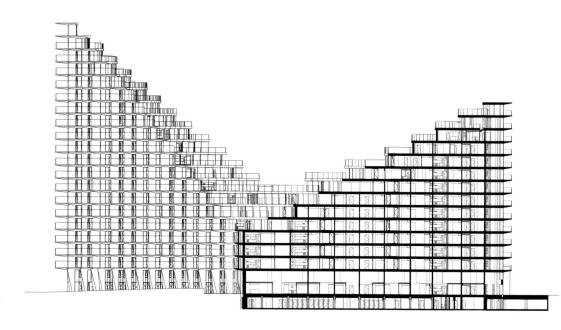

east-west section

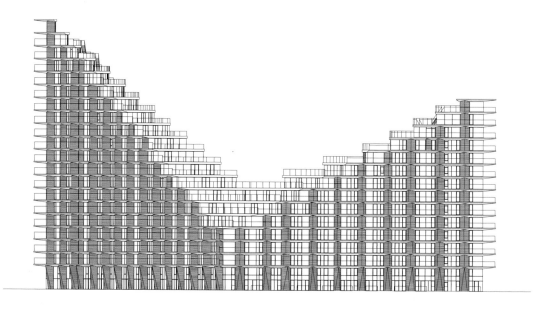

north elevation

0 1 2   5   10   15M

RASMUS HJORTSHØJ

317

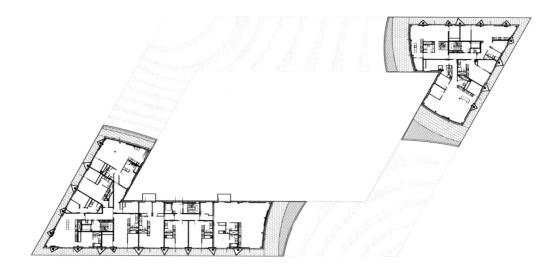

plan level 10

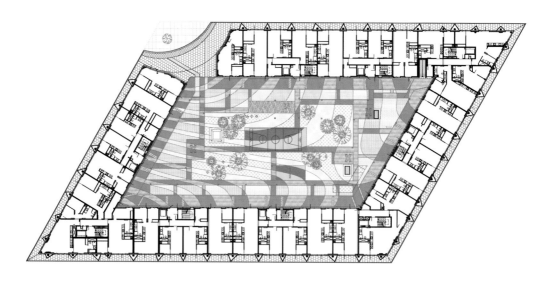

plan level 2

0 2 4　　10　　　　20　　　　30M

RASMUS HJORTSHØJ

RASMUS HJORTSHØJ

RASMUS HJORTSHØJ

RASMUS HJORTSHØJ

RASMUS HJORTSHØJ

RASMUS HJORTSHØJ

RASMUS HJORTSHØJ

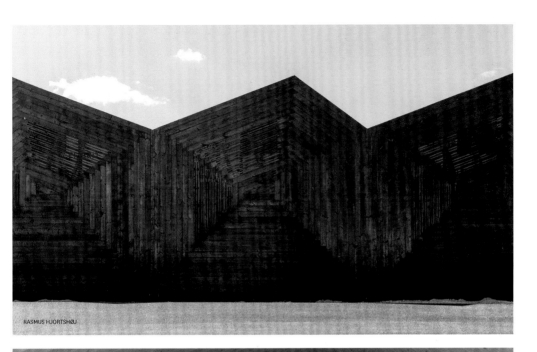

RASMUS HJORTSHØJ

SØREN MARTINUSSEN

GARE DU PONT DE BONDY

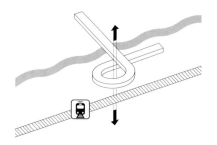

The Gare du Pont de Bondy continues the Parisian tradition of utilizing bridges as social spaces and cultural landmarks. Located at the encounter between the communities of Bondy, Bobigny, and Noisy-le-Sec, the station is conceived as both bridge and tunnel wrapped around a giant atrium, connecting the riverbank to the train landing. The deepest train tunnels will now open directly to the Parisian sky, and all three surrounding neighborhoods will be united in a single inclusive loop—a new architectural hybrid of urban infrastructure and social space.

Paris, FRANCE
10,000 M² | Urbanism
2030

GOWANUS ZIGGURAT

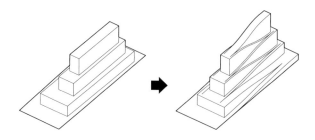

Located along the Gowanus Canal, the design is organized around a ramp ascending from the canal's edge to a ziggurat of spaces for leisure, culture, retail, working, and living. The building is organized according to the depth of space for each program. Starting from the ground floor with retail space, slimming down to accommodate office space, rental apartments, and condos. The building naturally creates a series of stepping structures that culminate in a rooftop park. The ramp gradually increases in pitch as it ascends with the lower slopes along the public levels easily accessible by bicycle and the steeper slopes at the top providing private residences with a pedestrian path and gardens. To reinforce the experience of rising up the building, the vegetation corresponds and adapts to the changing elevations, with water-friendly willow trees near the canal to mountaintop firs at the peak. Visitors, workers, and residents will be able to literally climb the façade by bike or on foot. Real world King Kong 2.0.

Brooklyn, New York, USA
78,000 M²
Mixed-Use

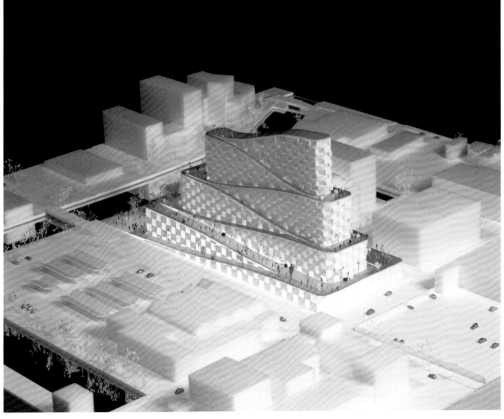

333

CAPITASPRING

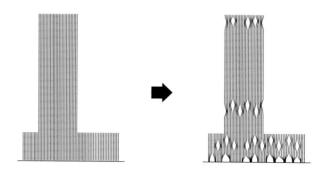

Capitaspring is located in the heart of Singapore's financial district on the site of a 1980s car complex and a hawkers' market. Entirely defined by zoning rules, street walls, and setback requirements, the volume is a complex composition of polygonal shapes. The program, too, is strictly defined—offices sit on top of residences that in turn rest on a podium of food markets and parking. Due to the unique character of Singapore's urbanism—both extremely dense and extremely green— we decided to make the design a vertical exploration of tropical urbanism. At grade, the street is closed to form a new linear park. An urban room invades the footprint like a public plaza sheltered from the tropical sunlight and showers. Above, a vertical park is inserted in the middle of the tower in the form of a spiraling promenade ascending among tropical tree trunks and canopies. On top, an urban forest allows visitors to enjoy the lushness of the summit. From the outside, the façade looks like a classic tower in a pinstripe suit. The linear regularity of the curtain wall breaks open to reveal the park programs within. Like a vision of a future in which city and countryside, culture and nature can coexist, and urban landscapes can expand unrestricted in the vertical dimension.

SINGAPORE
93,000 M² | Commercial
2021

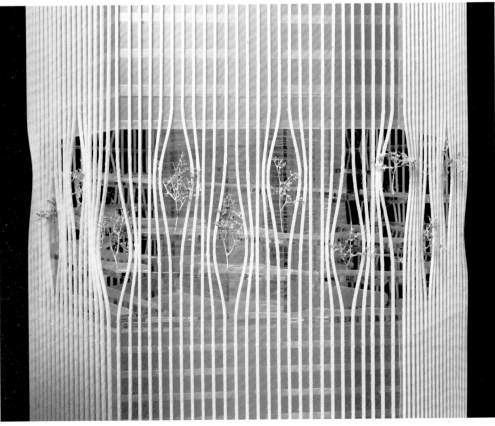

337

VERTICAL
OASES

The Dubai Creek Harbor Observation Tower lifts the oasis into the air, creating a string of floating islands at every 100M of altitude like an archipelago in the sky. As a counterbalance to the striking landmark Burj Khalifa, the tower invests minimal amounts of material to create a maximal presence on the skyline, and uses minimal amounts of steel to create the maximum amount of space in the sky. Using tensile cables from long-span bridges and telecommunication towers, the tower orchestrates the structural forces into a single 800M spire surrounded by an array of spiraling cables. Distilled into a single vertical vector, the tower comprises the necessary elevators and stairs into the most conceivably slender cross section. Like a diagram of forces solidified in the skyline, or a sculpture made of structural imagery rather than physical mass, it could be a true landmark of the third millennium.

Dubai, UAE
80,000 M²
Observation Tower

MIAMI PRODUCE

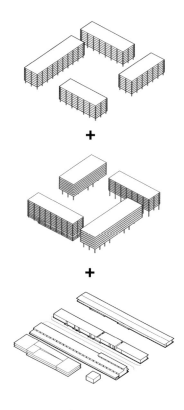

Located in the center of the industrial district of Allapattah, Miami Produce is conceived as a three-dimensional urban framework. A block of interconnected volumes with large industrial-sized floor plates will host urban farming, restaurants, storefronts, co-working offices, co-living apartments, and educational programming. At the ground floor, a series of existing warehouses will be converted into a vibrant public realm while preserving the industrial spirit of the neighborhood. Between the warehouses, three public spaces will exhibit a variety of landscapes of diverse microclimates and extend the building programs outdoors. A stack of new linear buildings floats above the existing warehouses, generating a large urban courtyard at the center. A forest of columns with varying dimensions depending on loads and heights create a permeable perimeter around the site. On top of each building, programmed roofscapes will extend the public realm vertically to capture stunning views of greater Miami. The resultant composition is a vertical overlay of three neighborhoods, one on top of the other, forming a new hybrid between industry and agriculture, office park and residential city block.

Miami, Florida, USA
125,000 M²
Housing

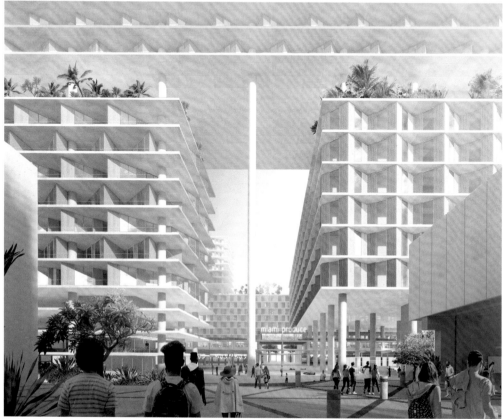

THE SYMBIOTE

A city may have a church, a museum, or a city hall. Public buildings with public programs and public spaces—inside and out. But 99 percent of the city is where we live, work, learn, and shop. Most of these buildings are based on the zero-sum game of using the total available area for their own private purposes. But if every building cared only for itself, the city would become a poor place of private spaces deprived of common ground. To turn our cities on, we need to activate the 99 percent for massive impact and not just stick to the one percent of public landmarks.

Hosting is the gift of carving out space to welcome a public parasite. The active solicitation of trespassers. Every chance an architect has to build represents an opportunity to create a framework that is more inviting, more engaging, more accommodating to the public than the status quo. A cultural institution that creates a public room at its heart—or a public passage at its center. A theater that liberates the ground and opens the roof to form outdoor arenas. A home for LEGO where the ground and roof become public squares and cascading playgrounds. A city block on the sea that opens up like a drawbridge to funnel ships inside. An incubator that draws the public along the longitudinal and vertical axes. An urban project that dissolves the monolithic podium into a voxelated landscape of peaks and valleys, caves and canyons. A Parisian district that turns the city block inside out and upside down. And finally, a Milanese pair of high-rises united by a catenary shading a sheltered plaza underneath.

Hosting architecture is the accommodation of the parasitic program as a welcome symbiote. As many activities that used to require public space have migrated online —shopping, education, and social interaction—the public realm is losing ground from logistical necessity. The remaining reason to leave the comfort of your touch screen is the thrill of casual coincidence and human interaction. As the programs inside the buildings transform and change over time, it becomes the parasitic program that keeps the destination alive. Rather than the traditional front door on Main Street, the most prominent address becomes the space within, underneath, or above. The house that hosts turns generosity into a survival strategy. The trespasser becomes the ultimate occupant.

LEGO HOUSE

LEGO is a company that has succeeded in making people around the world believe that LEGO comes from their home country. But it actually comes from our home country. Imagine our excitement when we were invited to design the home of the brick. Centrally located in the heart of Billund, LEGO House is designed to be as inviting and engaging as LEGO is itself. 21 overlapping blocks are placed like individual buildings, intersecting to create a continuous journey inside and out. On top, a roofscape of interconnected playgrounds is open for anyone to climb. Below, a public square is illuminated through the cracks and gaps between the volumes above. The plaza appears like a column-free urban cave, publicly accessible from all four corners, allowing visitors and citizens of Billund to roam freely through the building. The overlapping galleries above are color coded in LEGO's primary colors, so navigating through the exhibitions becomes a journey through the color spectrum. Through systematic creativity, children of all ages are empowered with the tools to create their own worlds and inhabit them through play. It is probably the only museum where you are encouraged to touch the artifacts. Below ground, the vault holds the most treasured LEGO sets of all time. Even if the LEGO House is a pilgrimage for builders of all ages and nationalities, it is first and foremost a welcoming public space for the citizens of Billund, the Children's Capital of the World. The climbable roofs and walkable squares extend the public realm of the town, affirming LEGO's commitment to its community.

Billund, DENMARK
12,000 M² | Culture
2017

IWAN BAAN

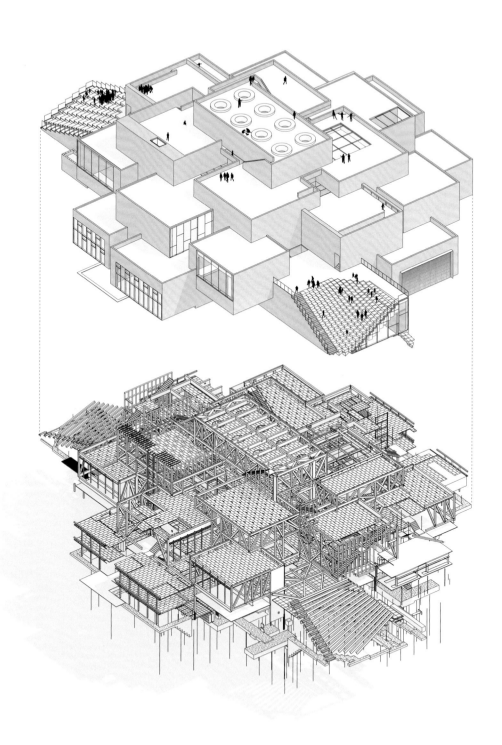

exploded axonometric

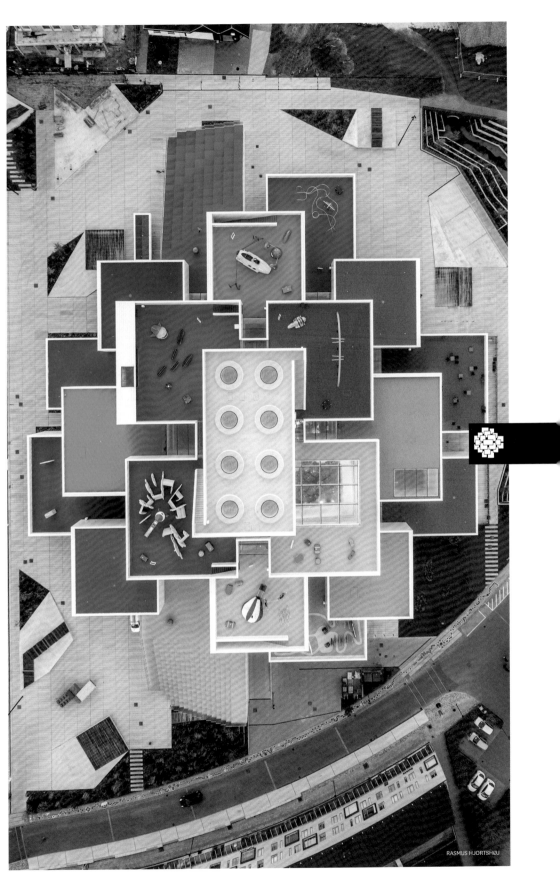

RASMUS HJORTSHØJ

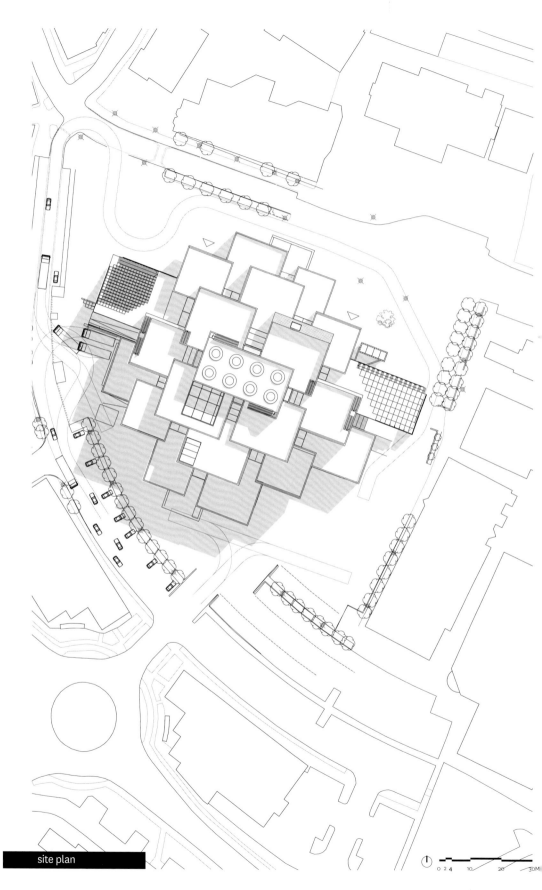

site plan

IWAN BAAN

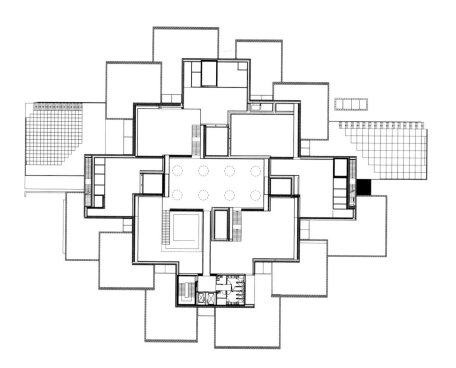

plan level 3

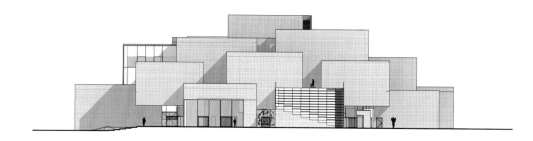

east elevation

longitudinal section

0 4 8   20   40   6om

IWAN BAAN

RASMUS HJORTSHØJ

IWAN BAAN

IWAN BAAN

RASMUS HJORTSHØJ

CAT HUANG

IWAN BAAN

MÉCA

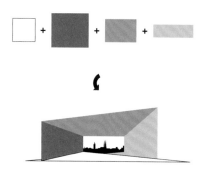

The Maison de l'Économie Créative et de la Culture en Aquitaine, MÉCA, creates a literal framework for the celebration of contemporary art, film, and performances. Centrally located between the River Garonne and Saint-Jean train station, MÉCA brings together three regional arts agencies: FRAC for contemporary art; ALCA for cinema, literature, and audiovisuals; and OARA for performing arts. The building is conceived as a single loop of public institutions. The riverfront promenade lifts off from the ground, covering a shared lobby below. The theater and mediateques form the two pillars that carry the skylit attic for the visual arts. The three institutions frame a central space, an urban living room for the life of the city as well as outdoor events for visual, narrative, or performance arts. As the promenade becomes façade, the concrete pavers become façade tiles. By pulling them apart, the gaps expand into windows, bringing daylight and views to the spaces within. Inside, the modest budget allowed us to pursue a Corbusian austerity in materials, with practically every surface finished in concrete, including a spiraling story pit sunken in the floor of the foyer. On the bleachers leading to the urban room, artist Benoît Maire created a bronze statue of a giant Hermes head. Located on the edge of the urban room, half the head has been sliced away as if the same gesture that created the hole in the building also cut away half of Hermes. For the art piece as well as for the architecture, the most exciting part, is the part that is absent.

Bordeaux, FRANCE
18,000 M² | Culture
2019

LAURIAN GHINITOIU

LAURIAN GHINITOIU

LAURIAN GHINITOIU

LAURIAN GHINITOIU

LAURIAN GHINITOIU

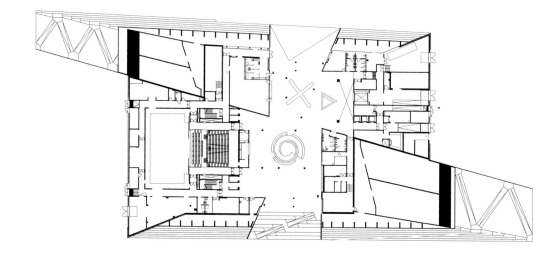

ground floor plan

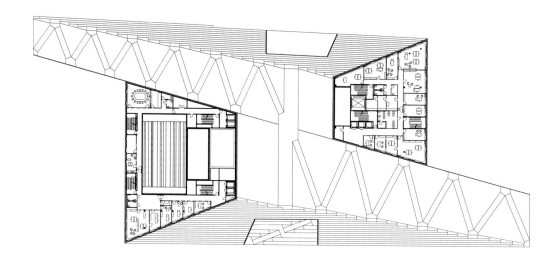

plan level 1

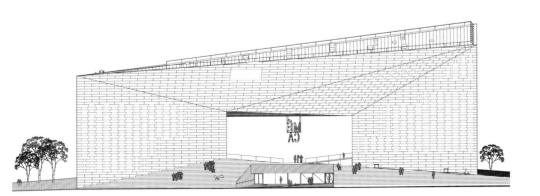

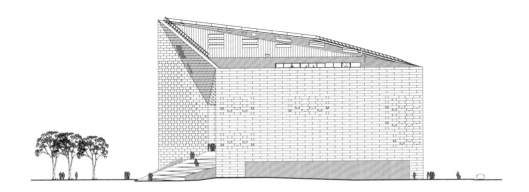

0 2 4   10   20   30M

LAURIAN GHINITOIU

LAURIAN GHINITOIU

LAURIAN GHINITOIU

FLORENT MICHEL

LAURIAN GHINITOIU

LAURIAN GHINITOIU

LAURIAN GHINITOIU

LAURIAN GHINITOIU

LAURIAN GHINITOIU

LA PORTE

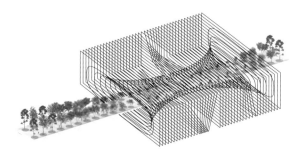

Located at the key pedestrian access point to EuropaCity, La Porte exhibition hall acts as a portal allowing the public to flow freely between the neighborhood and the new train station. A tree-lined pedestrian bridge passes through the building on its way across the urban boulevard. Rather than a square tunnel through the building, the gateway is conceived as a smooth transition from one façade to the other, turning the surface of the museum inside out. In the direction of the bridge, the building will consist of a procession of 43 parallel concrete frames that change in scale, from generous to intimate as you pass through. Similarly, the species of trees will range from big to bonsai and back again. The façade will seem to cave in like a loophole from front to back. Viewed from the front, the building is opaque and enigmatic. As people pass through, it turns out to be an entirely transparent space with works of art in all directions. The passageway becomes a promenade through an art archive. The building's insides will be exposed on the outside, and its main façade will be the space within it.

Gonesse, FRANCE
34,000 M²
Culture

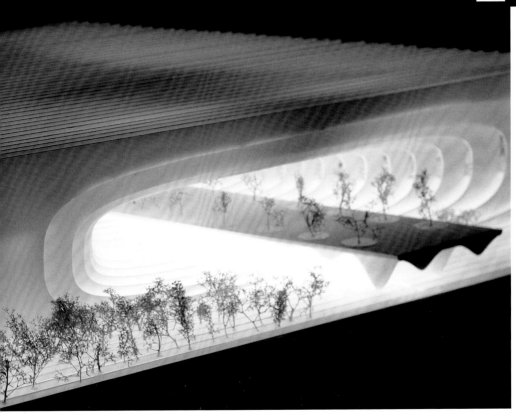

ALBANIAN NATIONAL THEATER

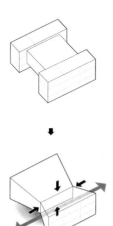

The New National Theater of Albania is conceived as two buildings connected by an auditorium: one building for the audience and one for the performers. Located prominently on the cultural axis in a mostly pedestrian neighborhood, the building envelope is compressed and lifted in the center, creating connections and public plazas on both sides of the theater at street level. Underneath, the auditorium arches up from the ground, creating an entrance canopy for the audience as well as the performers. Above, the roof sags down, mirroring the archway, forming an open-air amphitheater with a backdrop to the city's skyline. The two main façades open up to reveal the interior activities to the public outside. One side reveals the foyer, lounge, bar, and restaurant as well as the two experimental stages like rooms in a dollhouse. The other side reveals the entire section of the backstage, side stages, under stage, and fly tower, exposing the theatrical machinery to bypassing citizens. The geometry of the pinch point is resolved by folding the façade into a rippled surface, like a traditional lampshade or a rippled dress. The main public gesture that allows passage, opens for access, and creates the open-air auditorium, also becomes the ornament for the otherwise purely performance-based architecture.

Tirana, ALBANIA
9,300 M²
Culture

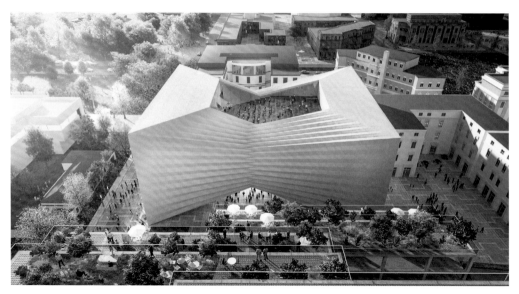

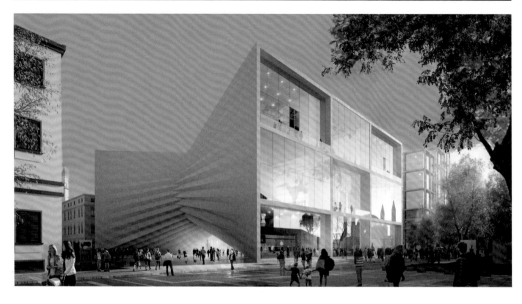

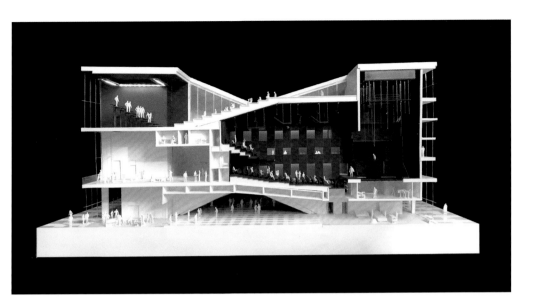

SLUISHUIS

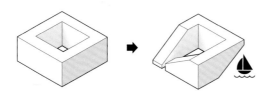

Sluishuis is designed as a traditional Amsterdam perimeter block floating in the IJmeer Lake. Toward the city, the building volume kneels down to invite visitors to climb its roof and enjoy the view of the new neighborhoods on the IJmeer. Toward the water, the building rises from the lake, creating a gate for boats to enter and dock in the courtyard marina. Sluishuis becomes a building inside the port, with a port inside the building. The marina extends outward with a promenade of public programs around its perimeter that continues into the water, forming an archipelago of mini islands. A public passage climbs the building's terraces, serving as a small rooftop street that eventually loops onto the top of the building. From one vantage point, the silhouette of the building appears as the bow of a boat reflecting the water below; from another, a vertical green community; and finally, as you approach and enter, as a new kind of hybrid city block inviting both city and harbor within.

Amsterdam, NETHERLANDS
46,000 M² | Housing
2022

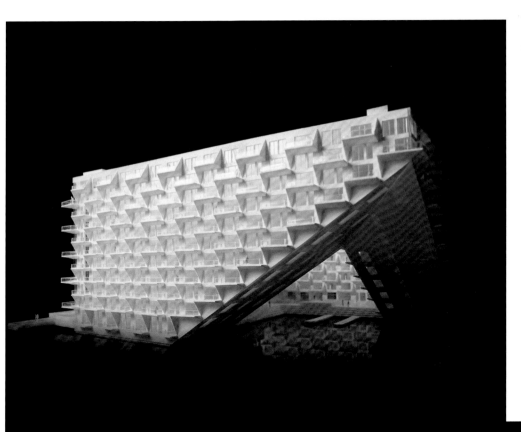

PARIS PARC

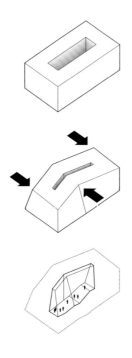

Paris Parc is wedged in between Parisian architectural
icons of all eras: Institut du Monde Arabe, Campus Jussieau,
and Notre Dame. It is conceived as the imprint of the pressures
of its hyper-saturated urban context. It is conceived as a chain
of reactions to the various external and internal forces acting
upon it: inflated to allow light and air to enter into the heart of
the facility, compressed to ensure daylight and views for the
neighboring classrooms and dormitories, lifted to allow the
public to enter from both plaza and park, and finally tilted to
reflect to Parisians the spectacular view of the Paris skyline
and the Notre Dame. The facility is both park and building
at once. The central canyon extends a public space through
the building. The green space taken up by the footprint of the
building is replaced by the large roof garden, providing both
covered outdoor spaces for the restaurant and a gently sloped
meadow with panoramic views over the city. The iconic view of
the Notre Dame cathedral is not only enjoyable from the roof
garden, but the façade facing the Institute du Monde Arabe
is slightly angled like a periscope, allowing a mirror image
of the cathedral to be seen from eye level on the square. An
architecture of invitation, both visually and physically.

Paris, FRANCE
15,000 M² | Education
2021

OFF ARCHITECTURE

OFF ARCHITECTURE

OFF ARCHITECTURE

KING TORONTO

King Toronto is set in a transitional area of Toronto between the tall towers of the Central Business District to the east and the low-rise neighborhoods in the northwest. Located at the meeting point of three 20th-century neighborhood parks, the building is organized as a traditional perimeter block with a public park and plaza in the center. The plaza itself is defined by two distinct atmospheres: a lushly landscaped forest paired with an urban, hardscaped courtyard. Surrounding the plaza, King Toronto rises as sets of voxels extruded upward to create spaces for living, working, and shopping. The new urban tissue wraps around the existing heritage buildings like a new organic frame. Each voxel is set at the size of a room, rotated 45 degrees from the street grid to increase exposure to light and air. At the base, voxels lift to provide access across the courtyard. The roof surface undulates to allow sunlight to penetrate the street, creating spaces for green terraces for each unit in the process. The resulting urban volume is a radical alternative to the tower and podium prevalent in Toronto. It echoes some of Moshe Safdie's most revolutionary ideas from Habitat 67 in Montreal, but rather than a utopian experiment on an island, it is nested into the heart of the city. 50 years later, Habitat evolves from unique prototype to urban typology.

Toronto, CANADA
57,000 M² | Housing
2023

HAYES DAVIDSON

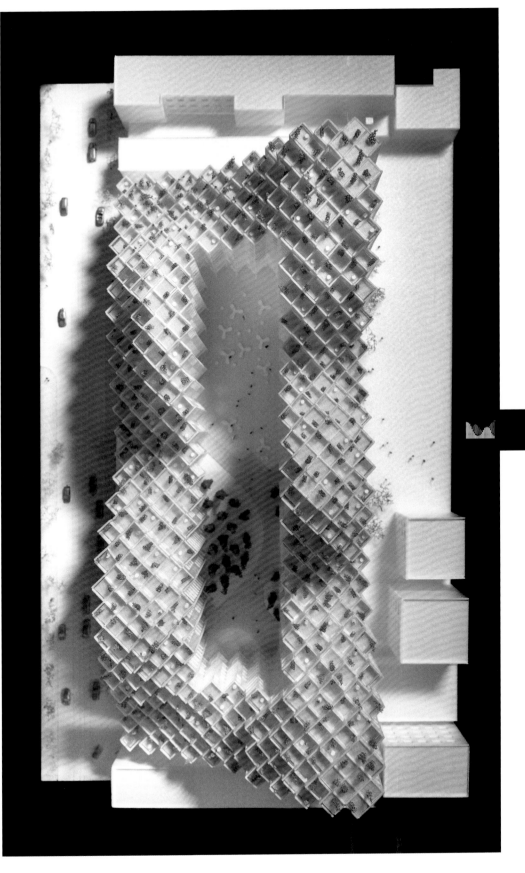

LE MARAIS
À L'INVERSE

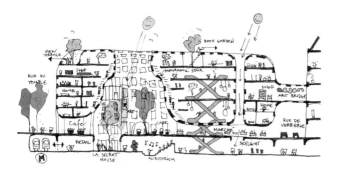

In the heart of Paris, Le Marais has a uniquely porous urban fabric. On the outside, it's a traditional Parisian neighborhood of city blocks. On the inside, it's a labyrinth of interconnected courtyards. Le Marais à L'inverse is conceived as the interior transformation of the urban courtyards expressed on the outside of the buildings. Le Marais turned inside out. Walls cave in to become gateways. Façades fold out to cover courtyards or loop around to become roofs. The façade extends as a bridge across the street to connect to its neighbor. A classic architecture of walls and windows is materialized in the local Parisian limestone, while a psychedelic physical and visual manipulation of the classic city fabric allows stone to take on a fluid form. Classicism on LSD. Salvador Dalí as an architect. At a glance, the new architecture blends seamlessly with that of its neighbors. On closer inspection, it's a social sculpture shaped by the flow of people passing between its streets, archways, courtyards, and rooftops.

Paris, FRANCE
6,500 M²
Mixed-Use

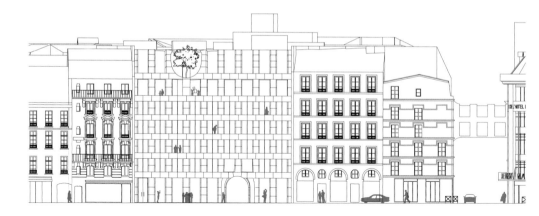

north elevation

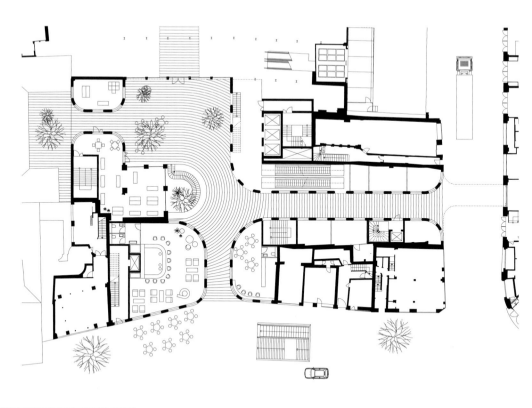

groundfloor plan

0 4 8   20   40M

397

IL PORTICO

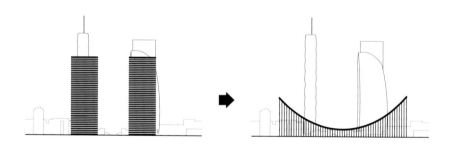

CityLife consists of three iconic towers surrounded by a green public realm. While the brief asked to design a fourth tower on the site, the presence of the three existing icons offered the opportunity to explore a different typology for the city. We proposed to create two individual buildings connected by a 140M-long hanging roof, forming a generous shaded public realm as the entrance to CityLife: The Portico. Rather than to compete with the existing context, our proposal seeks to complete it. The Portico will be an extension of the interior space to the exterior, allowing the climate to be enjoyed throughout the year. The Portico is created by a hanging structure, with a light roof and thin columns working in tension to prevent uplift. Two courtyards allow employees to enjoy a place of respite during the workday, while the large, central, covered public realm becomes a gift to the city of Milan. Under the sagging roofs, a cascading ring of amenities allows for interconnected workspaces, and extends into the rooftop bar overlooking the Alps and Monte Rosa. Throughout the urban history of Milan, an urban axis is symbolized by a set of twin buildings and a gate. The Portico is an evolution of that typology creating both a gateway to CityLife and a significant destination for Milan.

Milan, ITALY
53,500 M² | Commercial
2023

BEAUTY AND THE BIT

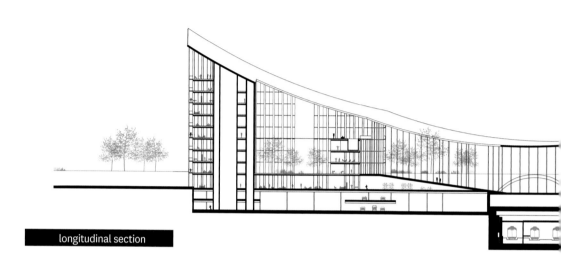

longitudinal section

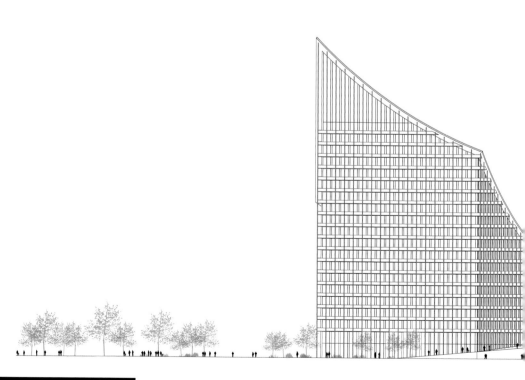

north-east elevation

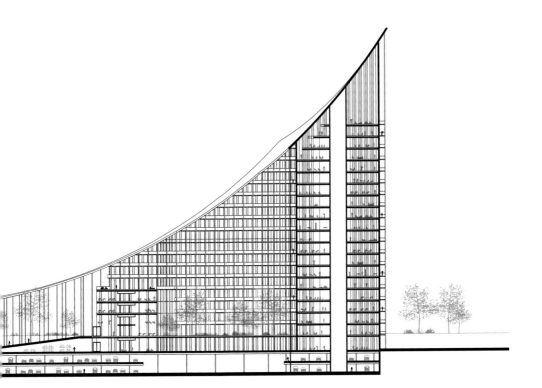

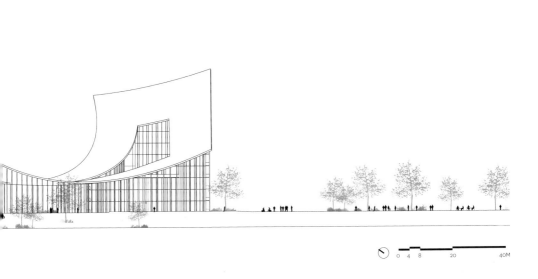

0 4 8   20   40M

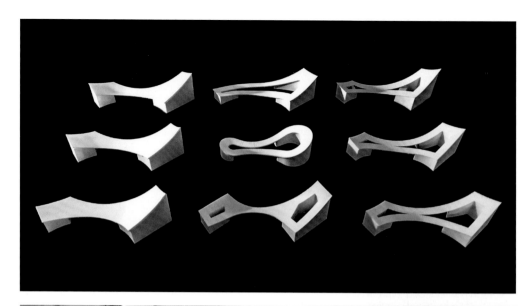

PARQUE DE LA INNOVACIÓN

We were invited to design two new city blocks at one of the main entrances to Buenos Aires. The zoning called for a dense development within two compact volumes capped at 100 meters of height framing a small public space. The result was like a tall urban wall with a small gap in it. We needed to break this mold. Less public space would mean more freedom but also less quality. We decided to do the opposite. Buenos Aires is a lively city with a vibrant social life, but to our surprise it only has two square meters of public green space per person compared to the nine square meters recommended by WHO. This was something we could address. The two blocks will be transformed into five towers. Each tower is given a different height to eliminate the sensation of a wall. The podium is reduced into semi-sunken pavilions, turning their roofs into green slopes. We erode the bases of each tower, diminishing the footprint and allowing a public park to expand. Toward the top, the towers erode in a similar way by creating a landscape of terraces for the people living and working there. The resulting complex provides a new park with a more than threefold increase in public green space, and an alpine architectural silhouette on the city's skyline. In a synergy of public and private interest, by offering the space to the public where it is the most in need, we earn the freedom to redistribute the lost density above.

Buenos Aires, ARGENTINA
220,000 M²
Mixed-Use

PRODUCTIZATION

The most prolific architect will realize maybe 100, at best 1,000, buildings in a lifetime. A drop in the ocean of the billions of square meters that go up all over the planet every year. Unable to scale, architecture remains boutique even at its upper limits of productivity. If we look at the increase in productivity in American manufacturing over the last three decades, the increase in value generated per worker is more than 150 percent. For construction, we see a flat line with a gentle decline. The main difference is that the construction industry has remained practically unaffected by the wave of automation that has flowed through manufacturing. And despite the apparent lack of innovation in the industry, each building is a prototype—always starting from scratch. The insistence on the original is the greatest hindrance for original architecture. By never repeating a design, we eliminate the forces of refinement and optimization that we find in manufacturing; the iPhone X, for example, is vastly superior to the iPhone 1 even if the design typology has remained the same.

By productizing architecture, we can deliver architectural impact at scale. We can reduce the architecture to the scale of furniture—a building to a product, prefabricated and fully functional straight of the truck. Or we can design manufactured elements, like the architectural equivalent of LEGO, which allow for almost infinite variability in their reassembly. We can create the classic original architectural prototype, and redeploy it in multiple cities across the world, their uniqueness intact due to geographical separation. Finally, by freeing ourselves from the greatest strength and weakness of architecture—its intrinsic connection to real estate, fixed assets—we may be able to imagine buildings and cities like products. Liberated from terra firma and gravity, floating on water, deployable like a fleet of prefabricated neighborhoods waiting to dock for a year, a decade, or a century. Architects are rich in ideas, but often poor in impact. Thoughts without action. Vision without mission. Productization can unleash the power of manufacturing on architecture to deliver impact at scale, finally merging the best of both worlds: custom-tailored sustainable design at great numbers, high quality at low cost. The original as the new standard.

URBAN RIGGER

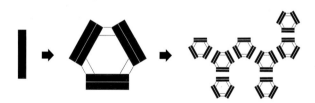

Copenhagen's harbor remains an underutilized and underdeveloped area at the heart of the city. By introducing a building typology optimized for harbor cities, we can introduce a housing solution that will keep students in the middle of town. The standardized container system has been developed to allow goods to be transported anywhere in the world in a complex network of operators at a very low cost. By making use of the standard container system, we offer the framework for an extremely flexible building typology. Stacking nine container units in a hexagon, twelve student homes frame a communal courtyard and rest on top of a shared pontoon. The resulting homes have waterfront views and direct access to the clean water of Copenhagen, so residents can jump out of their windows for a swim. Each floating collective is like a tiny human-made ecosystem: A heat pump draws all hot water for showers and heating from the harbor water and PV panels atop one of the containers provide electricity for the students and their homes. In addition to mass production, Urban Rigger homes also have the advantage of buoyancy and mobility. If the conditions change in Copenhagen, the units are easily detached and can be towed to the next urban development area in town—a fleet of deployable homes that are always ready to draw the anchor and temporarily colonize the next frontier.

Copenhagen, DENMARK
680 M² | Housing
2016

DAVID RASMUSSEN

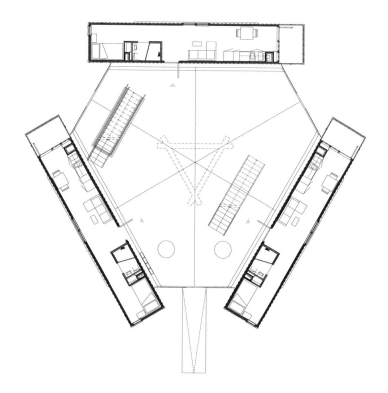

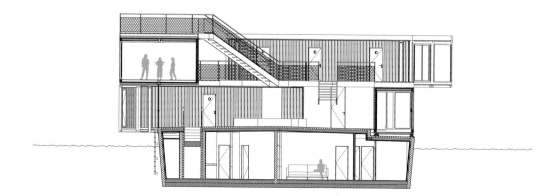

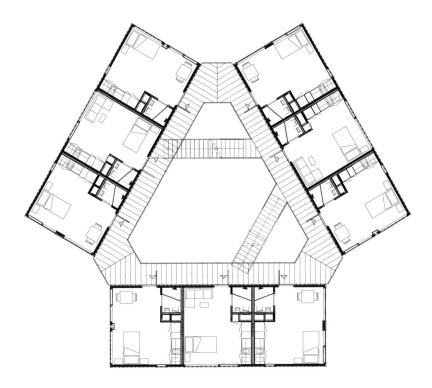

0 0,5 1　　2,5　　　　5M

LAURENT DE CARNIERE

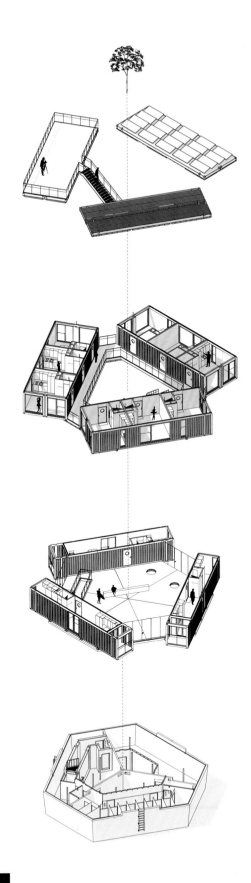

exploded axonometric

LAURENT DE CARNIERE

LAURENT DE CARNIERE

LAURENT DE CARNIERE

URBAN RIGGER APS

WEGROW

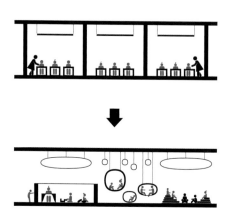

WeGrow's first location in New York City facilitates a transformative and holistic approach to learning that's less prescriptive and more intuitive. A field of super-elliptic objects forms a learning landscape that's dense and rational, yet free and fluid. Modular classrooms, tree houses, and a vertical farm promote an inclusive and collaborative teaching environment. Partitions inside the school are shelves raised to the level of the child but no higher, allowing natural light to reach deep inside the building. Acoustic clouds made of felt reflect patterns in nature—fingerprints, corals, or the Moon—and illuminate with Ketra bulbs that shift in color and intensity based on the time of day. Nature's qualities are repeated throughout WeGrow to create calm settings for focused study: the mushroom shelves, the magic meadow, the soft pebbles, and reading hives form an organic learning environment. The framework for learning evolves as life and curricula evolve, giving the children the agency to shape their learning and environment through play and experimentation.

New York, USA
1,830 M² | Education
2019

DAVE BURK

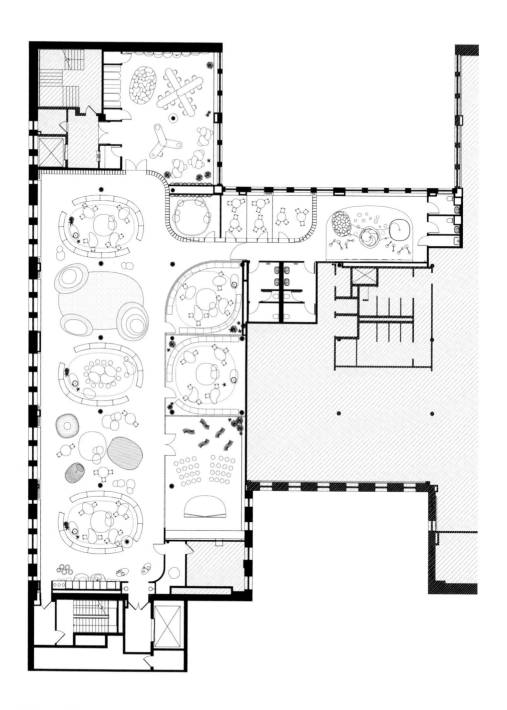

floor plan

0 0.5 1   2.5   5   10M

KATELYN PERRY

DAVE BURK

LAURIAN GHINITOIU

LAURIAN GHINITOIU

LAURIAN GHINITOIU

LAURIAN GHINITOIU

427

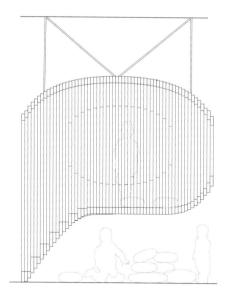

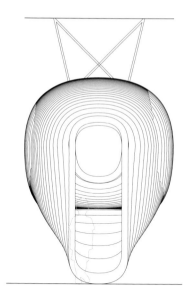

0   0,1 0,2   0,5   1   1,5M

KATELYN PERRY

429

KATELYN PERRY

KLEIN HOUSE

Klein House is a building scaled down to a product, sized to be delivered on site in modules made of 100 percent recyclable materials. Future homeowners can purchase, tailor, and build the house in any location for any purpose, from weekend getaways to a guest room or a music studio to a creative retreat. The design is an evolution of the traditional A-frame cabin, known for its pitched roof and angled walls, which are easy to construct and exceptionally durable in harsh climates. By rotating the structure 45 degrees, the lowest part of the house is transferred to two corners, maximizing the ceiling height inside. Klein House becomes a more spacious version of the A-frame, resulting in a crystal-like shape with an ever-changing appearance—from certain angles it almost looks like a cube, and from others it looks like a tapered spire or a classic silhouette. Generous frameless windows and marine-grade canvas stretch over the structure to create a seamless, weatherproof enclosure. The interior offers cozy comfort while being fully immersed in nature. The exposed timber frame and dark insulating cork bring nature inside, while accentuating views out to the wilderness. A small fireplace is nestled in one corner, while the off-grid equipment is tucked in the back, supporting a fully reliable and self-powered home.

New York, USA
17 M² | Housing
2018

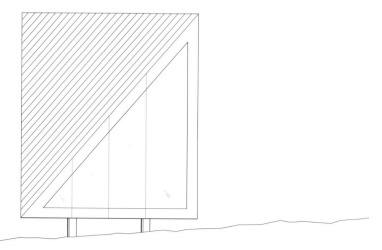

elevation

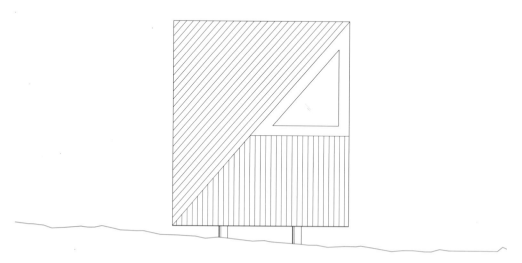

elevation

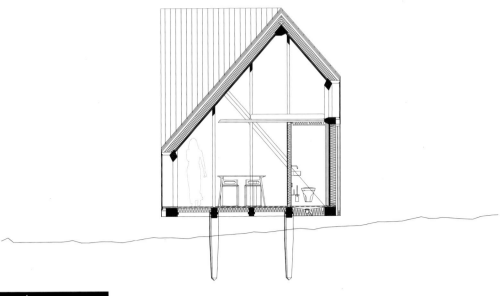

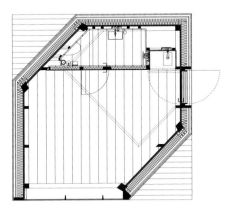

0   0.3 0.6   1.5   3M

435

MATTHEW CARBONE

MATTHEW CARBONE

MATTHEW CARBONE

MATTHEW CARBONE

DORTHEAVEJ 2

Prefabrication with room-sized modules has the conventional weakness of doubling all surfaces as they get assembled—wall against wall, floor against ceiling. By pulling the modules apart, we eliminate the flaw of redundancy and, as a bonus, we create extra-tall kitchens and dining rooms. The resulting checkered pattern becomes the trademark of Dortheavej. Conceived as a porous wall, the building gently curves in the center, creating space for a public plaza toward the street on the south side and an intimate green courtyard toward north. On the street level, the building opens up to allow the residents and general public to pass seamlessly into the courtyard. All materials are chosen for economic efficiency: exposed concrete ceilings, construction fence guardrails on the balconies, pine timber façades. The result is a free and flexible, elegant and organic architecture, that can be customized and adapted to many different sites, and hopefully evolve into an increasingly refined design as iterations and generations of designs pass by.

Copenhagen, DENMARK
6,800 M² | Housing
2018

RASMUS HJORTSHØJ

443

south elevation

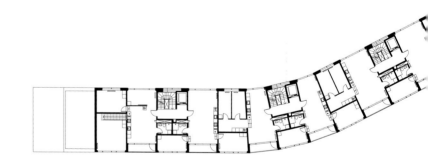

plan level 3

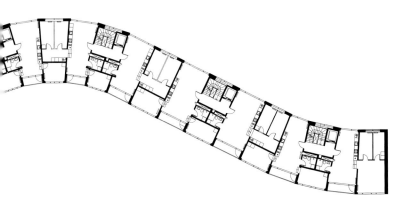

RASMUS HJORTSHØJ

RASMUS HJORTSHØJ

RASMUS HJORTSHØJ

RASMUS HJORTSHØJ

RASMUS HJORTSHØJ

KAKTUS TOWERS

  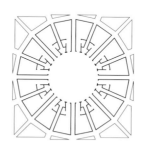 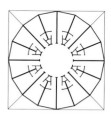

Kaktus is our first attempt at mass-produced modular homes. A wedge-shaped unit is mirrored to form a pair. And multiplied by eight to form a hexadecagonal floor plan. Wedge-shaped balconies are mirrored and repeated to form a square outline. A spiral stair wrapped around a central elevator creates a compact core, and the entire assembly can be stacked infinitely. By mounting the same balconies differently on each floor, we create the perception of a complex, customized sculptural tower, even if every unit is made from the same elements. Maximum variation with total repetition. As we repeat the project across Denmark, Norway, Sweden, Germany, England, and Ireland, we encounter the opportunity to enhance and refine from 1.0 to 1.3 to 2.0. Ironically, typological repetition becomes our ticket to product innovation.

Copenhagen, DENMARK
26,100 M² | Housing
2021

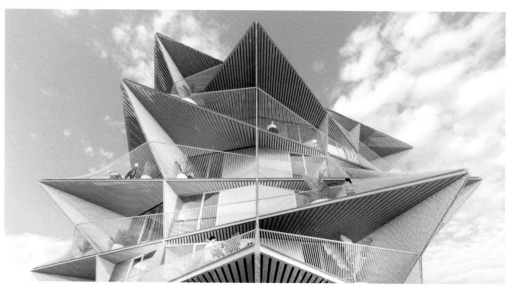

BIOPHILIA

There is a widening divide between people and all other forms of life. Cities are becoming monocultures. They are increasing in human population but declining in biodiversity. Living systems have a lot to offer cities. Where dead things decay, living things grow. Palaces turn to ruins while fields grows into forests. What if we could design cities to grow rather than deteriorate? Growing breaks down the traditional distinctions between city and countryside through hedonistic sustainability—environments designed to thrive ecologically while improving the quality of life for human inhabitants. Rather than relying on reduction and sacrifice in order to be green, grown cities will simultaneously be more desirable and more sustainable.

Imagine a restaurant where the food is not merely prepared and consumed, but also grown. A zoo designed for animals and humans alike, like the most biodiverse neighborhood in the town. Finally, a floating city designed from scratch to address every Sustainable Development Goal of the United Nations. All the energy harvested from the elements: the thermal mass of the ocean, the flow of the currents and tides, the force of the waves, the energy and heat of the sun, and the power of the wind. Water collected and cleaned locally in a mixture of organic and mechanical systems. The food locally sourced and grown, fish- and plant-based. Waste is recycled, digested, and composted, put to new use or harvested for energy. Rather than a city designed around a street grid or a building layout, an urban design that starts with the available renewable resources and the orchestrated flow of resources through the city. Free to grow organically by adding floating island after island, to form an urban archipelago of interconnected cells, reconfigurable like a sliding puzzle, growing like a culture in a petri dish. In our future, we will design with and for living tissue, for the cohabitation of all life forms. Human-made ecosystems, grown rather than built.

PANDA HOUSE

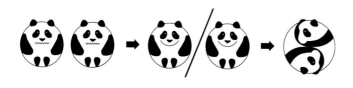

To our surprise, the main design challenge in creating the Danish home for two Giant Pandas, Mao Sun and Xing Er, in the heart of the Copenhagen Zoo, is that the two have to be completely separated. Apart from the few days a year when the female is in heat, the two Giant Pandas will fight—even Pandas have a hard time cohabitating. The obvious solution became a circular habitat divided into two separate areas—one for him and one for her—appearing like a yin and yang symbol from above. By raising and lowering the edges, we create the necessary protection between Pandas and guests in the least visible way possible. A restaurant offers the guest to dine with a Panda. The material palette is authentic yet familiar: concrete cast with bamboo formwork, fencing made from tubular corten pipes evoking bamboo, mega terrazzo made from river boulders mirroring the black-and-white patterns of Panda fur. The final result is a stylized habitat saturated with natural and cultural elements from the Panda's Scandinavian and Asian homes.

Copenhagen, DENMARK
2.450 M² | Mixed-Use
2019

RASMUS HJORTSHØJ

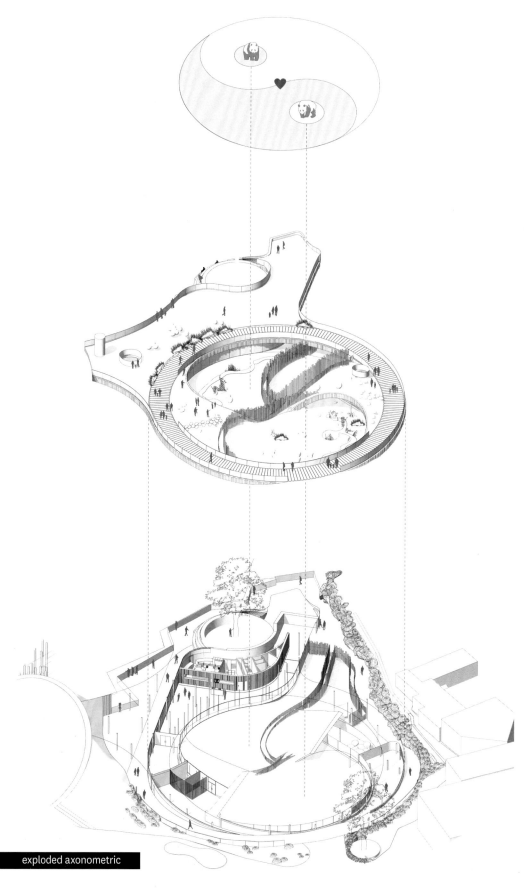

exploded axonometric

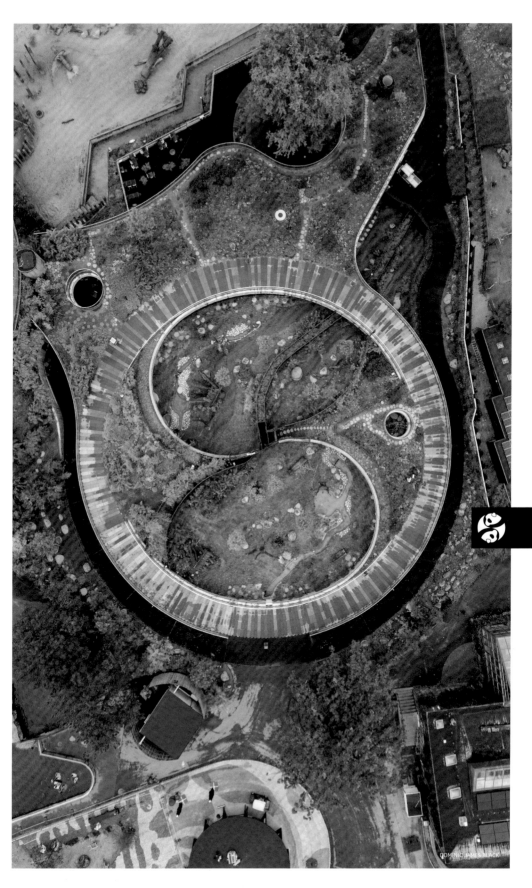

DOMINIC JAMES BLACK

459

RASMUS HJORTSHØJ

RASMUS HJORTSHØJ

RASMUS HJORTSHØJ

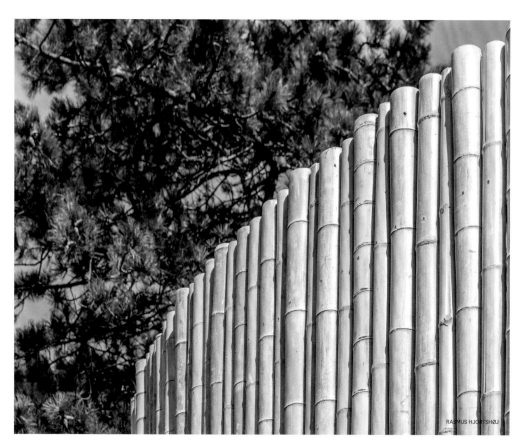

RASMUS HJORTSHØJ

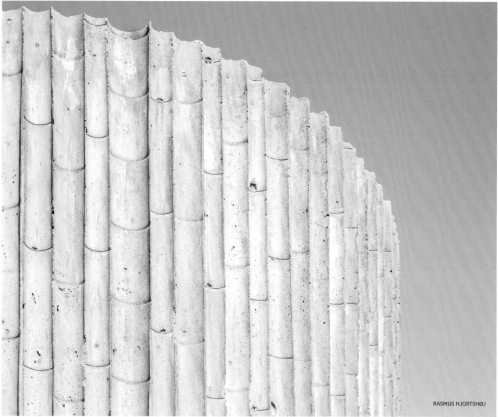

RASMUS HJORTSHØJ

RASMUS HJORTSHØJ

RASMUS HJORTSHØJ

RASMUS HJORTSHØJ

RASMUS HJORTSHØJ

NOMA 2.0

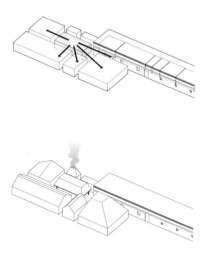

Noma 2.0 is built in Christiania on the protected site of an old fortification once used to store mines for the Royal Danish Navy. The design dissolves the traditional idea of a restaurant into its constituent parts and reassembles them to put the chefs at the heart of the restaurant. A collection of separate yet connected buildings are tailored to their specific needs and are densely clustered around the kitchen. Designed like a panopticon, the kitchen allows the chefs to oversee the staff and guest areas, while every guest can follow what would traditionally happen behind-the-scenes. Each building within the building is connected by glass-covered paths that reveal the changes in weather, daylight, and seasons—making the natural environment integral to the culinary experience. The raw shell of the historic warehouse is preserved and used for back-of-house functions, including the prep kitchen, fermentation labs, fish tanks, terrarium, ant farm, and break-out areas for staff. Guests have the opportunity to walk through each of the surrounding buildings and to experience a variety of Nordic materials and building techniques: The barbecue is a giant walk-in steel chimney, and the lounge looks and feels like a room-size cozy fireplace made entirely of brick—inside and out. Three greenhouses serve as food production, arrival lounge, and experimental kitchen. A permaculture garden designed and planted by Piet Oudolf serves as a garden for the senses, transforming the former military facility into an urban farm for the production, preparation, and consumption of the new Nordic cuisine.

Copenhagen, DENMARK
1.290 M² | Culture **noma**
2018

RASMUS HJORTSHØJ

469

noma

RASMUS HJORTSHØJ

east elevation

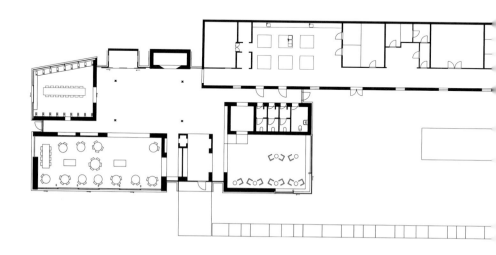

ground floor plan

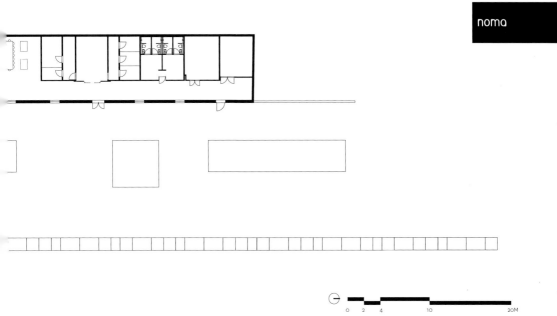

noma

0 2 4   10   20M

SØREN AAGAARD

RASMUS HJORTSHØJ

noma

RASMUS HJORTSHØJ

RASMUS HJORTSHØJ

noma

RASMUS HJORTSHOJ

RASMUS HJORTSHØJ

RASMUS HJORTSHØJ

noma

RASMUS HJORTSHØJ

RASMUS HJORTSHØJ

RASMUS HJORTSHØJ

noma

RASMUS HJORTSHØJ

RASMUS HJORTSHØJ

RASMUS HJORTSHØJ

RASMUS HJORTSHØJ

RASMUS HJORTSHØJ

RASMUS HJORTSHØJ

noma

RASMUS HJORTSHØJ

OCEANIX CITY

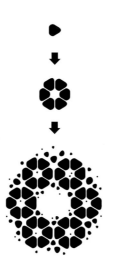

By 2050, 90 percent of the world's largest cities will be
exposed to rising seas. As part of UN-Habitat's New Urban
Agenda, we propose a vision for the world's first sustainable
floating community for 10,000 residents. Designed as a human-
made ecosystem, Oceanix City is anchored in the UN Sustainable
Development Goals, channeling flows of energy, water, food, and
waste to create a blueprint for a modular maritime metropolis.
Oceanix City is designed to grow, transform, and adapt
organically over time, evolving from neighborhoods to cities with
the possibility of scaling indefinitely. Modular neighborhoods of
two hectares create thriving self-sustaining communities of up to
300. All built structures in the neighborhood are kept below seven
stories to create a low center of gravity and to resist wind. Every
building fans out to shade internal spaces and the public realm,
providing comfort and lower cooling costs while maximizing
roof area for solar capture. Communal farming is at the heart of
every platform, allowing residents to embrace sharing culture
and zero-waste systems. Below sea level, biorock floating reefs
and seaweed, oyster, musell, scallop, and clam farming clean
the water and accelerate ecosystem regeneration. Residents
can easily walk or boat through the city using electric vehicles.
All communities regardless of size will prioritize locally sourced
materials for building construction, including fast-growing
bamboo that has six times the tensile strength of steel, a negative
carbon footprint, and can be grown on the neighborhoods
themselves. Floating cities can be prefabricated onshore and
towed to their final site, reducing construction costs. This, paired
with the low cost of leasing space at sea, creates an affordable
model of living. These factors mean that affordable housing can
be rapidly deployed to coastal megacities in dire need. The first
Oceanix Cities are calibrated for the most vulnerable tropical and
subtropical regions around the globe.

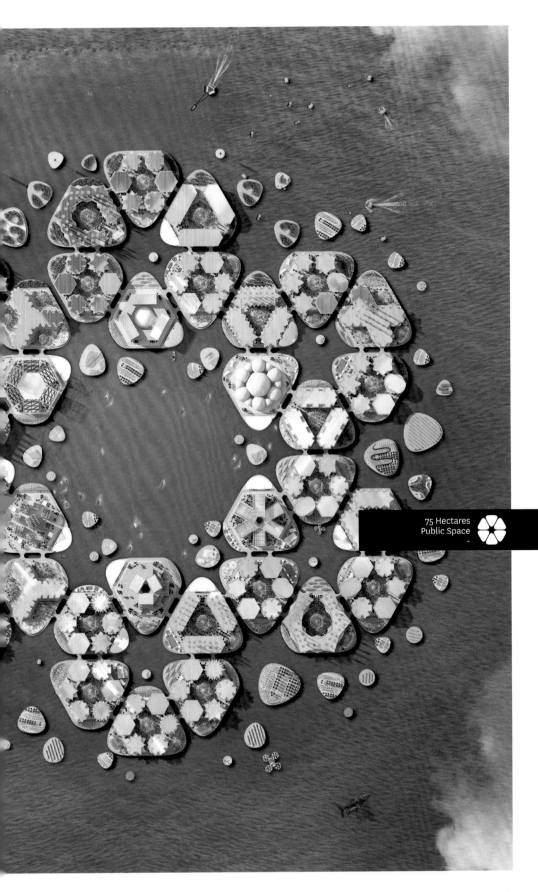

75 Hectares
Public Space

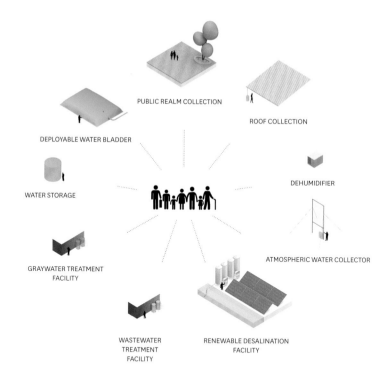

PUBLIC REALM COLLECTION

ROOF COLLECTION

DEPLOYABLE WATER BLADDER

DEHUMIDIFIER

WATER STORAGE

ATMOSPHERIC WATER COLLECTOR

GRAYWATER TREATMENT
FACILITY

WASTEWATER
TREATMENT
FACILITY

RENEWABLE DESALINATION
FACILITY

water kit of parts

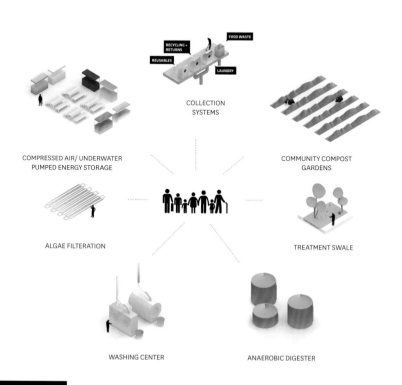

RECYCLING +
RETURNS

FOOD WASTE

REUSABLES

LAUNDRY

COLLECTION
SYSTEMS

COMPRESSED AIR/ UNDERWATER
PUMPED ENERGY STORAGE

COMMUNITY COMPOST
GARDENS

ALGAE FILTERATION

TREATMENT SWALE

WASHING CENTER

ANAEROBIC DIGESTER

waste kit of parts

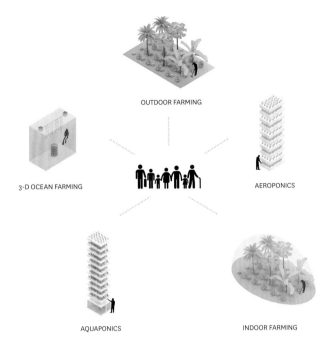

OUTDOOR FARMING

3-D OCEAN FARMING

AEROPONICS

AQUAPONICS

INDOOR FARMING

food kit of parts

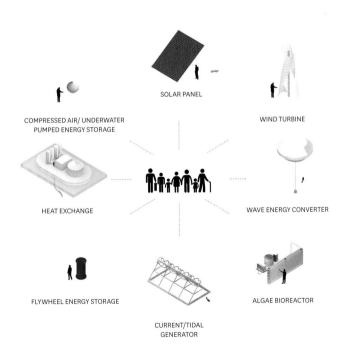

SOLAR PANEL

WIND TURBINE

COMPRESSED AIR/ UNDERWATER
PUMPED ENERGY STORAGE

HEAT EXCHANGE

WAVE ENERGY CONVERTER

FLYWHEEL ENERGY STORAGE

CURRENT/TIDAL
GENERATOR

ALGAE BIOREACTOR

energy kit of parts

city block – 300 people | 2HA

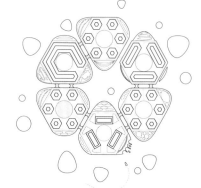

neighborhood block – 1,650 people | 12.2 HA

city – 10,000 people | 75HA

COLLECTIVE INTIMACY

Architecture is losing its monopoly on offering places for social interaction. Social media and massive multiplayer online role-playing games are the new public arenas, disassociated from physical space. Architecture was once where people gathered for memorable events. The Agora for public discourse and the Arena for public spectacle. Now it happens wherever possible online. Human bonding may be the biggest challenge facing architecture and humanity today.

Architecture bridges the gap between space and experience through collective intimacy. It provides spaces for participation, not just consumption. It's pure presence at minimum mass, like a reflective orb hovering above the desert to become a shaded destination by day, and a nocturnal mirage by night. A structure that is a market below and an amphitheater above. A wall of homes that frames a communal park at its heart. And a ballpark that brings the ball game back to the park, where the field is open to residents the vast majority of the year. A collectively intimate architecture that creates bonds between residents and visitors, between players and spectators, between the game and life. Passive spectacle becomes active participation. The Arena becomes Agora. In the future, we won't have to choose between watching and doing. And we won't have to choose between live and life—virtual and actual reality—since life will make them inseparable in ubiquitous augmented reality.

THE ORB

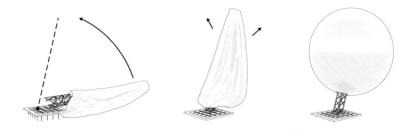

    Scaled to 1/500,000th of the Earth's surface, the inflatable metallic sphere is a source of social gravity and shade for a temporary city in the Nevada desert attended by more than 70,000 people each year. The planetlike sculpture is an inflated spherical mirror, constructed of the same fabric as NASA weather balloons and supported by a 32M-long inclined steel mast, baseplate, and foundation anchors. The Orb's material is designed to easily inflate and deflate, leaving no trace, in the spirit of the festival mantra. Because of The Orb's curvature, it will reflect the space and people around it, showing the social energy and exchange from an entirely new perspective—essentially turning public life into public artifact, and like gravity drawing people to its center. It becomes a mirror for earth lovers—reflecting the passing daytime, evolving life, and other artworks beneath it—a new planet to sci-fi fans, a wayfinder for travelers, or just a huge disco ball for those who love to party. During the day, The Orb will provide shade, and as the Sun sets, the light emitted by Burners and art cars underneath The Orb will reflect onto its belly to serve as a beacon in the night and a destination in the desert.

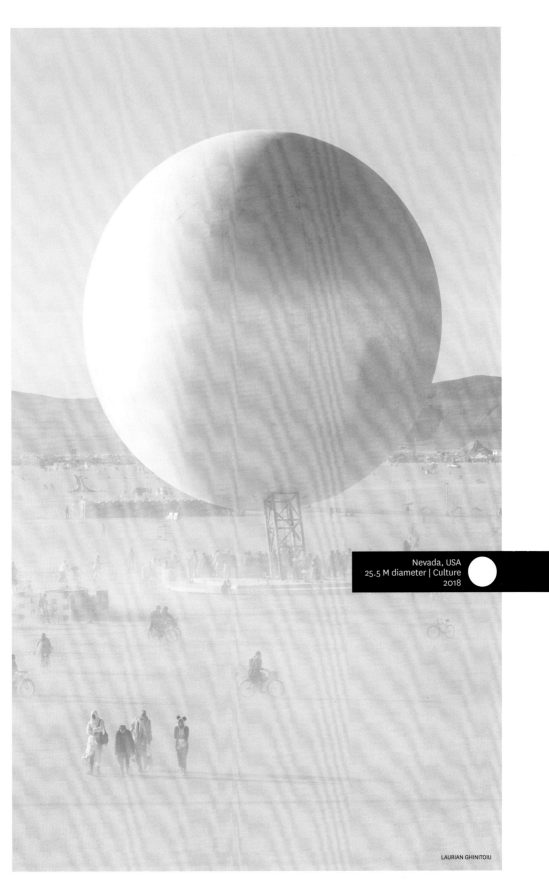

Nevada, USA
25.5 M diameter | Culture
2018

LAURIAN GHINITOIU

JAMEN PERCY

499

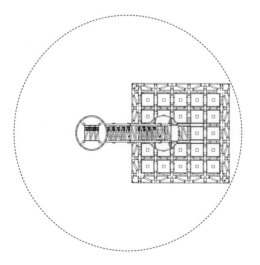

plan

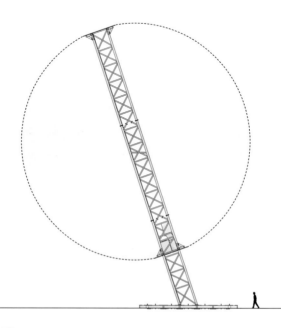

section

0 2 4 10M

ALEX MEDINA

LAURIAN GHINITOIU

LAURIAN GHINITOIU

SHAWN ORTON

MA NING

79&PARK

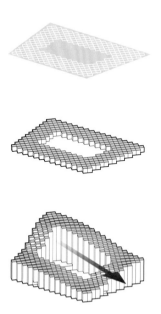

79&Park is a porous residential structure located at the edge of Stockholm's national park Gärdet. The wood-clad volume is comprised of 3.6×3.6m modules organized around an open courtyard. One corner is lifted up to 35 meters in order to maximize the inflow of sunlight as well as views of Gärdet and the free port. The modules cascade down to the building's lowest profile at just seven meters, making 79&Park appear like a gentle hillside, seamlessly blending with the forests around it. The zigzagging façade alternates between open and closed to regulate for privacy, views, thermal exposure, and glare. As a result, depending on the vantage points the building can appear all glazed or entirely wooden. The organic expression and cedar-cladding continues into the green courtyard, where residents and visitors are met by variously sized plateaus that create small activity pockets. Nearly all of the 169 units have unique layouts, appealing to a diverse group of residents across all age groups and walks of life. All dwellings have access to private and shared roof terraces planted with a rich variety of vegetation. The abundance of niches and gardens provides a plethora of meeting places around, within, and on top of the structure, making the entire structure a social condenser for its resident population.

Stockholm, SWEDEN
25,000 M² | Housing
2018

LAURIAN GHINITOIU

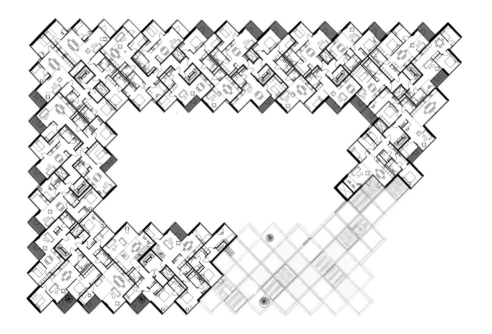

plan level 3

west elevation

plan level 5

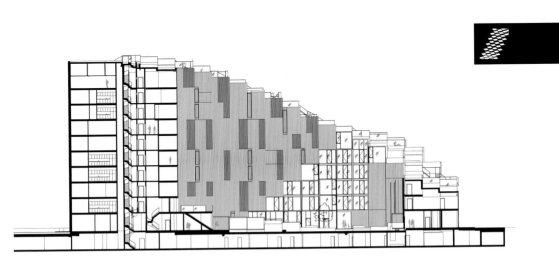

longitudinal section

0 1 2   5   10   15M

LAURIAN GHINITOIU

LAURIAN GHINITOIU

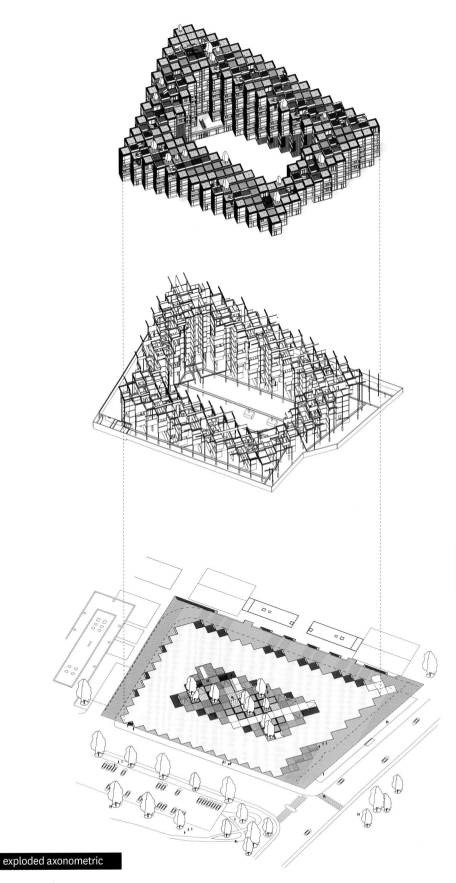

exploded axonometric

ERIC LEPVANDER

LAURIAN GHINITOIU

LAURIAN GHINITOIU

LAURIAN GHINITOIU

LAURIAN GHINITOIU

LAURIAN GHINITOIU

DUBAI EXPO
PLAZA

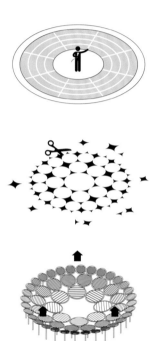

Dubai Expo Plaza and Pavilion is to be the heart of the 2020 Dubai World Exhibition welcoming people of all nations, religious beliefs, languages, and cultures into one space. The plaza will consist of two complementary spaces. One space is a contemporary interpretation of the Souk, the vast shaded public space where people gather during the day. Tall slender columns mushroom at the top forming a continuous canopy of interconnected discs. Each disc tilts toward the center, collectively rising toward the greater perimeter, and forming a shallow dish-like roof that lifts up at the edges to receive visitors from all directions. Above, the discs come together to form an arena for nocturnal performances. The central stage will be built on hydraulic pistons so it can rise from below like a three-dimensional curtain draw. People will access the discs to view performances through the gaps from the square below. Dubai Expo Plaza and Pavilion is the ultimate symbol of the spirit of the World's Fair, representing unity from plurality: Out of many, we come together as one.

Dubai, UAE
20,000 M²
Culture

OAKLAND A'S BALLPARK

As the last remaining sports team in Oakland, the A's new home returns the game to its roots as the natural meeting place for the community. An elevated tree-lined promenade frames the ballpark on all sides. The ballpark dips down to meet the public square and opens the field to the water and the city. The perimeter park connects a series of social spaces for fans watching the sport on game days and extends the urban fabric with a neighborhood park that will be in use 365 days a year, putting the "park" back in "ballpark." The ballpark is carefully placed within its urban surroundings to create the most intimate baseball experience for 35,000 people, all arranged in the closest configuration possible to the home plate. On game days as well as the 284 non-game days every year, the stadium functions as an agora, a space for people to participate in public life, parks, restaurants, and working spaces that are part of the ballpark complex. Rather than an empty venue, the Oakland A's new circular park will be the natural social center for the newest neighborhood in town.

Oakland, California, USA
36,000 M²
Body Culture

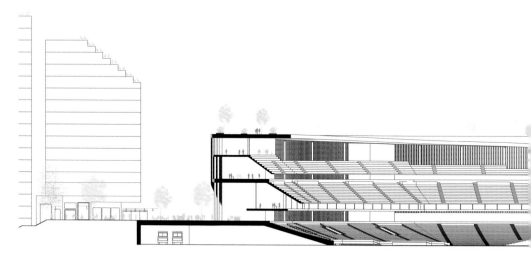

cross section

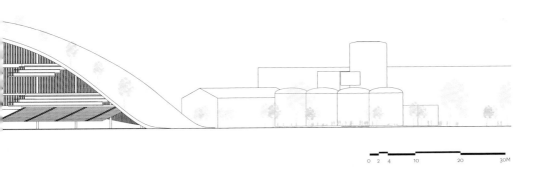

MINDPOOL

Humankind's ability to collaborate through the exchange of ideas and services may be the secret sauce to our success as a species and our future survival. Physical space is the ultimate platform for human interaction. The more distracted we are by our digital omnipresence and social media, the more critical the physical pooling of talent, ideas, and skills becomes for our social well-being and our creative productivity.

The frontier of innovation requires the pooling of human resources in a paradoxical combination of deep diving and surface skimming. To accommodate this oscillation between focus and exchange we must find ways to pool people together without drowning them in the crowd. In our work with Google, we have explored ways to maximize the informational friction between people to ensure that sparks of knowledge will fly from one to another. On one hand, bringing thousands of talents together in a continuous environment. On the other, ensuring a manageable amount of people are in your daily circle. Allowing openness and freedom for teams to expand and contract across an unrestricted territory, simultaneously restraining visual and acoustic noise.

Where the old productivity paradigm was about efficiency, speed, and repetition, creative productivity requires the pooling of people with different skills to flow together in one place to learn new things and try new activities. To open up behavior, we must dissolve the traditional typologies of offices and corridors into new work habitats such as hangars and canopies, platforms and patios, medinas and playas. In our future, pooling will travel beyond the work environment to include all forms of human intercourse. Pooling people, ideas, views, spaces, activities, plants, animals, materials, impressions, sensations, knowledge, care, opinions, expressions, love, and community becomes the ultimate power of formgiving. Architecture is the art of accommodation. It gives social structures built form. It solidifies human relationships in stone and steel. But once materialized, it has the power to separate or connect, bar or bridge: an empty void or a pool of people.

GLASIR

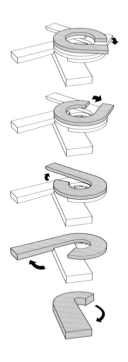

Glasir is designed to merge three different schools into one integrated landscape for learning. The high school, the business school, and the technical school will retain their individual autonomies and identities. Shaped by the internal needs of the students and teachers, Glasir is conceived as a stack of five individual levels that wrap around a central courtyard: one for each of the three institutions, one for food and faculty, and one for physical exercise and gatherings. The building is organized like a vortex, with each level opening up and extending in all directions. Due to the steep slope of the site, the main entrance of the school is in the middle of the building accessible from a bridge. Cascading across several levels, the stepped topography merges the multistory building into a single entity. Designed as an extension and interpretation of the natural landscape, the indoor courtyard with terraced steps provides generous, flexible spaces for group meetings and social events, as well as auditorium seating for performances and announcements. The inner façades between the classrooms and courtyard are clad in colored glass, providing an intuitive overview of the different functions within the building. The exterior glass façades are mounted in a sawtooth shingle that allow the straight elements to form a soft circular shape. Over time, grass planted on the rooftops will slowly grow to allow the education center to disappear into the Faroese fells.

Tórshavn, FAROE ISLANDS
19,200 M² | Education
2018

RASMUS HJORTSHØJ

535

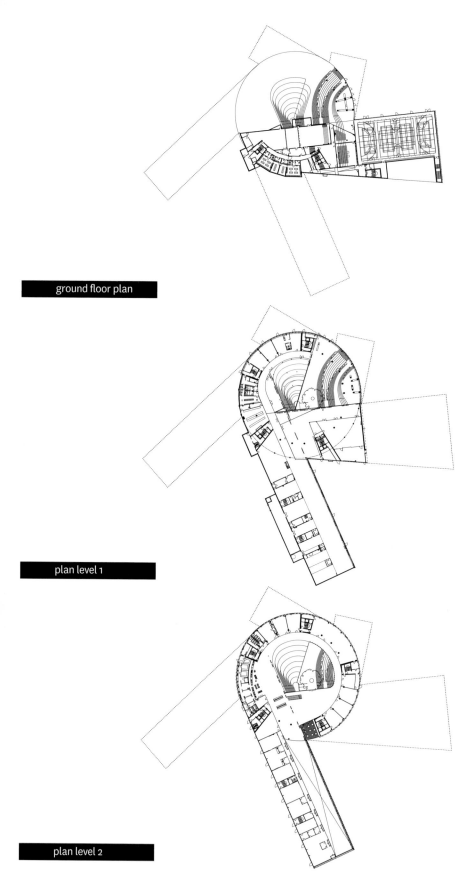

ground floor plan

plan level 1

plan level 2

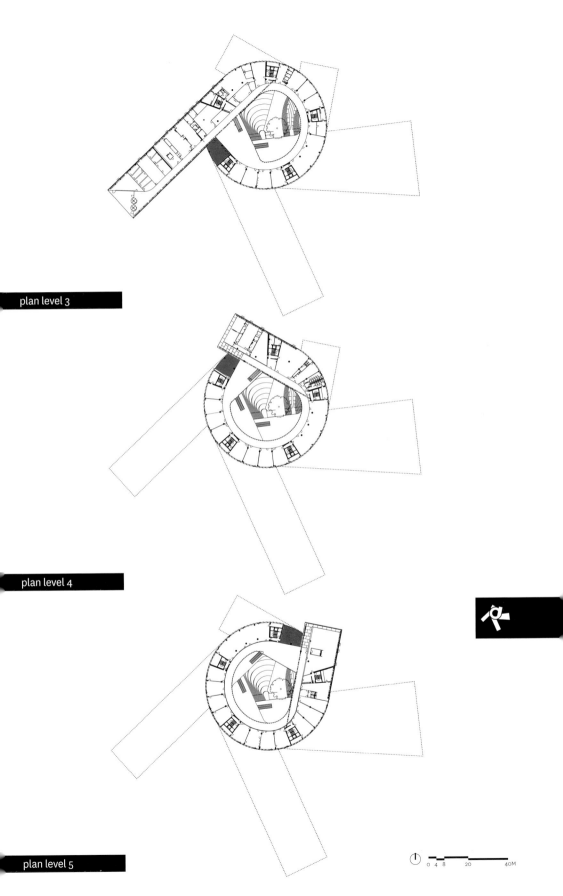

plan level 3

plan level 4

plan level 5

0 4 8   20   40M

RASMUS HJORTSHØJ

RASMUS HJORTSHØJ

538

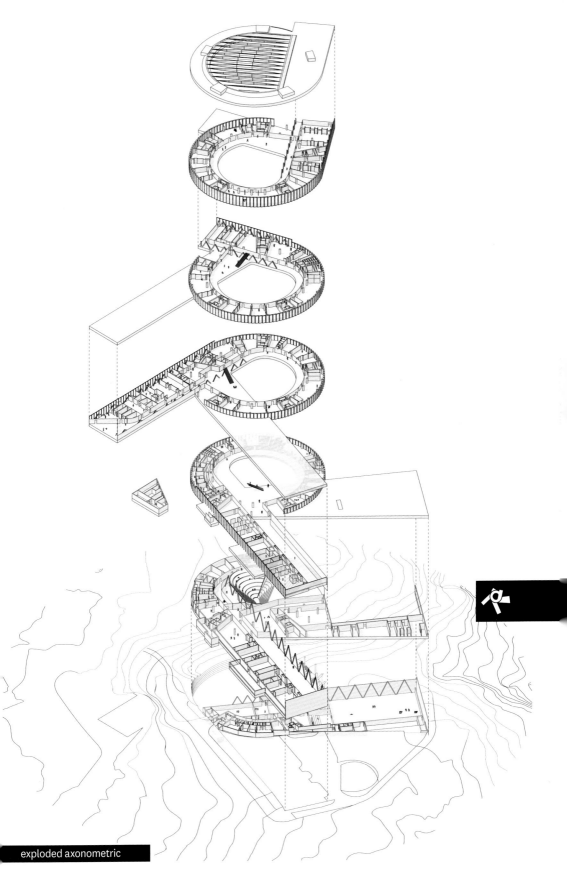

exploded axonometric

north elevation

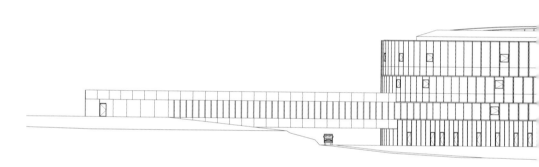

southwest elevation

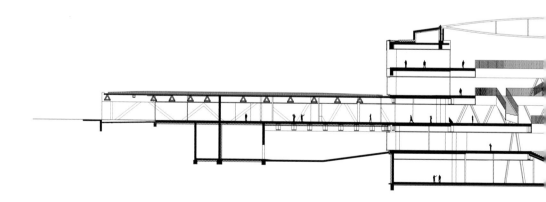

longitudinal section

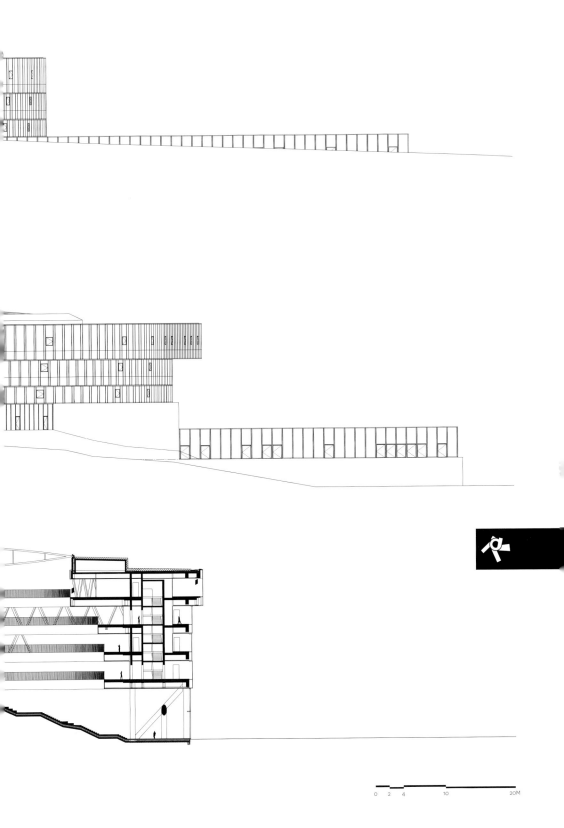

0 2 4 10 20M

RASMUS HJORTSHØJ

RASMUS HJORTSHØJ

RASMUS HJØRTSHØJ

GONÇALO PACHECO

GONÇALO PACHECO

RASMUS HJORTSHØJ

RASMUS HJORTSHØJ

GOOGLE BAYVIEW + CHARLESTON EAST

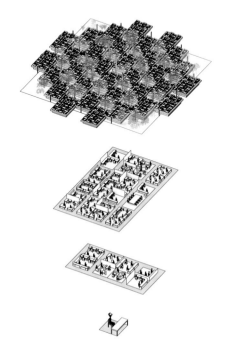

Google, like a hermit crab, has always moved in and out of existing buildings rather than building its own offices. Google's first new-build headquarters needed to provide a physical framework for the organizational architecture that they already have: teams of 25 people, neighborhoods of 100-150, and communities of up to 500 people. Typically, office support functions clutter focus areas and break up continuity between colleagues. By organizing each neighborhood into platforms, colleagues are connected on a single floor plate for focusing, with communal parks and plazas arranged in between. The towns are covered by a single tensile canopy clad in photovoltaics. The draped sheets of PV shingles extend beyond the buildings to shade the façade and cover the outdoor activities. Clerestory windows flood the vast open space in daylight. Each platform and team has its own human-scale architecture of furniture, and space-defining elements allowing great freedom for individual Googlers to hack, adapt, and transform the space over time. The Google campus harvests solar energy, treats storm- and gray water, and is home to the largest geothermal installation in North America. Like a hangar rather than an office building, the future workspace of Google is made from ordinary materials—steel tubes, PV panels, and CLT slabs—used in an extraordinary way.

California, USA
56,000 M² | Commercial
2020

exploded axonometric

CHRISTOPHER MCANNENY

GOOGLE CARIBBEAN

Rooted in the same principles as Mountain View and Bayview, the Caribbean Campus attempts to achieve similar performance criteria at a more competitive price point. The same for less. Straddling the West Channel waterway, the two sibling office buildings stagger out of the landscape, forming ascending zigzagging roof gardens. Walking paths and bike lanes from the Bay Trail meander up the roofscape, allowing Googlers to walk or bike to their desks. Under these gardens, cascading floor plates form an interconnected space for Googlers, flooded with double-height northern light, views of the San Francisco Bay, and instant access to nature. Quadruple-height porches punctuate the south side, spilling life out onto the drive lane—the new social street for the neighborhood. The Google hillside campus is the seed for an emerging neighborhood that combines an innovative workplace, nature, and three-dimensional pathways into a new kind of human-made social landscape.

Sunnyvale, California, USA
96,800 M²
Commercial

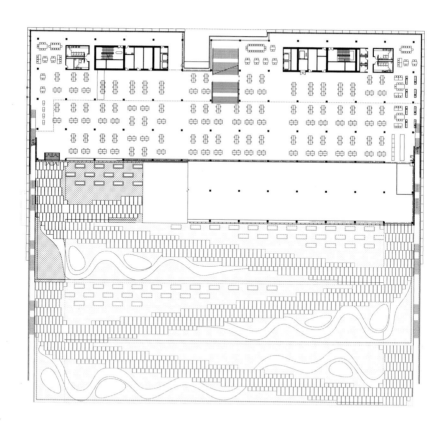

plan level 2

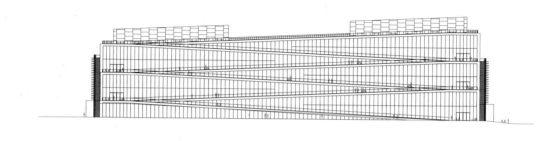

north elevation

0   5   10   25   50M

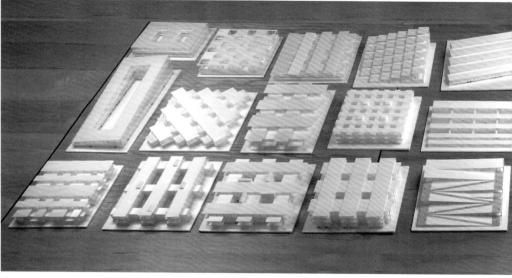

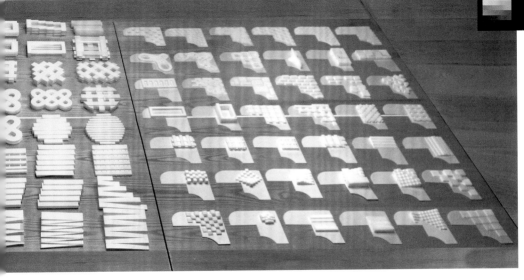

THE SPIRAL

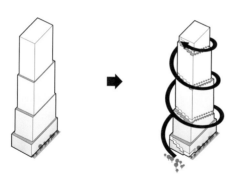

The Spiral will punctuate the northern end of the High Line, where the linear park will appear to carry through into the tower. Forming an ascending ribbon of green spaces, the tower will extend the High Line to the skyline. The Spiral combines the classic ziggurat silhouette of the premodern skyscraper with the slender proportions and efficient layouts of the modern high-rise. Designed for the people that occupy it, The Spiral ensures that every floor of the tower opens up to the outdoors, creating hanging gardens and cascading atria that connect the open floor plates from the ground floor to the summit into a single uninterrupted workspace. The string of terraces wrapping around the building expand the daily life of the tenants to the outside air and light. The Spiral sets a new standard for the contemporary workplace, where nature becomes an integrated part of the work environment while spatial features are continuously adaptable to the changing needs of the tenants and their organizations.

New York, USA
265,000 M² | Commercial
2023

SQUINT OPERA

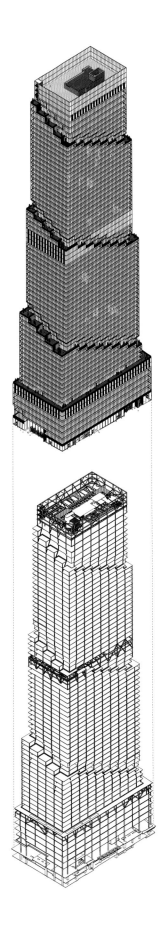

BIG HQ

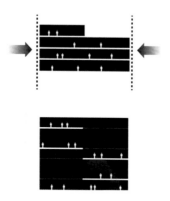

The new BIG HQ is architecturally anchored in Copenhagen harbor's heritage of warehouses and factories. The small footprint at the end of the pier became the main design dilemma: how to organize a single work environment for all of us when we would have to be split between a minimum of four levels. In a counterintuitive decision, we split all the floors in half and doubled the amount of levels. A series of half floor plates overlap to create a cascading environment of interconnected levels that unite the entire eight-story building visually and physically into a single space. The floor plates are carried by 20M-long concrete beams stacked on top of each other, which make the exterior façade appear as a checkerboard of interchanging solid beams and transparent windows. Each floor has direct access to a balcony connected to the balcony above and below, forming a continuous ribbon of outdoor spaces, spiraling from the roof to the quayside like a mountain path. The ribbon doubles as the additional fire escape freeing up the interior from the obstruction of the traditional core. A single stone column of eight different types of rock—ranging from dense granite at the bottom to a porous limestone at the top—form a totem pole to gravity at the heart of the open space. An open stair ricochets from level to level all the way from the basement to the penthouse. Upon entering the main entrance, BIGsters and guests will find themselves in a dramatic Piranesian space, where the inner life of the building reveals itself through diagonal views all the way up to the top floor.

Copenhagen, DENMARK
4,710 M²
Office

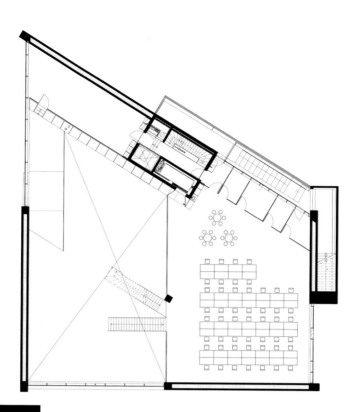

plan level 1

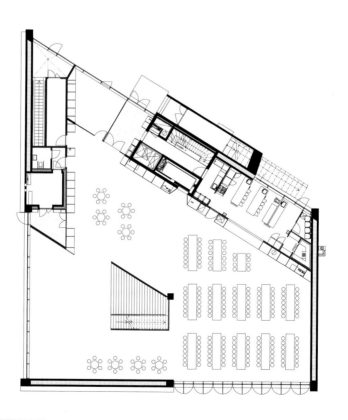

ground floor plan

0   3   6   15M

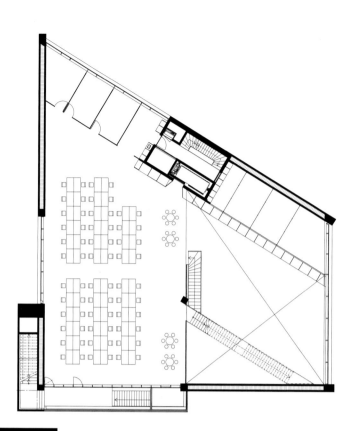

plan level 4

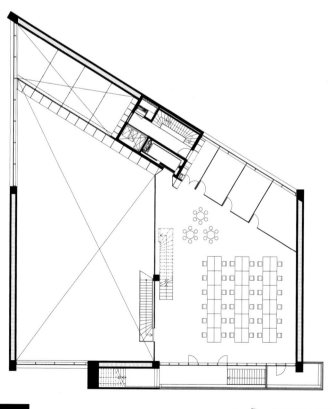

plan level 3

0   3   6   15M

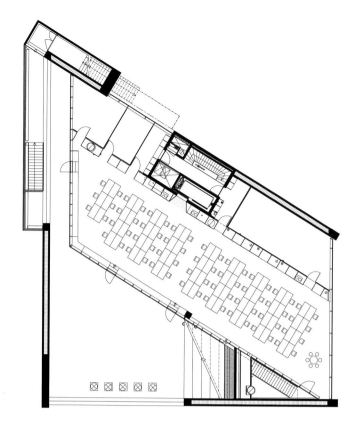

plan level 6

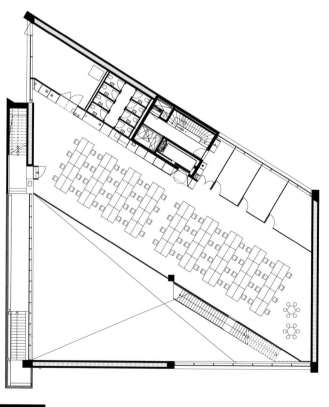

plan level 5

0   3   6   15M

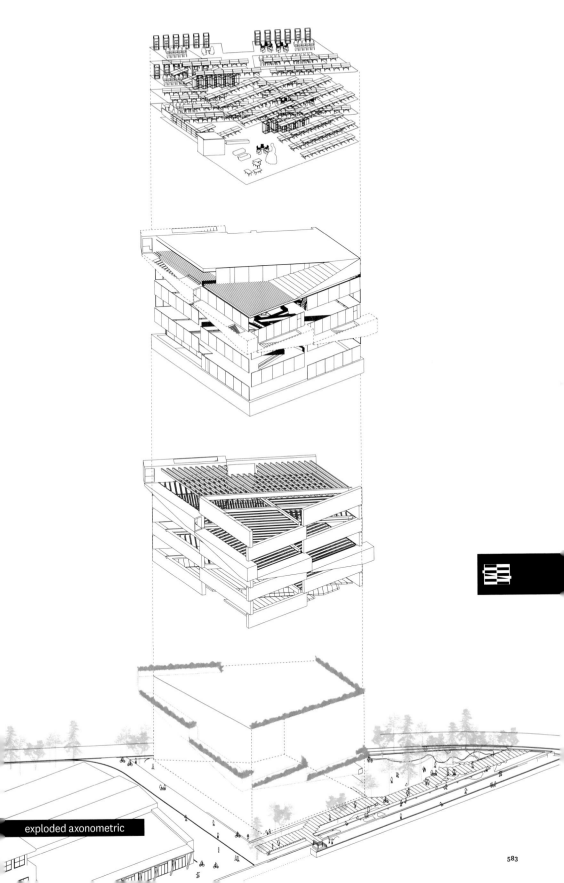

exploded axonometric

BIG LEAP

"Talent can hit a target no one else can hit. Genius can hit a target no one else can see," according to Schopenhauer. By that definition Leonardo da Vinci was undeniably a genius in his capacity to see and hit targets in fields as diverse as architecture, anatomy, astronomy, aerodynamics, and the arts. He was possibly also the last Renaissance man: The last single individual with the bandwidth and talent to master all the arts and sciences.

Today, the escalating complexity of the world and the accelerating speed of change exceed any individual's capacity to comprehend. For architects operating today, the Golden Ratio is no longer the standard—rather, the UN's 17 Sustainable Development Goals are. From a single elegant equation, we are now held to multidimensional success criteria with almost infinite variables. If understanding precedes action—then singular individuals are inevitably left incapacitated and paralyzed. Since sustainability is inherently a question of complex systems, circular design, and holistic thinking, no single person holds the solution. Architects must team with scientists, engineers with biologists, politicians with entrepreneurs, to combine skill sets and perspectives, knowledge and sensibility, to match the complexity of the challenges we face. Future formgivers won't be defined by their individual talents or singular skill sets—but rather by their capacity to pool the skills of the many to give our future form. To act with impact today the individual talent must become a collective genius. The "I" must become a "we."

At BIG we have grown organically over the last two decades from a founder, to a family, to a force of 500. For our next transformation the gradual growth must become a BIG LEAP: Bjarke Ingels Group of Landscape, Engineering, Architecture, and Production. A plethora of in-house professional perspectives may allow us to see what no one else can—what none of us would be able to see on our own. The sum of our individual talents becomes our collective creative genius. A small step for each of us becomes a BIG LEAP for all of us.

Under the umbrella of BIG LEAP, we may stand a chance to tackle the future of making, sensing, sustaining, thinking, healing, and moving. As the scale and complexity of our challenges have escalated, we have found ourselves forced to navigate the confluence of multiple fields of knowledge, in territories as diverse as artificial intelligence, augmented reality, urban metabolism, longevity, robotic enhancement, and interplanetary migration. As our presence and impact on the planet escalates to having planetary side effects in the form of climate change, rising sea levels, plastic patches the size of countries, the scope of our responsibility must rise along with it. As architects, we can apply holistic architectural thinking at the scale of the building, the neighborhood, the city, the country, the region. Inevitably, our thinking can and must rise to the scale of the planet. The last three projects constitute the very early beginnings of the application of the power of formgiving at the planetary scale:

1.   A permanent station on the Moon.
2.   A sustained city on Mars.
3.   And a holistic master plan for our entire planet. Earth.

Ada Gulyamdzhis, Adam Robert Poole, Adam Tomasz Busko, Adrianna Karnaszewska, Agla Egilsdottir, Agne Rapkeviciute, Agnieszka Wardzińska, Agnieszka Magdalena Trzcińska, Agustin Perez-Torres, Aikaterini Apostolopoulou, Aileen Koh, Aina Medina Gironés, Ákos Márk Horváth, Alana Goldweit, Alberto Mennegazzo, Albina Saifulina, Alda Sol Hauksdóttir, Alejandra Cortes, Alessandro Zanini, Alex Bogdan Ritivoi, Alexander Højer Bøegh, Alexander Matthias Jacobson, Alexandra Gezelle, Alexandru Malaescu, Alice Nielsen, Allen Dennis Shakir, Allison Wicks, Alvaro Velosa, Amanda Lima Soares Da Cunha, Amir Mikhaeil, Ana-Maria Vindfeldt, Anders Kofod, Anders Holden Deleuran, Anders Bruntse, Andre Enrico Cassettari Zanolla, Andrea Zalewski, Andrea Angelo Suardi, Andrea Megan Hektor, Andreas Bak, Andreas Buettner, Andreas Klok Pedersen, Andreea Gulerez, Andres Romero Pompa, Andrew Lasbrey, Andrew Peter Young, Andrew Robert Coward, Angel Barreno Gutiérrez, Anja Sønderby Nørgård, Anna Lockwood, Anna Maria Pazurek, Anna Natalia Krzyzanowska, Anne Brown Frandsen, Anne Katrine Sandstrøm, Anne-Charlotte Wiklander, Anne-Sophie Kernwein, Annette Birthe Jensen, Anushka Pramod Karnawat, Aran Coakley, Ariana Szmedra, Ariana Ribas, Ariel Diaz, Ariela Osuna, Artemis Antonopoulou, Athena Morella, August Queitsch Frimann, Autumn Visconti, Barbora Hrmova, Bartosz Kobylakiewicz, Beat Schenk, Beatrice Melli, Beatrise Steina, Benjamin Caldwell, Bernardo Schuhmacher, Bich Tran Le, Biqin Li, Bjarke Koch-Ørvad, Bjarke Bundgaard Ingels, Blake Smith, Borko Nikolic, Brandon Cappellar, Brian Lee Bo Ying, Brian Yang, Bryan Hardin, Buster Christensen, Cæcilie Lærke Hansen, Callum Nolan, Camilla Handrup Miehs, Camille Inès Sophie Breuil, Camilo Leonardo Sandoval Acosta, Carl Pettersson, Carl Macdonald, Carlos Ramos Tenorio, Carlos Castillo Simanca, Carmen Salas Ruiz, Carmen Philippine Wientjes, Casey Tucker, Casey Crown, Catherine Po-Ching Huang, Catherine Stéphanie Boramy Lun, Cathleen Clarke, Cecilie Søs Brandt-Olsen, Celeste Ulrikka Maffia Trolle, Chao-Yang Jason Wu, Charlotte Kjærgreen Silsbury, Cheng-Huang Lin, Chi Yee Corliss Ng, Chi Yin Stepehn Kwok, Chia-Yu Liu, Ching Man Boni Iven, Choong-Il Joseph Kim, Christian Salkeld, Christian Cueva, Christopher Tron, Christopher William Falla, Claire Irene Thomas, Claudia Micula, Claudia Bertolotti, Cristian Teodor Fratila, Cristina Medina-Gonzalez, Cristina Giménez, Dagmara Anna Obmalko, Dalma Ujvari, Daniel Sundlin, Daniel Ferrara Bilesky, Danna Lei, Danyu Zeng, Davi Weber, David Iseri, David Holbrook, David Carlinfanti Zahle, Deborah Campbell, Derek John Lange, Dimitrie Grigorescu, Dominic Black, Dominik Mroziński, Dominyka Voelkle, Dong-Joo Kim, Dora Jiabao Lin, Douglas Breuer, Duncan Horswill, Dylan Hames, Eddie Chiu Fai Can, Eduardo Javier Sosa Trevino, Elisabetta Costa, Elizabeth Mcdonald, Ella Coco Murphy, Elnaz Rafati, Emmett Walker, Enea Michelesio, Eric Wen Tung Li, Erik Kreider, Eskild Schack Pedersen, Eszter Oláh, Eva Seo-Andersen, Ewa Zapiec, Ewa Bryzek, Ewelina Purta, Everett Hollander, Fabian Lorenz, Faye Nelso, Federica Fogazzi, Fernando Longhi Pereira da Silva, Filip Kubiny, Filip Jacek Rozkowski, Finn Nørkjær, Florencia Kratsman, Francesca Portesine, Francisco Alberto Castellanos Martinez, Francois Ducatez, Frederik Lyng, Frederik Skou Jensen, Frederik Wolfgang Mathiasen, Freja Jerne Fagerberg, Friso Van Dijk, Gabriel Jewell-Vitale, Gabrielle Nadeau, Gary Polk, Gaurav Janey, Gayathri Achuthankutty, Geetika Bhutani, Geoffrey Eberle, George Edward Entwistle, Gerard William O'Connell, Gerhard Pfeiler, Giovanni Simioni, Gitte Lis Christensen, Giulia Frittoli, Gonzalo Auger Portillo, Gonzalo Ivan Castro Vecchiola, Gregory Pray, Gualtiero Mario Rulli, Guillaume Evain, Gulnar Qubatov, Gustav Krarup, Gustav Albert Perez Nordahl, Gül Ertekin, Hanna Ida Johansson, Hannah Buckley, Hanne Halvorsen, Haochen Yu, Harry George Andrews, Hector Romero, Heidi Pedersen, Heidi Lykke Sørensen, Helen Shuyang Chen, Helle Holst Eriksen, Henriette Helstrup, Henrik Jacobsen, Hsiao Rou Huang, Hung-Kai Liao, Hyojin Lee, Høgni Laksafoss, Ioannis Gkasialis, Ioannis Gio, Ipek Akin, Irie Annik Meree, Isabel Narea, Isabel Maria de Carvalho Alves da Silva, Isabella Marcotulli, Isela Liu, Ivana Moravová, Jacek Baczkowski, Jacob Karasik, Jagoda Helena Lintowska, Jakob Sand, Jakob Henke, Jakob Laustrup Lange, Jakub Fratczak, Jakub Kulisa, Jakub Mateusz Wlodarczyk, James Hartman, Jamie Maslyn Larson, Jan Magasanik, Jan Leenknegt, Jane Ehrbar, Janie Louise Green, Janina-Ioana Spilcea, Jean Valentiner Strandholt, Jean-Sébastien Pagnon, Jeffrey Andrew Bourke, Jelena Vucic, Jenna Dezinski, Jennifer Ng, Jennifer Kean Proudfoot, Jennifer Yong, Jennifer Amanda Zitner, Jens Majdal Kaarsholm, Jeppe Langer, Jeppe Zhang Andersson, Jeremy Siegel, Jeremy Zitner, Jesper Kanstrup Petersen, Jesper Bo Jensen, Jesper Boye Andersen, Jesse Castillo, Jessica Wells, Jesslyn Guntur, Jialin Yuan, Jin Seung Lee, Jinho Lee, Ji-Young Yoon, Joanna Targowicz, Joanne Chen, João Albuquerque, Johanna Linnea Jakobsson, Jonathan Udemezue, Jonathan Otis Navntoft Russell, Joos Jerne, Jordan Doane, Jordan Felber, Jose Lacruz Vela, Joseph Kuhn, Joseph Baisch, Joshua Woo, Joshua McLaughlin, Josiah Poland, Juhye Kim, Julia Novaes Tabet, Julian Ocampo Salazar, Julie Kaufman, Julie Ma, Juras Lasovsky, Kai-Uwe Bergmann, Kalliopi Caroline Bouros, Kam Chi Cheng, Kamila Abbiazova, Kamilla Heskje, Kaoan Hengles De Lima, Karim Muallem, Karolina Lepa-Stewart, Karoline Tolsøe, Kathleen Cella, Kathryn Lauren Chow, Katrine Juul, Kayeon Lee, Kekoa Jean Charlot, Kelly Neill, Ken Chongsuwat, Kevin Cui, Kevin Hai Pham, Kilmo Kang, Klaudia Szczepanowska, Kongphob Amornparatasin, Kristian Hindsberg, Kristian Mousten, Kristian Ulrik Palsmar, Ksenia Zhitomirskaya, Laj Karsten Rasmussen, Lars Thonke, Lasse Ryberg Hansen, Laura Wätte, Laura Kovacevic, Laura Alberte Liebst Abildgaard, Lauren Michelle Connell, Laurène Marie Alice Lucy, Laurent De Carniere, Lawrence-Olivier Mahadoo, Leon Rost, Liliana Sabeth Cruz-Grimm, Liliane Wenner, Linda Dannesboe Sjøqvist, Lingyi Xu, Linqi Dong, Linus Saavedra, Lisa Nguyen, Lisbet Fritze Christensen, Lisha Wan, Lone Fenger Albrechtsen, Lorenz Krisai, Lorenzo Boddi, Lorenzo Maccacaro, Louise Baagøe Petersen, Louise Natalie Mould, Luca Pileri, Luca Senise, Luca Nicoletti, Luca Braccini, Lucas Coelho Netto, Lucas Stanley Carriere, Lucia Sanchez Ramirez, Lucian Tofan, Luciana Bondio, Ludmila Majernikova, Lukas Molter, Mackenzie Keith, Mads Bjarrum, Mads Engaard Stidsen, Mads Primdahl Rokkjær, Mads Hvidberg, Mads Christian Klestrup Pedersen, Mads Mathias Pedersen, Magdalena Mróz, Magni Waltersson, Maki Matsubayashi, Malgorzata Zielonka, Malka Logo, Mantas Povilaika, Marah Wagner, Marcos Anton Banon, Marcus Wilford, Margaret Tyrpa, Maria Acosta, Maria Sole Bravo, Maria Skotte, Maria Natalia Lenardon, Mariana De Soares E Barbieri Cardoso, Marie Lancon, Marie Hedegaard Jensen, Marina Cogliani, Marius Tromholt-Richter, Marjan Mostavi, Martha Kennedy, Martin Voelkle, Martin Sull, Martyna Kloda, Masa Tatalovic, Matea Mađaroš, Mateo Fernandez, Mathis Paul Gebauer, Matilde Tavanti, Matteo Dragone, Matteo Pavanello, Matteo Baggiarini, Matthew Oravec, Matthew Thomson, Mattia Di Carlo, Mauro Saenz de Cabezon Aguado, Maxwell Moriyama, May Dieckmann, Megan Van Artsdalen, Melissa Jones, Melissa Murphy, Melissa Andres, Melody Hwang, Mengyuan Li, Merve Kavas, Mette Brinch Lyster, Mher Tarakjian, Michael Leef, Michael James Kepke, Michael Rene Hansen, Michael Stephen Howard, Michela Cardia, Michelle Stromsta, Mike Yue Yin, Mikkel M. R. Stubgaard, Mikki Seidenschnur, Milan Holm Moldenhawer, Miles Treacy, Ming Ken Cheong, Min-jung Ku, Minyu Li, Mo Li, Monika Dauksaite, Morgan Day, My Duy Bui, Nana Lysbo Svendsen, Nandi Lu, Nanna Gyldholm Møller, Napatr Pornvisawaraksakul, Naphit Puangchan, Nasiq Khan, Natchaluck Radomsittipat, Nawapan Suntorachai, Neha Sadruddin, Nereida Trujillo, Neringa Jurkonyte, Nicholas Reddon, Nick Beissengroll, Nicolas Michael Kastbjerg, Nicolas Vincent Robert Carlier, Nicole Salden Venøbo, Nikolaos Romanos Tsokas, Ningnan Ye, Nojan Adami, Norbert Nadudvari, Nynne Brynjolf Madsen, Ole Elkjær-Larsen, Oliver Siekierka, Oliver Thomas, Oliver Nybakk, Ombretta Colangelo, Otilia Pupezeanu, Paige Greco, Palita Tungjaroen, Parinaz Kadkhodayi-Kholghi, Patrick Nyangkori, Patrick Hyland, Paul Clemens Bart, Paula Madrid, Paula Domka, Paula Gonzalez, Paula Joanna Tkaczyk, Paulina Panus, Pauline Lavie, Pawel Marjanski, Per Bo Madsen, Pernille Patrunch, Pernille Kinch Andersen, Peter Sepassi, Peter Badger, Peter Mortensen, Peter David, Petros Palatsidis, Phillip Macdougall, Phillipa Seagrave, Pia Møller-Holst, Pin Wang, Polina Galantseva, Ruhiya Veerasunthorn, Raphael Ciriani, Rasam Aminzadeh, Richard Elbert, Richard Garth Howis, Richard Steven Keys, Rihards Dzelme, Rita Sio, Robert Grimm, Robert Ryan Harvey, Roberto Fabbri, Ross James O'Connell, Rron Bexheti, Ruhiya Melikova, Ruo Wang, Ruth Maria Otero Garcia, Ryan Duval, Ryan Hong, Ryohei Koike, Samuel Michael Collins, Sanam Salek, Sang Ha Jung, Santa Krieva, Sara Najar Sualdea, Sarah Leth Dalley, Sarah Green-Lieber, Sarah Asli, Sarkis Sarkisyan, Sascha Leth Rasmussen, Sau Wai Stephanie Hui, Sean Franklin, Sean Shamloo Rezaie, Sean O'Brien, Sebastian Claussnitzer, Seda Yildiz, Seo Young Shin, Seongil Choo, Seonhwan Kim, Sera Eravci, Sergiu Calacean, Seunghan Yeum, Shane Dalke, Sheela Maini Søgaard Christiansen, Shu Zhao, Sijia Zhou, Sijia Zhong, Sille Foltinger, Simon Scheller, Simone Grau, Siqi Zhang, Siva Sepehry Nejad, Snorre Emanuel Nash Jørgensen, Sofia Fors Adolfsson, Sofya Borlykova, Sophie Lee Peterson, Sorcha Burke, Soren Grunert, Stanisław Daniel Rudzki, Steen Kortbæk Svendsen, Stefan Plugaru, Stephanie Mauer, Stine Sandstrøm Christensen, Sue Biolsi, Sung Ho Choi, Susie Kang, Søren Martinussen, Søren Aagaard, Søren Dam Mortensen, Tal Mor, Taliya Nurutdinova, Tamilla Mahmudova, Tara Abedinitafreshi, Taylor Hewett, Terrence Chew, Théo Hamy, Thomas Christoffersen, Thomas Smith, Thomas McMurtrie, Thomas Calvert, Thomas Hoff Schmidt, Thor Larsen-Lechuga, Tillmann Marc Pospischil, Timo Harboe Nielsen, Tine Kaspersen, Tobias Hjortdal, Tomas Rosello Barros, Tomas Karl Ramstrand, Tommy Bjørnstrup, Tony-Saba Shiber, Tore Banke, Tracey Coffin, Tracy Sodder, Trine Emilie Sørensen, Troels Soerensen, Tyler John Koraleski, Tyrone James Cobcroft, Ulla Hornsyld, Valentino Gareri, Wei Lesley Yang, Veronica Watson, Veronica Varela, Weronika Siwak, Wesley Thompson, Victor Mads Moegreen, Viktoria Millentrup, Wilbur Franklin Sharpe III, William Jackson, William Herb, William Henry Campion, Vincent Katienin Konate, Vinish Sethi, Vladislav Saprunenko, Won Ryu, Xavier Delanoue, Xi Zhang, Xingyue Huang, Xuechen Kang, Yara Rahme, Yasmin Bianca Kobori Belck, Yen-Jung Alex Wu, Yeong JoonKo, Yi Lun Yang, Yiling Emily Chen, Ying Yi Cai, Youngjin Yoon, Yu Inamoto, Yuanxun Xu, Yue Hu, Yuejia Ying, Yueying Wan, Yushan Huang, Ziad Shehab, Zirui Pang, Ziyu Guo, Zuzanna Hanna Sliwinska.

589

CITY OF NEW HOPE

The Moon was formed around 4.5 billion years ago out of debris thrown into orbit by a massive collision between a smaller proto-Earth and another planetoid. This collision resulted in a quite similar terrestrial composition. The absence of a significant atmosphere leaves the Moon subject to a constant bombardment of asteroids, giving it the cratered appearance we are all familiar with and making it challenging to inhabit even though it is the only other body in the solar system that humans have visited.

Many consider the Moon a good outpost for a base of operations to enable journeys deeper into the solar system thanks to its low gravity. The discovery of water in the lunar regolith adds the potential for local food and fuel production. The discovery of subterranean lava tubes offers abundant protection from radiation and asteroids as well as enhanced thermal stability. The proximity to Earth allows for a short commute (48 hours) and little delay in communications (2.5s), allowing for close contact and remote operations.

The City of New Hope is a vision for a long-term human outpost anchored in commercial activities for Earth and space-oriented satellites, science, quantum computing, mining, and tourism. The physics at the lunar surface including the very low gravity and the month-long day cycle offers an opportunity to reimagine the way we work, play, live, and grow—on the Moon. This will be the new space frontier allowing us to rewrite the clichés of what a space-faring society will look and feel like.

DATA

Gravity	0.166 g
Pressure	3×10^{-15} atm
Day	29 days 12 hours 44 minutes
Year	354 days 8 hours 48 minutes
Surface Temperature	−173 to 116 °C
Magnetic Field	✖ 1% of Earth
Radiation	✖ 380 mSv/year
Surface Wind	no atmosphere
Light Intensity	100%
Metals	✔
Carbon	✔ trace quantities from solar wind
Water	✔ deposits in the pole and soil
Geothermal	✖
Travel Time from Earth	48 hours

*The Moon only has **1/6th gravity**
compared to that of the Earth.*

0.166 g

3,474 km

SIZE | GRAVITY

PRESSURE 3x10⁻¹⁵ atm

ATMOSPHERIC PRESSURE

*The Moon's magnetic field is significantly weaker
than the Earth's and the absence of a dipole
would signal the absence of an active mantle.*

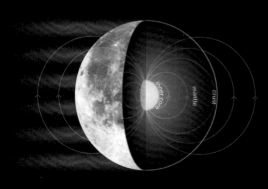

MAGNETIC FIELD

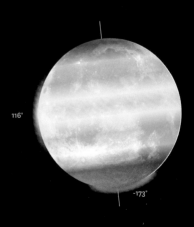

116°

-173°

SURFACE TEMPERATURE

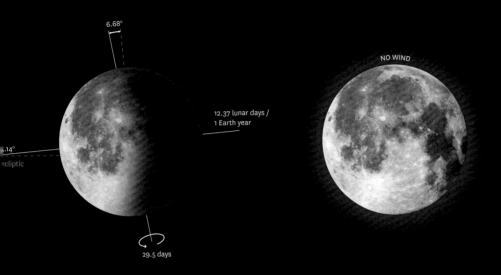

6.68°

12.37 lunar days /
1 Earth year

.14°
ecliptic

29.5 days

AXIAL TILT | DAY/YEAR

NO WIND

**WIND SPEED AT LOW & HIGH
ALTITUDE**

*There is almost **zero atmosphere** on the Moon,
making the environment ideal for astronomy research.*

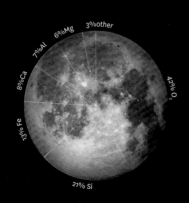

3%other

6%Mg

7%Al

8%Ca

42%O₂

13% Fe

21% Si

SURFACE MATERIAL COMPOSITION

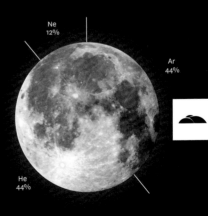

Ne
12%

Ar
44%

He
44%

ATMOSPHERE COMPOSITION

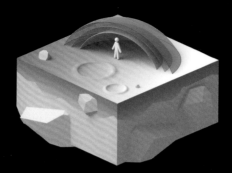

PROTECTION

*The Moon requires almost as much protection for human survival as outer space does—if not more due to lunar dust. Layers of **protection for pressure, temperature, radiation, and meteorites** are necessary for survival.*

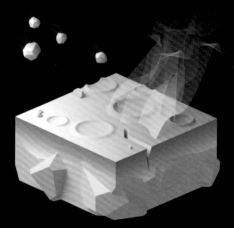

CLIMATE

*Meteorites, solar storms, temperature swings, and moonquakes occur on the lunar surface. About **180 meteorites hit the Moon every year.** When solar storms occur, they can be fatal without proper shelter. For the majority of the lunar cycle, the surface temperature is too cold or hot for human survival. **Moonquakes are less energetic than Earth 5.5 Richter, but last very long** (one hour).*

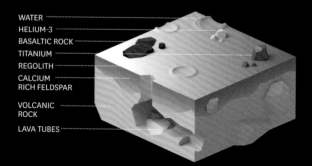

WATER
HELIUM-3
BASALTIC ROCK
TITANIUM
REGOLITH
CALCIUM
RICH FELDSPAR
VOLCANIC
ROCK
LAVA TUBES

RESOURCES

*Lunar regolith is very fine and abrasive resulting from its long history of impacts with meteors. **Water can be found in frozen form** on permanently shaded craters at the poles, and present in low concentrations over much of the Moon's surface. The abundance of **Helium-3 could be used for nuclear fusion and fission reactors**. In addition, lava tubes are also considered a valuable resource as they offer protection from radiation, extreme temperature swings, and meteor impacts.*

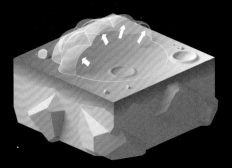

PRESSURE

The atmospheric pressure is equivalent to **10,000KM above Earth sea level**. Having very low atmospheric pressure at surface level creates very large forces when introducing a human minimum of 0.5 ATM inside. The magnitude of the pressure difference is much higher than gravity, pushing the shape into a sphere. As a result of the pressure stabilization, **inflatable structures have the advantage of covering long spans without columns**.

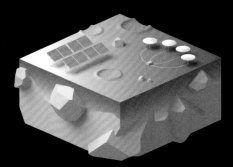

ENERGY GENERATION

The tenuous atmosphere means that electricity can be harvested with solar panels at a higher efficiency than on Earth. In addition, Helium-3 and Thorium nuclear fusion could be used in reactors and as rocket fuel.

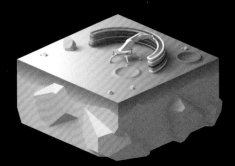

3D-PRINTING

Having a limited amount of people to set up a new base can be compensated by **robots doing most of the brute-force work**. Local resources can be excavated and processed to create printable materials in order to construct pressurized spaces for habitation.

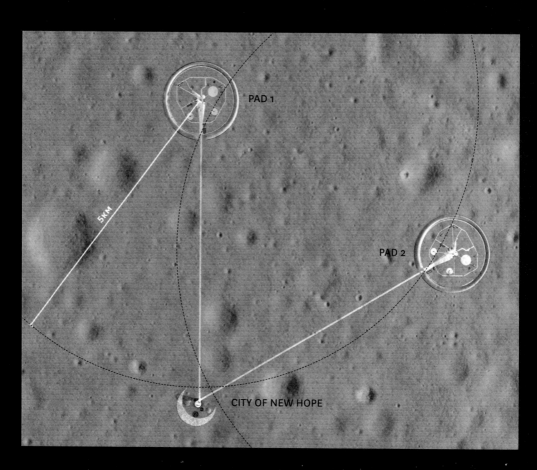

PAD 1

5KM

PAD 2

CITY OF NEW HOPE

Surface infrastructure is manufactured predominately with in situ resources (energy production, communications satellite, automated industrial space) provides the necessary means to sustain a long-term settlement within the lava tube below.

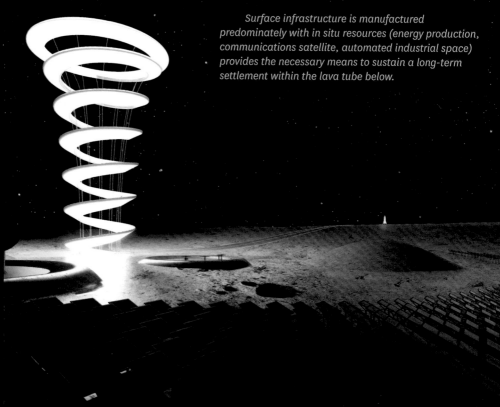

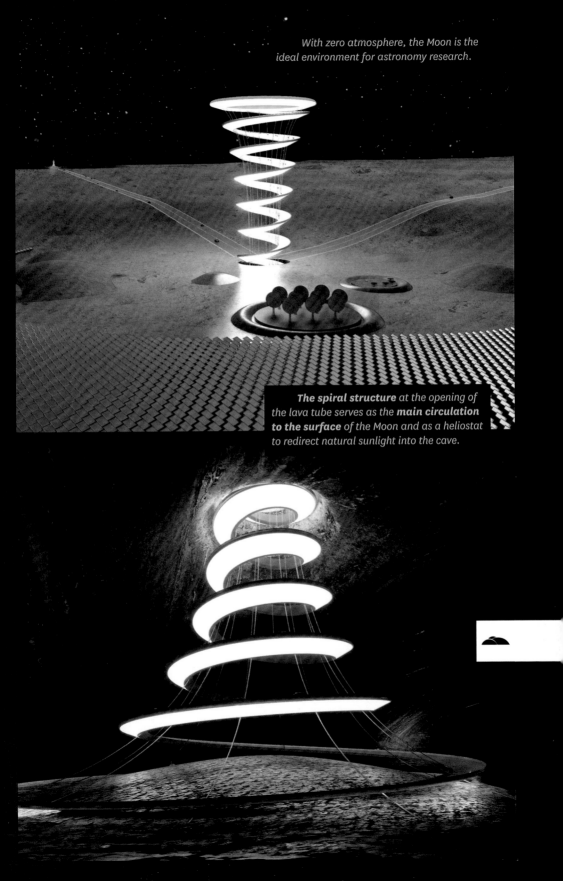

With zero atmosphere, the Moon is the ideal environment for astronomy research.

The spiral structure at the opening of the lava tube serves as the **main circulation to the surface** of the Moon and as a heliostat to redirect natural sunlight into the cave.

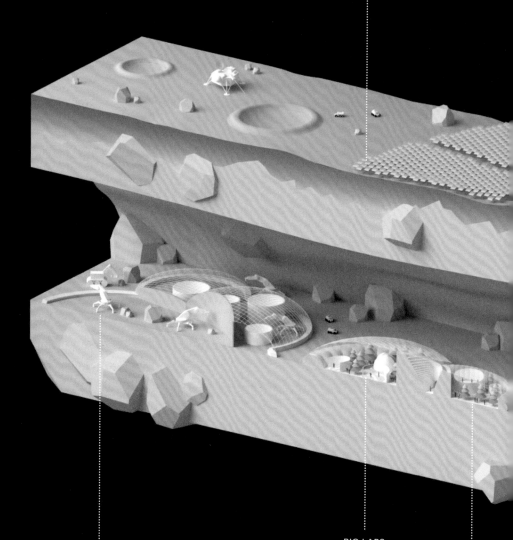

SOLAR PANELS

BIO LABS

DOMES UNDER
CONSTRUCTION

INDUSTRIAL
SPACE

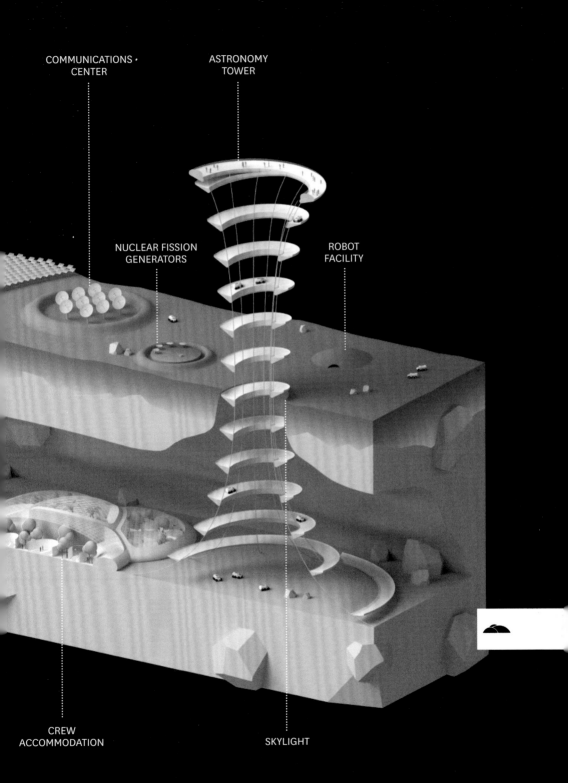

COMMUNICATIONS ·
CENTER

ASTRONOMY
TOWER

NUCLEAR FISSION
GENERATORS

ROBOT
FACILITY

CREW
ACCOMMODATION

SKYLIGHT

ground floor plan

0 5 10   20   40M

Eating together is one of the most special moments for many astronauts living in the International Space Station.

The living quarters simulate the circadian cycle to account for the two-week daylight cycle on the Moon.

With the reduced gravity compared to the Earth, people will have the ability to **jump around 3M-high**!

The hub provides facilities that support sports, music, and art in space to sustain a healthy mental wellness for inhabitants—especially for long-term missions.

Modern vertical farming creates up to **70 times** the yield of traditional farming per m². Aeroponics saves up to 95 percent of the water of traditional farming. With new LED lighting, energy costs can be reduced compared with first-generation vertical farming.

3D-printed structures using lunar regolith provide the functional spaces for people to work and collaborate.

*The central oasis not only provides most of the food production for the Innovation Hub, it also creates a **natural respite for the inhabitants**.*

MARS SCIENCE CITY

Mars is our immediate neighbor one spot farther away from the Sun. It is often referred to as The Red Planet due to the iron oxide prevalent on its surface. Surprisingly, at nightfall fine-grain dust particles in the thin atmosphere turn the Martian sunsets blue.

Due to its rotational period as well as its axial tilt relative to the ecliptic plane, its season and day cycles are extremely similar to Earth's. It is the home to the highest mountain in the Solar System, Olympus Mons, a staggering three times taller than Mt. Everest, and it is also home to Valles Marineris, one of the largest canyons in the Solar System. Mars has two tiny moons, Phobos and Deimos, the Greek gods of fear and terror.

Mars is a terrestrial planet with a thin atmosphere, with Moon-like impact craters as well as Earth-like valleys, deserts, and polar ice caps. Since the 1960s, we've visited Mars frequently. We've had eyes in the sky, witnessing ice forming and melting on the poles, craters, frozen lava flows, dried-out archipelagoes, landslides, dust devils, mountain ranges, and frost in the mornings. We've had wheels on the ground, already leaving tire tracks and litter.

The Mars Science City is a prototypical test site for a sustained city on Mars. Using the same techniques as on the Moon: robotic construction, excavation, 3D printing, and inflatable membranes, we aim to build a campus on Earth to host education and engineering, science and agriculture, conferences and exhibitions related to interplanetary exploration and settlement. Working and living there will allow us to gain experience with climate control, safety, quality of construction, and resilience of the human-made ecosystems that will be invaluable when we finally go to Mars. Part academic, part commercial, and part exhibition, it will act as a Martian embassy on Earth—the first foothold of our neighbor planet on Terran soil.

DATA

Gravity	0.39 g
Pressure	0.006 atm
Day	24 hours 40 minutes
Year	687 Earth days
Surface Temperature	–140 to 30 °C
Magnetic Field	✖ minor
Radiation	✔ 110 mSv/year
Surface Wind	0–90 km/h
Light Intensity	43%
Metals	✔
Carbon	✔
Water	✔ water-ice and underground lakes
Geothermal	✔
Travel Time from Earth	6 months

0 AU   1   2

MERCURY   VENUS   EARTH   MARS   ASTERIOD BELT

MOON

3 months

5 months   5 months

When Earth and Mars are aligned
*it only takes **3 months** to get there...*

3   4   5

JUPITER

 GANYMEDE

 CALLISTO

EUROPA

IO

3 years

*The same time it took **Magellan to sail from South America to Guan** 500 years ago. The three-month commute didn't stop the Europeans from traversing the Pacific.*

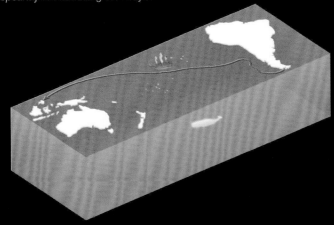

* planets not to scale

Gravity on Mars is really light! **A 100kg person will weigh 38kg upon arrival on Mars**—*an amazing 3-month diet!*

0.38 g

6,779 km

SIZE | GRAVITY

PRESSURE 6.36x10⁻³ atm

ATMOSPHERIC PRESSURE

Mars is temperate. **A Martian summer day by the equator is about 30°C,** *the same as a Danish summer. It does get a lot colder though...*

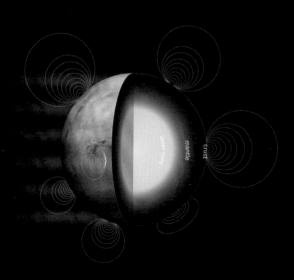

outer core

mantle

crust

MAGNETIC FIELD

30°

-140°

SURFACE TEMPERATURE

Mars has no global magnetic field like Earth—so **no protection from radiation.**

*Mars has the same seasonal tilt as Earth, which means that we will have **the same 4 seasons, only twice as long**—because the Martian year is twice as long.*

25°

355.5 Mars days /
1 Earth year

1.85°

ecliptic

24 hours 40 minutes

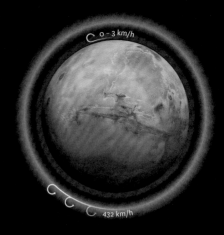

0 – 3 km/h

432 km/h

AXIAL TILT | DAY/YEAR

WIND SPEED AT
LOW & HIGH ALTITUDE

*And finally a cosmic coincidence: On Earth all living things have evolved to a 24-hour day cycle. **On Mars we will have the exact same day cycle**—only we get 40 minutes more to snooze every day!*

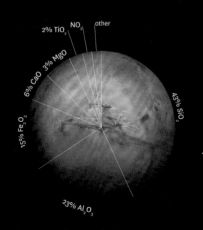

2% TiO_2 NO_2 other

3% MgO

6% CaO

15% Fe_2O_3

43% SiO_2

23% Al_2O_3

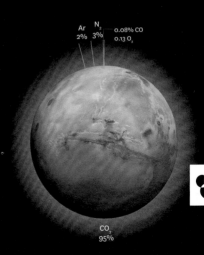

Ar N_2 0.08% CO
2% 3% 0.13 O_2

CO_2
95%

6.36 x 10^{-3} atm

SURFACE MATERIAL COMPOSITION

ATMOSPHERE COMPOSITION

So, what do we have on Mars?
*We have **regolith**. We can sort it and get **ice** that gets us **water**,*
*stones, and **sand**—so we can make **bricks**, **ceramics**, and **concrete**...*

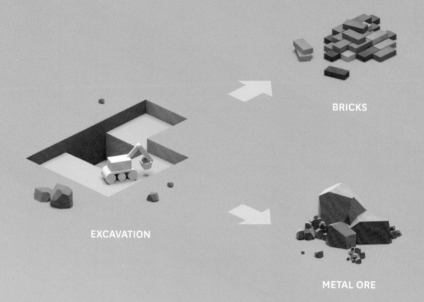

BRICKS

EXCAVATION

METAL ORE

REGOLITH

SURFACE MINING

WATER

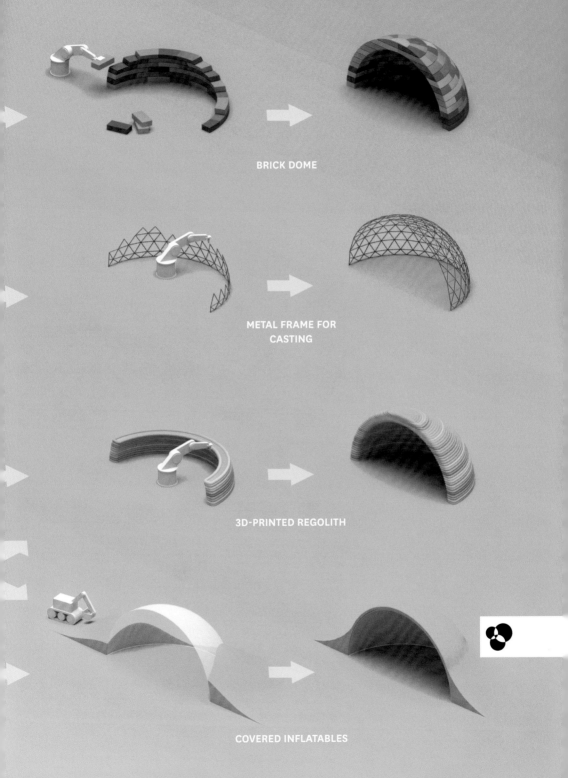

BRICK DOME

METAL FRAME FOR
CASTING

3D-PRINTED REGOLITH

COVERED INFLATABLES

*We can sort the sand further to make
aluminum and glass to make **technology**...*

*... and solar cells. Then we can **produce power;** with power and water, we can make **electrolysis** and split the water into **hydrogen** and **oxygen**. With the CO2-rich atmosphere on Mars, we can use a Sabatier reactor to create methane for **rocket propellant**—so we can **go back home.***

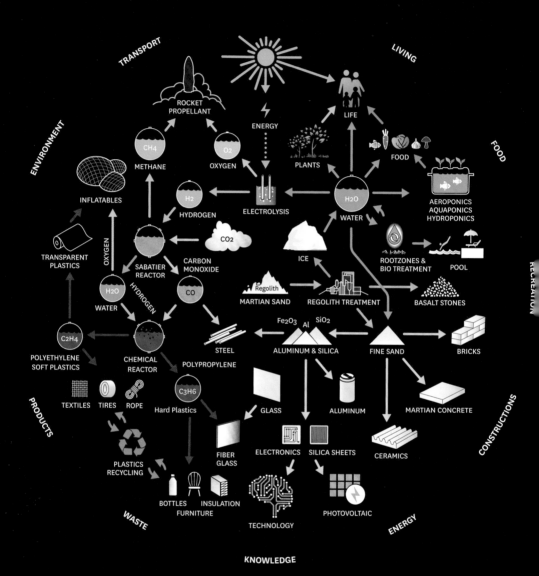

*The byproducts are **water** and **carbon monoxide**. Combined with the iron oxide, we can make **steel** and with further chemical reactors, we can make **hard and soft plastics**! We will of course recycle every single resource as they are so precious to us. The soft plastics wil give us **inflatable membranes**, so we can make pressurized environments where we can **grow plants**... and have rootzone gardens for water purification so we can even start enjoying the water. We can create **agriculture, hydroponics,** and **aquaponics** to grow food... **to sustain human life!***

*We have created an entire **human-made ecosystem** working with the ingredients that are already there plus the knowledge, creativity, and tools that we bring from Earth. Learning from Earth, we basically have 3 different ways to build:*

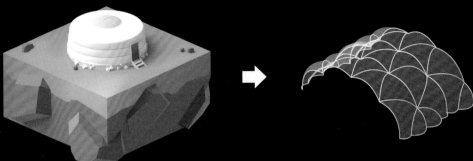

SEWING

INFLATABLES

YURT- MONGOLIA
Transportable building withstands strong winds
and low & high temperatures –35° to +40°C

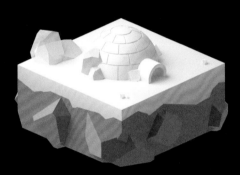

STACKING

3D-PRINTING

IGLOO - CANADA
Abundant snow and very low temperatures

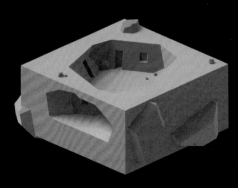

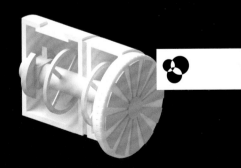

DIGGING

TUNNEL-BORING

TROGLODYTE - TUNISIA
Underground housing for high temperatures

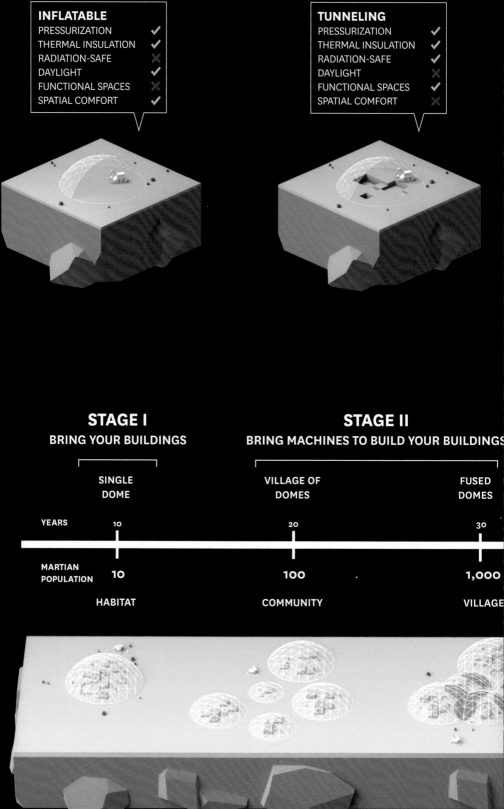

INFLATABLE

PRESSURIZATION	✓
THERMAL INSULATION	✓
RADIATION-SAFE	✗
DAYLIGHT	✓
FUNCTIONAL SPACES	✗
SPATIAL COMFORT	✓

TUNNELING

PRESSURIZATION	✓
THERMAL INSULATION	✓
RADIATION-SAFE	✓
DAYLIGHT	✗
FUNCTIONAL SPACES	✓
SPATIAL COMFORT	✗

STAGE I
BRING YOUR BUILDINGS

STAGE II
BRING MACHINES TO BUILD YOUR BUILDINGS

SINGLE
DOME

VILLAGE OF
DOMES

FUSED
DOMES

YEARS   10   20   30

MARTIAN
POPULATION   10   100   1,000

HABITAT   COMMUNITY   VILLAGE

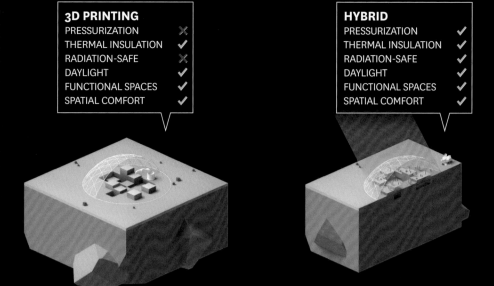

3D PRINTING

PRESSURIZATION	✗
THERMAL INSULATION	✓
RADIATION-SAFE	✗
DAYLIGHT	✓
FUNCTIONAL SPACES	✓
SPATIAL COMFORT	✓

HYBRID

PRESSURIZATION	✓
THERMAL INSULATION	✓
RADIATION-SAFE	✓
DAYLIGHT	✓
FUNCTIONAL SPACES	✓
SPATIAL COMFORT	✓

Inflatables are great for creating pressurized environments, but not really for shielding against radiation or meteors. ***3D-printed structures*** using local regolith provide shelter and privacy but insufficient protection—and finally ***excavated spaces*** provide full protection but no daylight. So no alternative works on its own, but ***combined they tick all boxes!***

STAGE III
BRING NOTHING

SINGLE TORUS	VILLAGE OF TORUSES	FUSED TORUSES
40	50	60
10,000	100,000	1,000,000
TOWN	CITY	METROPOLIS

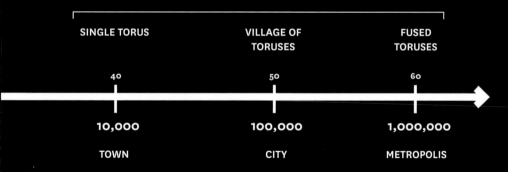

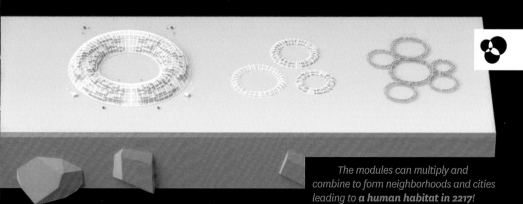

*The modules can multiply and combine to form neighborhoods and cities leading to **a human habitat in 2217!***

But even for an architect that is a pretty lazy timeline. So we're starting here on Earth in Dubai in a landscape visually similar to Mars, but a lot warmer.

2.30 km

3.24 km

EDUCATION

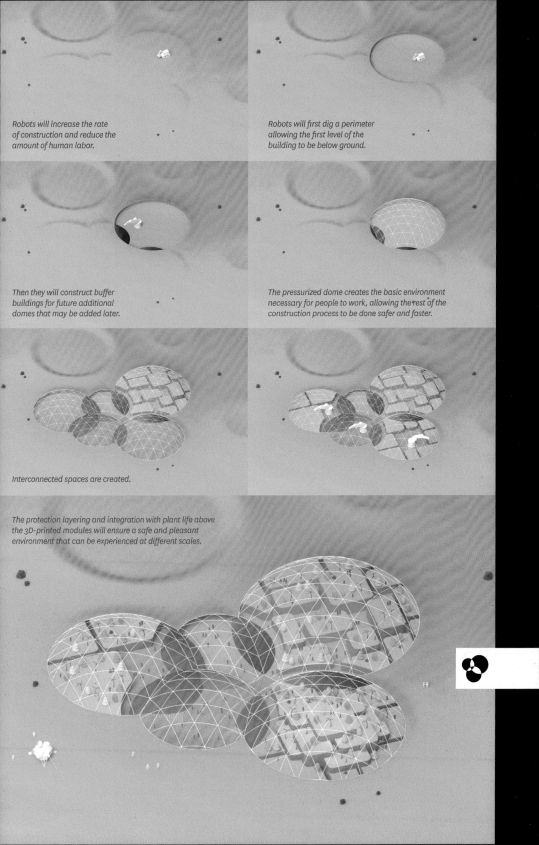

Robots will increase the rate of construction and reduce the amount of human labor.

Robots will first dig a perimeter allowing the first level of the building to be below ground.

Then they will construct buffer buildings for future additional domes that may be added later.

The pressurized dome creates the basic environment necessary for people to work, allowing the rest of the construction process to be done safer and faster.

Interconnected spaces are created.

The protection layering and integration with plant life above the 3D-printed modules will ensure a safe and pleasant environment that can be experienced at different scales.

People can walk the **3D-printed streets of a Martian town** and experience how living on Mars will be very different from living in a tin can. It turns out water is one of the best shelters for radiation—7 times better than regolith rock...

... imagine underground ballrooms washed in daylight, filtered through water and lily pads and swimming trouts.

*Lastly, is it even relevant to go to Mars, now that we have so many issues on Earth? If we look at the **17 sustainable development goals of the United Nations**, eight of them deal directly with the built or planned environment...*

DRINKING WATER ON EARTH

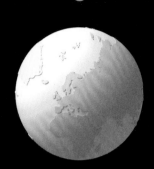

On Earth we have 1.5 billion cubic meters of water...

FOOD PRODUCTION ON EARTH

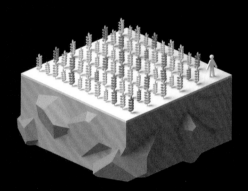

On Earth we have rather abundant agriculture...

ENERGY ON EARTH

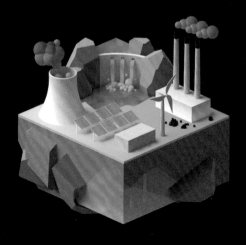

On Earth the main source of global warming is our reliance on fossil fuels...

DRINKING WATER ON MARS

· 5×10^6 km^3 of drinkable water

... on Mars we have only 5 million—so every drop counts!

FOOD PRODUCTION ON MARS

On Mars we have to be 10 times more efficient!

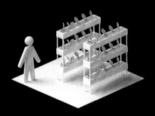

ENERGY ON MARS

On Mars there are no fossil fuels—because there are no fossils —so all power will be renewable.

The very same principles and technologies that will allow us to live on Mars are the ones that will make us great custodians on the planet we live on today.

The answer to our challenges here on Earth may very well be found on Mars!

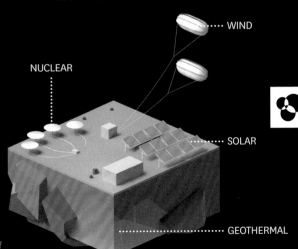

NUCLEAR

WIND

SOLAR

GEOTHERMAL

MASTERPLANET

Earth is the only astronomical object known to harbor life. About 71 percent of the Earth's surface is covered with water, mostly by oceans. The remaining 29 percent is land consisting of continents and islands. Within the first billion years of the Earth's history, life appeared in the oceans and began to affect Earth's atmosphere and surface. In the history of life on Earth, biodiversity has gone through long periods of expansion, occasionally punctuated by mass extinctions; over 99 percent of all species that ever lived on Earth are extinct. Over 7.7 billion humans live on Earth and depend on its biosphere and natural resources for their survival.

While the subject of climate change has reached peak awareness politically, there seems to be an absence of concrete proposals for how to address the problem on a global scale. Rather than the cacophony of reports and speeches, partial goals, and limited regulation that characterize the current efforts, we believe that we need to design a master plan for our entire planet. A tangible, actionable, executable master plan—pragmatic in its principles, utopian in its ambition. The Masterplanet.

Masterplanet is a project that aims to establish a master plan for achieving a carbon-neutral planet Earth, while addressing the fundamental challenges of energy, transport, industry, biodiversity, resources, pollution, water, food, and prosperous living conditions for a world with up to 10 billion inhabitants. The purpose of the project is to present an overview of what it would actually take to stop the net emission of greenhouse gasses, and to get an idea of the practical implications of the ultimate goal, a 100 percent sustainable human presence on planet Earth.

To do this, we approach the project in the same manner as we would approach a planning or architectural project of any scale: carefully identify the problem and opportunities, research the possible technological solutions, explore and benchmark multiple options of intervention, quantify the means and scope of work, resolve the basic planning implications, visualize the impact, break down the steps needed for realization, and propose a phasing and financing model. Included on these final pages is a preview of the Masterplanet—the framework to start rather than the plan itself. That will require an entire volume of its own.

DATA

Gravity	1 g
Pressure	1 atm
Day	24 hours
Year	365.24 days
Surface Temperature	-88 to 58 °C
Magnetic Field	100%
Radiation	✔
Surface Wind	up to 400 km/h
Light Intensity	100%
Metals	✔
Carbon	✔
Water	✔
Geothermal	✔
Travel Time from Earth	-

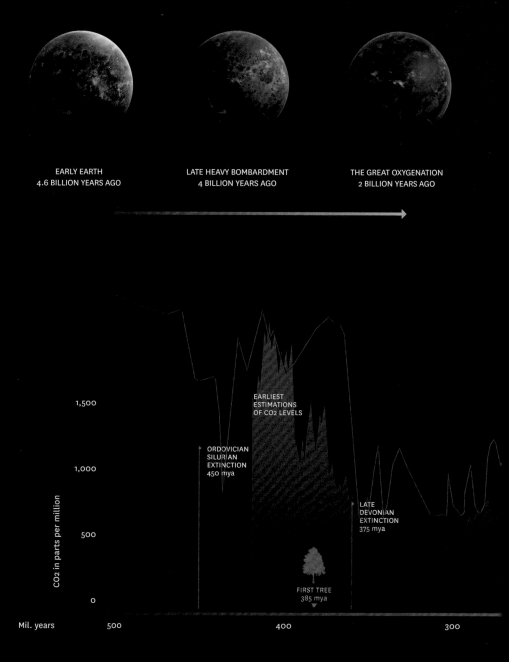

EARLY EARTH
4.6 BILLION YEARS AGO

LATE HEAVY BOMBARDMENT
4 BILLION YEARS AGO

THE GREAT OXYGENATION
2 BILLION YEARS AGO

Climate change has been part of the Earth's history since life began. Looking at Earth's past, we can see climate change is not a hypothetical, future threat, but a force that has shaped the planet, time and again. The very history of life is riddled with extinctions, ice ages, and blooms, all either caused by, or the cause of climate change.

Global Temperature
CO2 In Parts Per Million

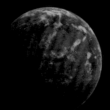

"SNOWBALL EARTH"
2 BILLION YEARS AGO

THE CAMBRIAN EXPLOSION
530 MILLION YEARS

THE ANTHROPOCENE
PRESENT DAY

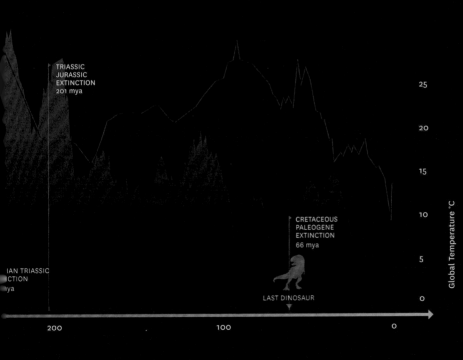

TRIASSIC
JURASSIC
EXTINCTION
201 mya

25

20

15

10

CRETACEOUS
PALEOGENE
EXTINCTION
66 mya

5

IAN TRIASSIC
CTION
ya

LAST DINOSAUR

0

Global Temperature °C

200

100

0

If we look back 500 million years, approximately the time span since the appearance of complex life, we see our planet has not been climatically static. Life as we know it, dominated by mammals, only goes back 66 million years, to the last extinction.

500 MILLION, 500 THOUSAND, 500 YEARS AGO

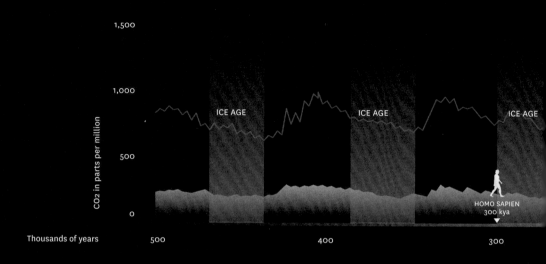

1,500

1,000

CO2 in parts per million

500

0

ICE AGE · · · ICE AGE · · · ICE AGE

HOMO SAPIEN
300 kya

Thousands of years · 500 · 400 · 300

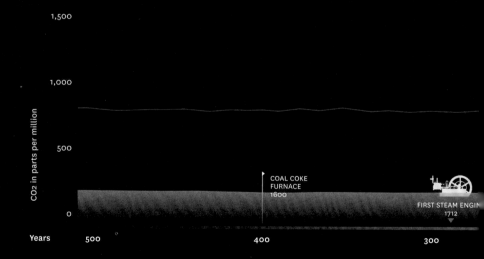

1,500

1,000

CO2 in parts per million

500

0

COAL COKE
FURNACE
1600

FIRST STEAM ENGIN
1712

Years · 500 · 400 · 300

Zooming in even closer to our time, we see that carbon dioxide levels are quite stable, and the recent increase, along with the increase in temperature, matches closely with the Industrial Revolultion. Although atmospheric CO2 has been as high as 415 parts per million before, this happened long before humanity and our current world.

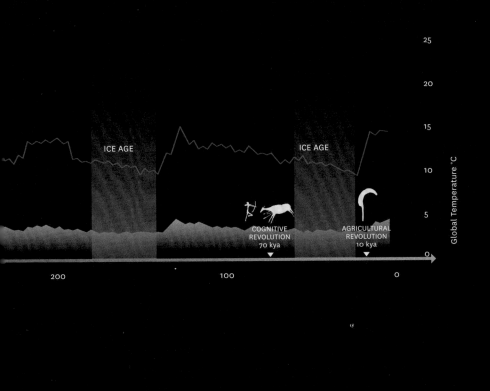

Global Temperature
CO2 In Parts Per Million

25

20

15

ICE AGE

ICE AGE

Global Temperature °C

10

5

COGNITIVE
REVOLUTION
70 kya

AGRICULTURAL
REVOLUTION
10 kya

0

200   100   0

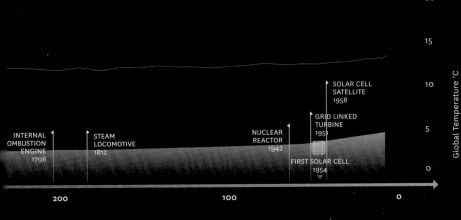

25

20

15

SOLAR CELL
SATELLITE
1958

10

GRID LINKED
TURBINE
1951

Global Temperature °C

INTERNAL
OMBUSTION
ENGINE
1798

STEAM
LOCOMOTIVE
1812

NUCLEAR
REACTOR
1942

5

FIRST SOLAR CELL
1954

0

200   100   0

GREENHOUSE GASSES

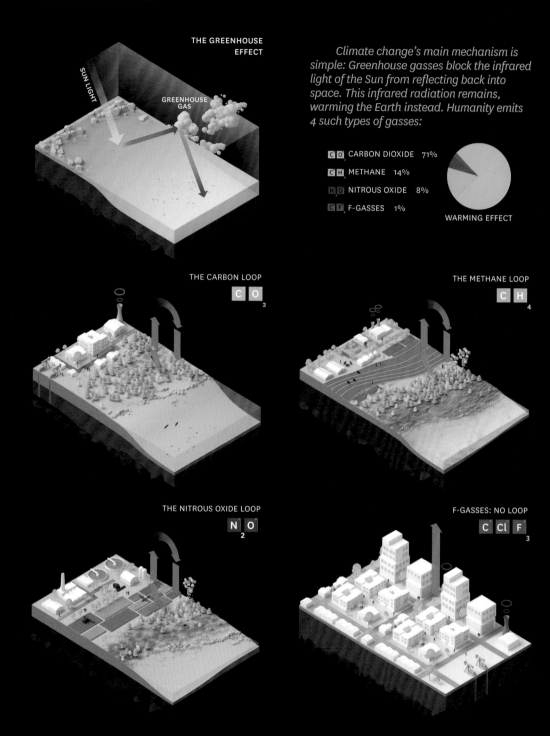

THE GREENHOUSE EFFECT

SUN LIGHT

GREENHOUSE GAS

Climate change's main mechanism is simple: Greenhouse gasses block the infrared light of the Sun from reflecting back into space. This infrared radiation remains, warming the Earth instead. Humanity emits 4 such types of gasses:

C O — CARBON DIOXIDE   71%

C H — METHANE   14%

N O — NITROUS OXIDE   8%

C F — F-GASSES   1%

WARMING EFFECT

THE CARBON LOOP CO_2

THE METHANE LOOP CH_4

THE NITROUS OXIDE LOOP NO_2

F-GASSES: NO LOOP $CClF_3$

Of the four gases humans produce, three are also naturally produced and absorbed by the Earth in cycles: Carbon Dioxide, Methane, and Nitrous Oxide. F-Gasses have no natural cycle of absorption and remain in the atmosphere for very long periods of time. The main greenhouse gas we are increasing is Carbon Dioxide.

CARBON DIOXIDE

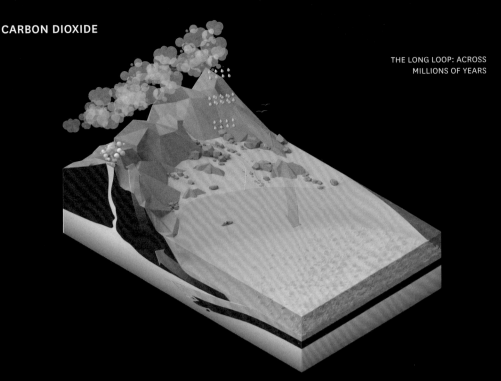

THE LONG LOOP: ACROSS
MILLIONS OF YEARS

THE SHORT LOOP: MEASURED
ON YEARLY BASIS

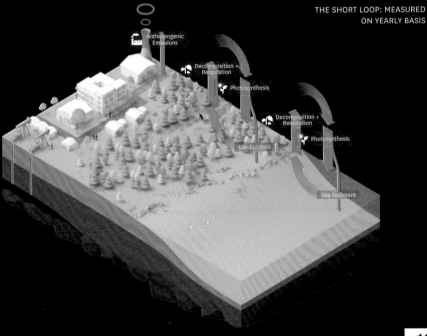

Anthropogenic
Emissions

Decomposition +
Respiration

Photosynthesis

Decomposition +
Respiration

Photosynthesis

Land Uptake

Sea Sediment

440
BIL /YEAR

Gt. CO2

PLANTS

36
BIL /YEAR

FOSSIL FUEL

3
BIL /YEAR

BREATHING
HUMANS

0.2
BIL /YEAR

VOLCANOES

Carbon circulates through nature in two natural loops. In the long-term loop, across eons, carbon gets trapped in sediments and is pushed toward, and melted into the Earth's mantle, only to be volcanically emitted again. The short loop is the yearly course of atmospheric CO2: absorbed by life-forms, and released though respiration, decomposition, and recently, through human emissions.

SECOND-ORDER EFFECTS:
ALBEDO SHINE

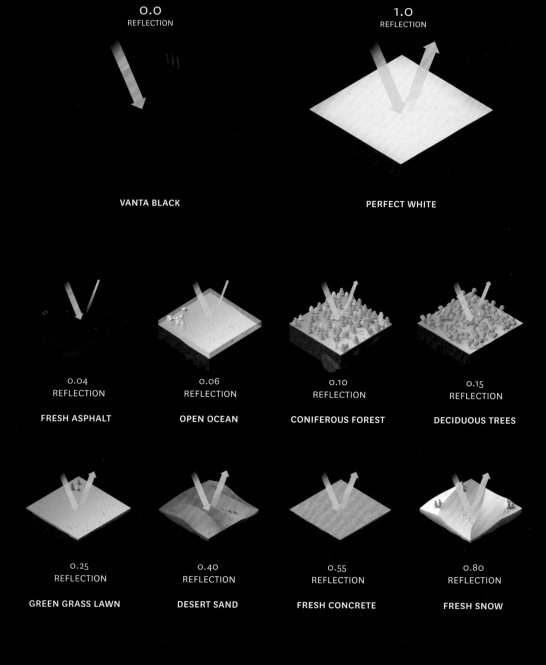

O.O
REFLECTION

VANTA BLACK

1.O
REFLECTION

PERFECT WHITE

0.04
REFLECTION

FRESH ASPHALT

0.06
REFLECTION

OPEN OCEAN

0.10
REFLECTION

CONIFEROUS FOREST

0.15
REFLECTION

DECIDUOUS TREES

0.25
REFLECTION

GREEN GRASS LAWN

0.40
REFLECTION

DESERT SAND

0.55
REFLECTION

FRESH CONCRETE

0.80
REFLECTION

FRESH SNOW

The complexity of Earth's atmospheric system is not constrained to the greenhouse effect, but is subject to second-order effects that can feed back and compound further warming. One such effect is Albedo shine, the degree of solar radiation absorbed by the Earth, depending on the surface's reflectivity. For example, snow (0.8 reflection) absorbs less heat than sea water (0.06 reflection).

IF THE PLANET WERE
ENTIRELY OCEAN

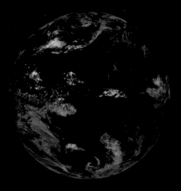

EARTH'S AVERAGE
TEMPERATURE:

27°C

CURRENT PLANET

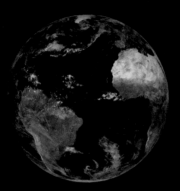

EARTH'S AVERAGE
TEMPERATURE:

15°C

IF A THIRD OF THE PLANET
WERE GLACIAL

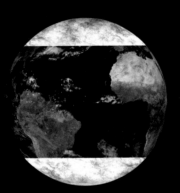

EARTH'S AVERAGE
TEMPERATURE:

0°C

Gradual disappearance of the ice that covers the poles forms a powerful feedback loop that further warms the Earth, absorbing more and more solar radiation. Second-order effects such as the albedo change of melting ice, the acidification of oceans, or the release of permafrost methane, make the change of Earth's temperature an even more unpredictable risk.

6 KM³

sized cube of
solid carbon (graphite)
every year

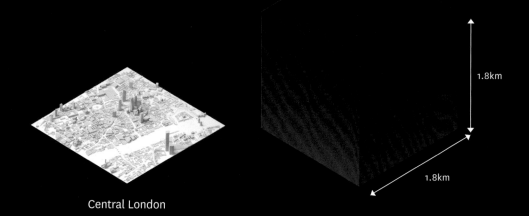

1.8km

1.8km

Central London

35,000

oil tanker ships
every year

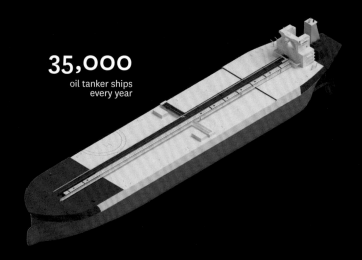

Carbon dioxide, the main anthropogenic greenhouse gas, is pushed into the atmosphere by humanity at a rate of 36,000 million tons every year, a quantity hard to fathom in terms of relatable, human scale. If we were to stack all this matter as one single cube of solid carbon, it would measure six cubic kilometers, standing at almost two kilometers height.

 157,000
Terawatt-hours per year

The world's primary energy
consumption in 2018

The greenhouse gasses accumulating in our atmosphere are primarily a result of our production of energy. Use of energy has been central to our progress and to the worldwide alleviation of poverty, yet, in its current form of production, it has also gradually become a threat to our environment. A critical time in humanity's history begins, as we must fundamentally rethink a key element of our prosperity so far. Over the next few pages, we will look at what a crucial role energy plays, within the natural world and within human systems. We will look at humanity's means of harvesting energy, and show the pathways from production to final uses.

LIFE'S EMBEDDED ENERGY

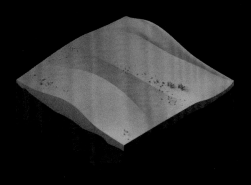

0 MWH PER HECTARE

DESERT

<26 MWH PER HECTARE

ARCTIC TUNDRA

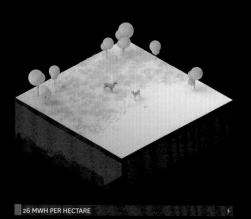

26 MWH PER HECTARE

PASTURE

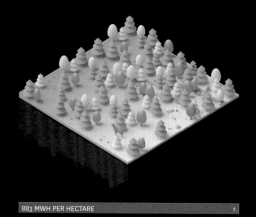

883 MWH PER HECTARE

DENSE FOREST

Life-forms crucially require energy to function. A hectare of dense forest, high in biodiversity, contains much greater embedded energy within its total biomass than a hectare of arctic tundra, which is populated only by simple life-forms. In general, the more biologically complex a natural environment is, the more energy it requires to absorb.

HOW TO STORE ENERGY: 100 KILOWATT HOURS

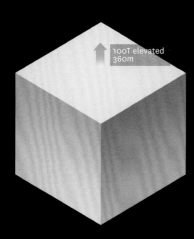

100T elevated 360m

GRAVITY
100T of concrete elevated
360M

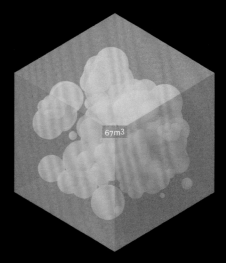

67m3

HYDROGEN
5.5 kg

WORKOUT
1,000 hrs on spin bike

CHEMICAL ENERGY
550 kg battery

13m3

NATURAL GAS
7.2 kg

COAL
40 kg

WOOD
60 kg

ROOFTOP PV
0.5 M^2 / 1 year

FOOD
178 Big Macs

FORMS OF ENERGY

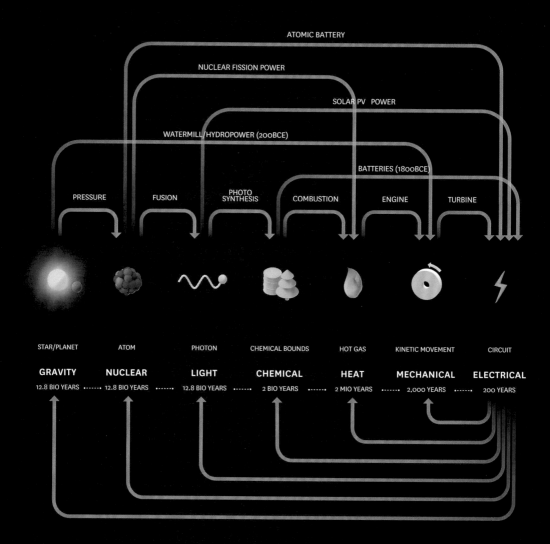

ATOMIC BATTERY

NUCLEAR FISSION POWER

SOLAR PV POWER

WATERMILL/HYDROPOWER (200BCE)

BATTERIES (1800BCE)

| PRESSURE | FUSION | PHOTO SYNTHESIS | COMBUSTION | ENGINE | TURBINE |

STAR/PLANET	ATOM	PHOTON	CHEMICAL BOUNDS	HOT GAS	KINETIC MOVEMENT	CIRCUIT
GRAVITY	**NUCLEAR**	**LIGHT**	**CHEMICAL**	**HEAT**	**MECHANICAL**	**ELECTRICAL**
12.8 BIO YEARS	12.8 BIO YEARS	12.8 BIO YEARS	2 BIO YEARS	2 MIO YEARS	2,000 YEARS	200 YEARS

With progressively more advanced technologies, humanity has been able to unlock and harvest exponentially more forms of energy throughout history. The gravitational and fusion energy that forms our Sun is ultimately radiated to Earth, as light radiation, and stored as chemical bonds inside life-forms. Humanity has since its inception harvested this form, first as wood and later as fossil fuel, to generate heat, mechanical movement, and ultimately electricity. With the advent of electricity fueling our technology, all other forms of energy became available to us. And with the advent of photovoltaic cells, we can further simplify the process, harvesting the Sun's light directly and unabated.

PRIMARY ENERGY SOURCES

THE SUN

SOLAR HEATING
FOSSIL FUEL ENERGY
WEATHER SYSTEMS

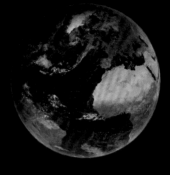

THE EARTH

GEOTHERMAL
ENERGY

THE MOON

TIDAL TURBINE
ENERGY

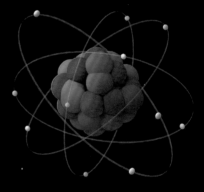

ATOMS

NUCLEAR ENERGY

Ultimately, all energy-producing means on Earth are limited to only four primary sources: the Sun (through solar radiation, its powering of weather systems, and the chemical energy it embeds in plants, current and fossilized), the Earth (through geothermal energy), the Moon (through tidal force), and finally, the radioactive decay of atoms.

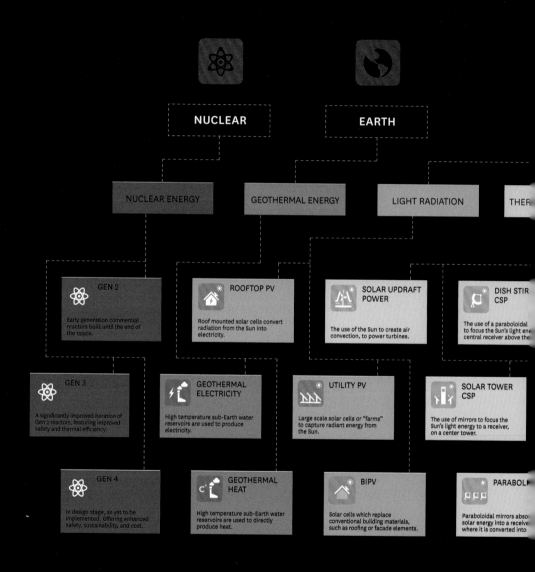

NUCLEAR

EARTH

NUCLEAR ENERGY

GEOTHERMAL ENERGY

LIGHT RADIATION

THER

GEN 2

Early generation commercial reactors built until the end of the 1990s.

ROOFTOP PV

Roof mounted solar cells convert radiation from the Sun into electricity.

SOLAR UPDRAFT POWER

The use of the Sun to create air convection, to power turbines.

DISH STIR CSP

The use of a paraboloidal to focus the Sun's light ene central receiver above the

GEN 3

A significantly improved iteration of Gen 2 reactors, featuring improved safety and thermal efficiency.

GEOTHERMAL ELECTRICITY

High temperature sub-Earth water reservoirs are used to produce electricity.

UTILITY PV

Large scale solar cells or "farms" to capture radiant energy from the Sun.

SOLAR TOWER CSP

The use of mirrors to focus the Sun's light energy to a receiver, on a center tower.

GEN 4

In design stage, as yet to be implemented. Offering enhanced safety, sustainability, and cost.

GEOTHERMAL HEAT

High temperature sub-Earth water reservoirs are used to directly produce heat.

BIPV

Solar cells which replace conventional building materials, such as roofing or facade elements.

PARABOL

Paraboloidal mirrors abso solar energy into a receive where it is converted into

We investigate and classify the broad spectrum of how the four primary sources, the Sun, the Earth, the Moon, and the radioactive decay of atoms, can be accessed by humanity, as ways of energy production.

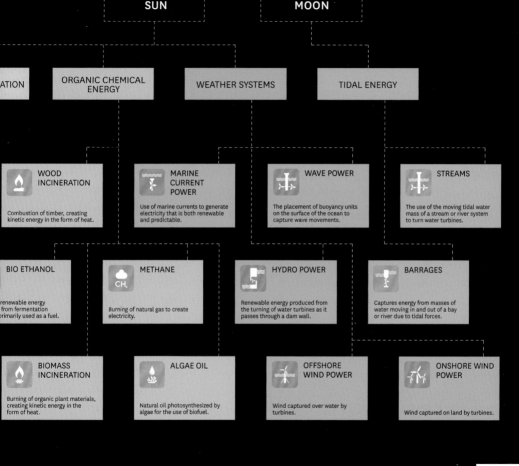

SUN	**MOON**

...ATION

ORGANIC CHEMICAL ENERGY

WEATHER SYSTEMS

TIDAL ENERGY

WOOD INCINERATION
Combustion of timber, creating kinetic energy in the form of heat.

MARINE CURRENT POWER
Use of marine currents to generate electricity that is both renewable and predictable.

WAVE POWER
The placement of buoyancy units on the surface of the ocean to capture wave movements.

STREAMS
The use of the moving tidal water mass of a stream or river system to turn water turbines.

BIO ETHANOL
...renewable energy ...from fermentation ...primarily used as a fuel.

METHANE
Burning of natural gas to create electricity.

HYDRO POWER
Renewable energy produced from the turning of water turbines as it passes through a dam wall.

BARRAGES
Captures energy from masses of water moving in and out of a bay or river due to tidal forces.

BIOMASS INCINERATION
Burning of organic plant materials, creating kinetic energy in the form of heat.

ALGAE OIL
Natural oil photosynthesized by algae for the use of biofuel.

OFFSHORE WIND POWER
Wind captured over water by turbines.

ONSHORE WIND POWER
Wind captured on land by turbines.

THE HISTORY OF ENERGY USE

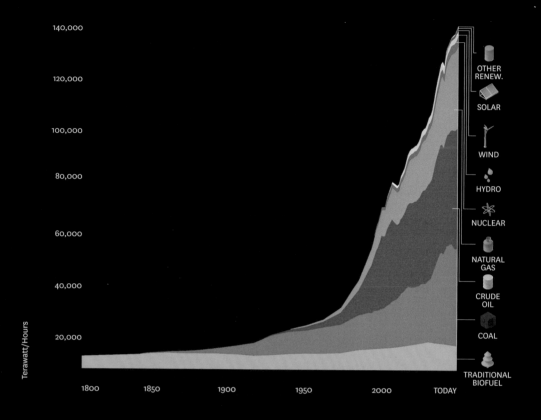

Terawatt/Hours

140,000
120,000
100,000
80,000
60,000
40,000
20,000

1800   1850   1900   1950   2000   TODAY

OTHER RENEW.
SOLAR
WIND
HYDRO
NUCLEAR
NATURAL GAS
CRUDE OIL
COAL
TRADITIONAL BIOFUEL

GLOBAL PRIMARY ENERGY, 2017

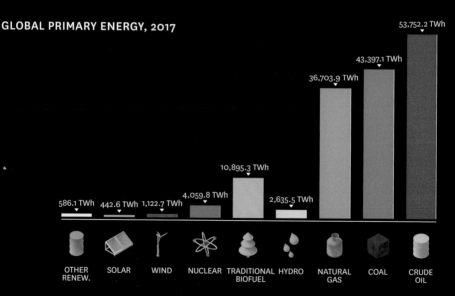

586.1 TWh — OTHER RENEW.
442.6 TWh — SOLAR
1,122.7 TWh — WIND
4,059.8 TWh — NUCLEAR
10,895.3 TWh — TRADITIONAL BIOFUEL
2,635.5 TWh — HYDRO
36,703.9 TWh — NATURAL GAS
43,397.1 TWh — COAL
53,752.2 TWh — CRUDE OIL

The greatest stride in human welfare and progress coincides with an equivalent increase in energy. Only recently, more developed nations started to succeed in decoupling economic growth from energy use.

CURRENT EMISSIONS BY COUNTRY

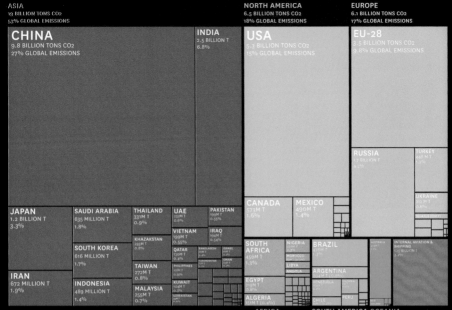

ASIA
19 BILLION TONS CO2
53% GLOBAL EMISSIONS

NORTH AMERICA
6.5 BILLION TONS CO2
18% GLOBAL EMISSIONS

EUROPE
6.1 BILLION TONS CO2
17% GLOBAL EMISSIONS

CHINA
9.8 BILLION TONS CO2
27% GLOBAL EMISSIONS

INDIA
2.5 BILLION T
6.8%

USA
5.3 BILLION TONS CO2
15% GLOBAL EMISSIONS

EU-28
3.5 BILLION TONS CO2
9.8% GLOBAL EMISSIONS

RUSSIA
1.7 BILLION T
4.5%

TURKEY
448 M T
1.2%

UKRAINE
212 M T

JAPAN
1.2 BILLION T
3.3%

SAUDI ARABIA
635 MILLION T
1.8%

THAILAND
331M T
0.9%

UAE
233M T
0.6%

PAKISTAN
199M T
0.55%

KHAZAKSTAN
283M T
0.8%

VIETNAM
199M T
0.55%

IRAQ
194M T
0.54%

SOUTH KOREA
616 MILLION T
1.7%

QATAR
130M T
0.4%

BANGLADESH

ISRAEL

TAIWAN
272M T
0.8%

PHILIPPINES

OMAN

IRAN
672 MILLION T
1.9%

INDONESIA
489 MILLION T
1.4%

MALAYSIA
255M T
0.7%

KUWAIT
104M T

UZBEKISTAN

CANADA
573M T
1.6%

MEXICO
490M T
1.4%

SOUTH AFRICA
456M T
1.3%

NIGERIA

MOROCCO

LIBYA

ANGOLA

BRAZIL
425M T
1.2%

ARGENTINA

VENEZUELA

EGYPT
219M T
0.6%

ALGERIA
133M T (0.4%)

CHILE

PERU

AUSTRALIA

INTERNAL AVIATION & SHIPPING
520 BILLION T
1.2%

AFRICA
1.3 BILLION TONS CO2
3.7% GLOBAL EMISSIONS

SOUTH AMERICA
1.1 BILLION TONS CO2
3.2% GLOBAL EMISSIONS

OCEANIA
0.5 BILLION TONS CO2
1.3% GLOBAL EMISSIONS

HISTORICAL CONTRIBUTIONS

NORTH AMERICA
457 BILLION TONS CO2
29% GLOBAL CUMULATIVE EMISSIONS

ASIA
457 BILLION TONS CO2
53% GLOBAL CUMULATIVE EMISSIONS

USA
399 BILLION TONS CO2
25% GLOBAL CUMULATIVE EMISSIONS

CANADA
32B T
2%

CHINA
200 BILLION TONS CO2
12.7% GLOBAL CUMULATIVE
EMISSIONS

JAPAN
62 BILLION T
4%

MEXICO
19B T
1.2%

INDIA
48B T
3%

SOUTH KOREA
16B T
1%

TAIWAN
8B T
0.5%

THAILAND
7B T
0.45%

UZBEKISTAN

SAUDI ARABIA
14B T
0.9%

MALAYSIA

PAKISTAN

NORTH KOREA

UAE

INDONESIA
12B T
0.8%

IRAQ

AZERBAIJAN

EU-28
353 BILLION TONS CO2
22% GLOBAL CUMULATIVE EMISSIONS

RUSSIA
101 BILLION TONS
6% GLOBAL CUMULATIVE EMISSIONS

VIETNAM

ISRAEL

SINGAPORE

IRAN
17B T
1%

KAZAKHSTAN
12B T
0.8%

QATAR

PHILIPPINES

SYRIA

KUWAIT

UKRAINE
25B T
1.25%

TURKEY
12.6B T
0.8%

SOUTH AFRICA
19.2B T
1.2%

ALGERIA

BRAZIL
14.7B T
0.9%

VENEZUELA

AUSTRALIA
17.4B T
1.1%

NIGERIA

COLOMBIA

EGYPT
7.6B T (0.35%)

ARGENTINA

CHILE

EUROPE
514 BILLION TONS CO2
33% GLOBAL CUMULATIVE EMISSIONS

AFRICA
43 BILLION TONS CO2
3% GLOBAL EMISSIONS

SOUTH AMERICA
1.1 BILLION TONS CO2
3.2% GLOBAL EMISSIONS

Dividing the yearly 36 billion tons of CO2 by country, we can see China currently contributes most. Yet looking from a historical perspective, the West has had the greatest cummulative share.

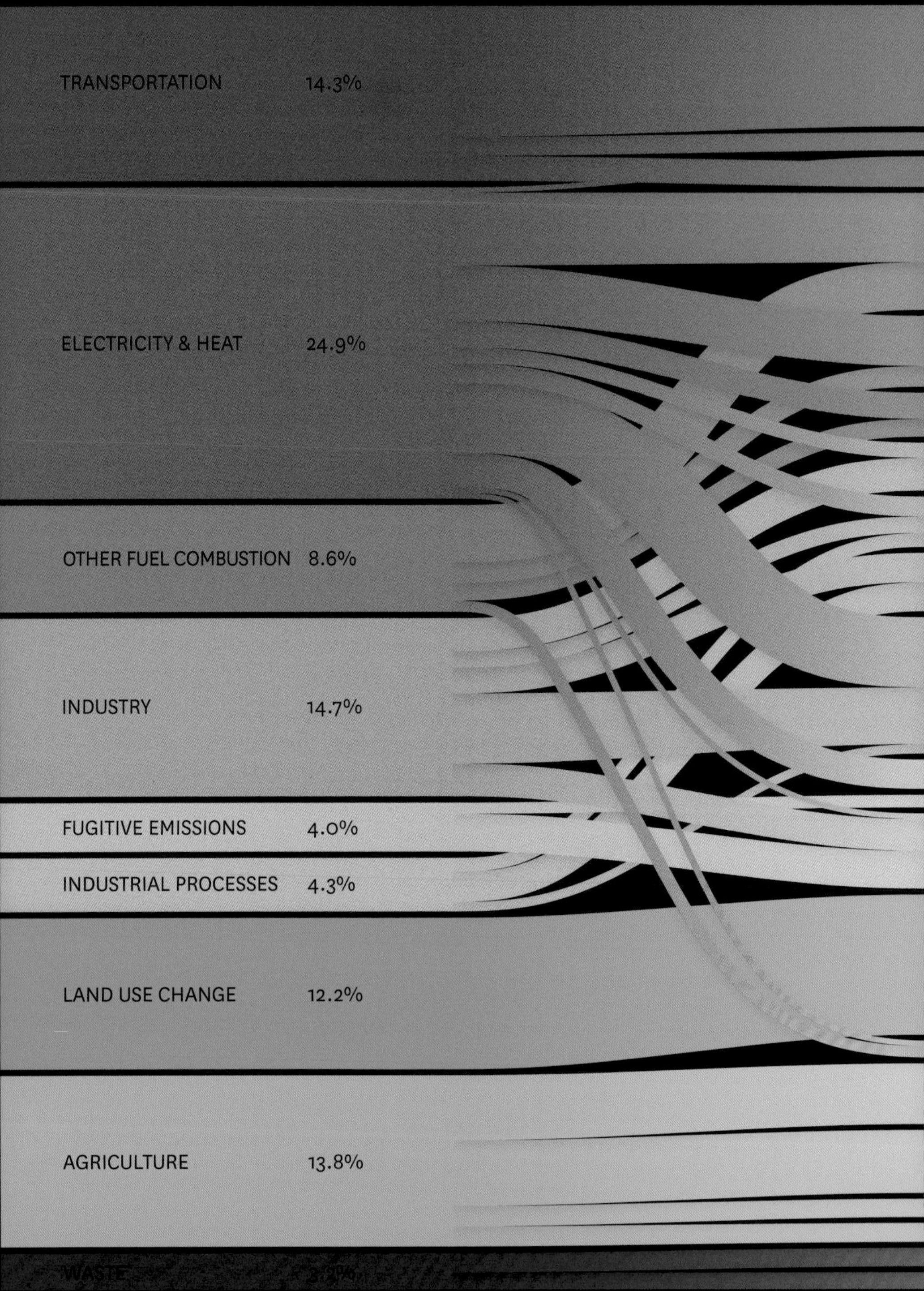

TRANSPORTATION 14.3%

ELECTRICITY & HEAT 24.9%

OTHER FUEL COMBUSTION 8.6%

INDUSTRY 14.7%

FUGITIVE EMISSIONS 4.0%

INDUSTRIAL PROCESSES 4.3%

LAND USE CHANGE 12.2%

AGRICULTURE 13.8%

WASTE 3.2%

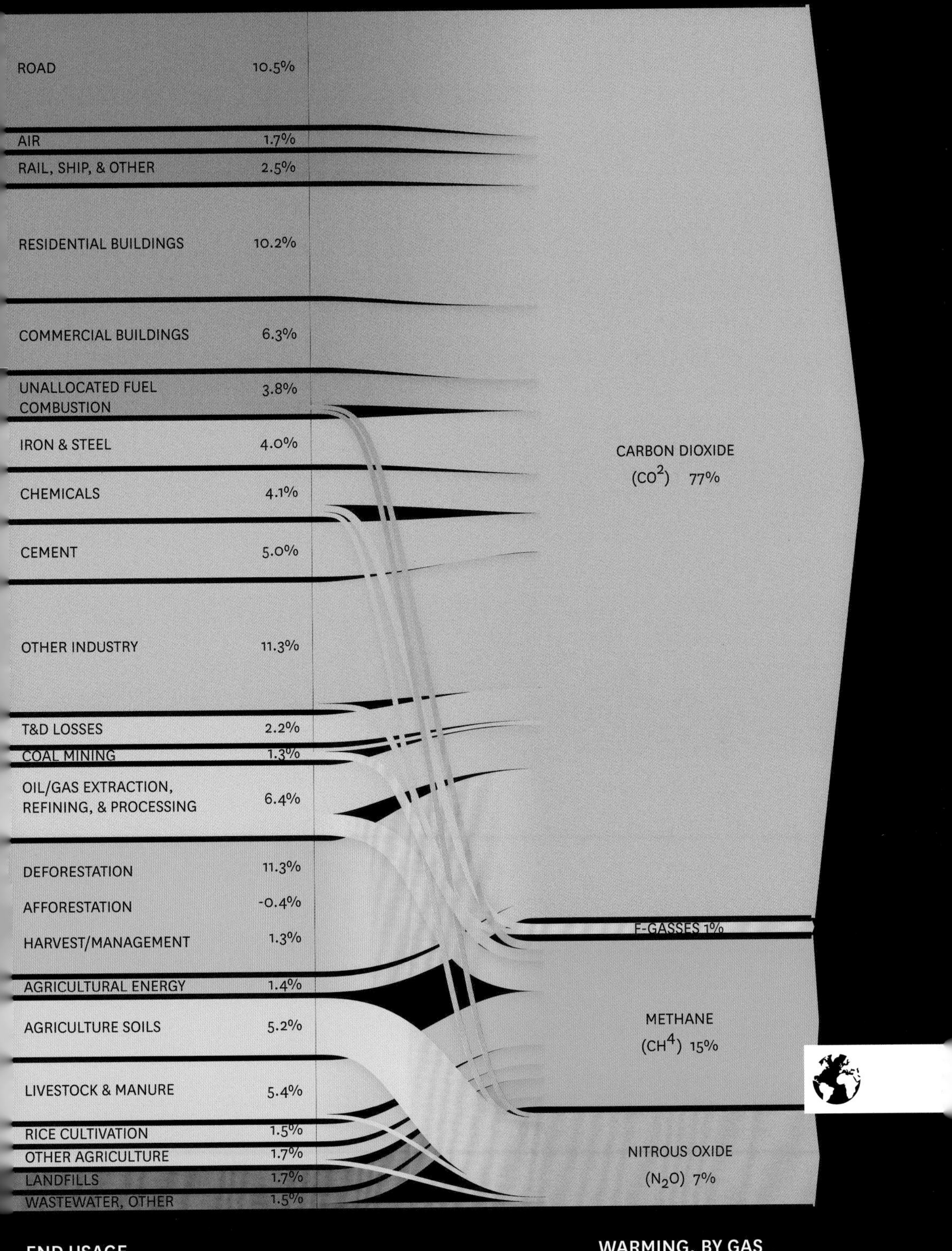

END USAGE		WARMING, BY GAS

ROAD — 10.5%

AIR — 1.7%

RAIL, SHIP, & OTHER — 2.5%

RESIDENTIAL BUILDINGS — 10.2%

COMMERCIAL BUILDINGS — 6.3%

UNALLOCATED FUEL COMBUSTION — 3.8%

IRON & STEEL — 4.0%

CHEMICALS — 4.1%

CEMENT — 5.0%

OTHER INDUSTRY — 11.3%

T&D LOSSES — 2.2%

COAL MINING — 1.3%

OIL/GAS EXTRACTION, REFINING, & PROCESSING — 6.4%

DEFORESTATION — 11.3%

AFFORESTATION — -0.4%

HARVEST/MANAGEMENT — 1.3%

AGRICULTURAL ENERGY — 1.4%

AGRICULTURE SOILS — 5.2%

LIVESTOCK & MANURE — 5.4%

RICE CULTIVATION — 1.5%

OTHER AGRICULTURE — 1.7%

LANDFILLS — 1.7%

WASTEWATER, OTHER — 1.5%

CARBON DIOXIDE (CO^2) 77%

F-GASSES 1%

METHANE (CH^4) 15%

NITROUS OXIDE (N_2O) 7%

THE 5 KEY SOURCES OF CLIMATE CHANGE

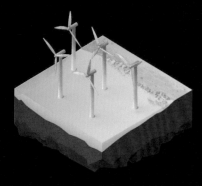

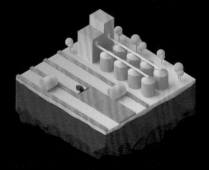

24.9%

ENERGY
Electricity, Heat Production

26%

FOOD
Agriculture, Land Usage

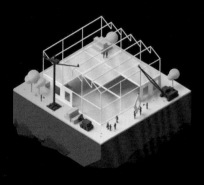

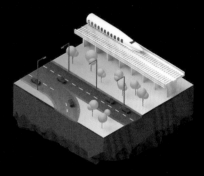

23%

INDUSTRY
Construction, Manufacturing, Industrial
Processes

14.3%

TRANSPORT
Land, Sea, and Air

We can break up humanity's greenhouse gas emissions into four key areas of activity.
These are: Transport, Energy (Electricity and Heat production), Food (Agriculture and
the related Land Usage Changes), and Industry. We will individually analyze each of these
sectors, finding the main challenges, possibilities, and crucial questions going forward.

In addition, we would like to study six other areas that are not direct sources of
greenhouse gas emissions, yet we consider as holding crucial questions for any sustainable
future of humankind. How humanity will deal with Health, Biodiversity, Water, Pollution,
primary Resources, and finally Architecture and Urbanism, will shape our near future world
beyond the struggle of climate change.

THE 5 KEY STRUGGLES BEYOND CLIMATE CHANGE

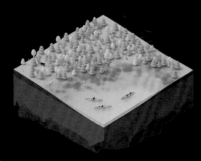

BIODIVERSITY
Species and Habitat Loss

RESOURCES
Extraction and Recycling

POLLUTION
Air, Soil, and Water

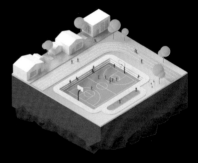

HEALTH
Global health risks and major threats to
humanity

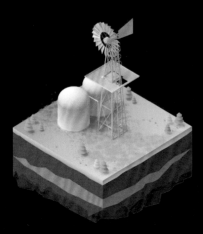

WATER
Water use and scarcity

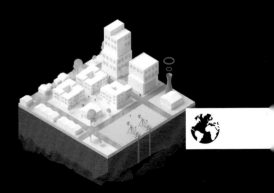

ARCHITECTURE AND URBANISM
Architecture, Cities, Regional Planning

DIRECT SOLAR RADIATION
ACROSS AFRICA

1 kWh/M² daily   10 kWh/M² daily

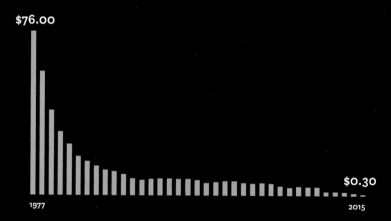

$76.00

$0.30

1977   2015

SOLAR PV PANEL
PRICE TIMELINE

Can the world be fully powered by 100% renewable energy?

Although renewable technologies exist today, the problems of mass deployment, energy storage, and particularly intermittence—dependence on the Sun shining and the wind blowing—pose problems that foretell a full upheaval in the way humanity harvests energy.

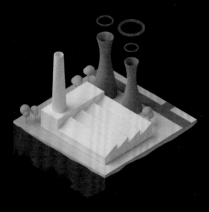

`820 gCO2eq/ kWh`

FOSSIL FUELS: COAL

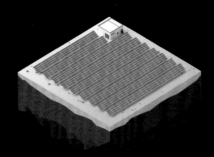

`48 gCO2eq/ kWh`

SOLAR PV

`38 gCO2eq/ kWh`

GEOTHERMAL

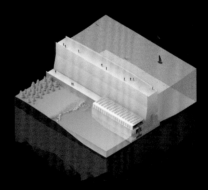

`24 gCO2eq/ kWh`

HYDRO

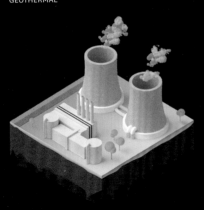

`12 gCO2eq/ kWh`

NUCLEAR

`12 gCO2eq/ kWh`

WIND

PRODUCTION METHODS BY
LIFE-CYCLE EMISSIONS

A world of expansive photovoltaic fields, endless, open ocean, floating wind farms, tide barrages, and geothermal plants, is a world vastly different from our own. As energy storage may not be able to cover the intermittence that the natural world subjects us to, possibilities might soon arise for a global grid, an internet of energy, to provide worldwide interconnection.

AIR TRANSIT ACROSS
NORTH AMERICA

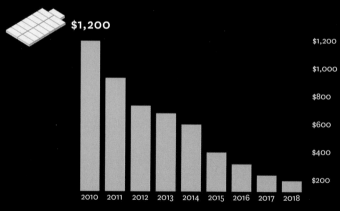

$1,200

$1,200

$1,000

$800

$600

$400

$200

2010 2011 2012 2013 2014 2015 2016 2017 2018

LITHIUM BATTERIES
PRICE TIMELINE

The revolution in electric cars is on its way. But what about the ships, planes, and vehicles we can't electrify?

With all land, sea, and air movement of freight and passengers needing to take place with zero carbon emissions, what are the solutions and implications of a fully renewable world transport?

2,500 TWh

SEA TRANSPORT

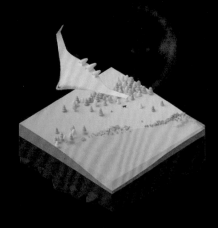

2,777 TWh

AIR TRANSPORT

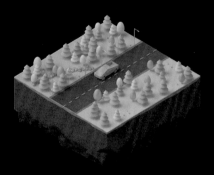

13,333 TWh

LIGHT ROAD TRANSPORT

6,389 TWh

HEAVY ROAD TRANSPORT

LIGHT
ROAD
13,333

HEAVY
ROAD
6,389

SEA
2,500

AIR
2,777

RAIL
555

**TRANSPORT ENERGY EXPENDITURE:
26,000 TERAWATT HOURS / YEAR**

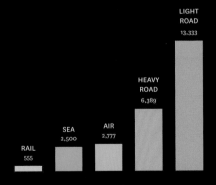

555 TWh

RAIL TRANSPORT

The highest energy expenditure within transport concerns light-duty vehicles, with over a billion cars, motorcycles, and mopeds currently in the world. Thus, a timely electrification of personal vehicles is the most pressing and high-yielding challenge. Yet humanity is also dependent on global shipping and air travel, fields in which alternatives such as hydrogen-powered seafarers or high-speed rail, might be the required solutions.

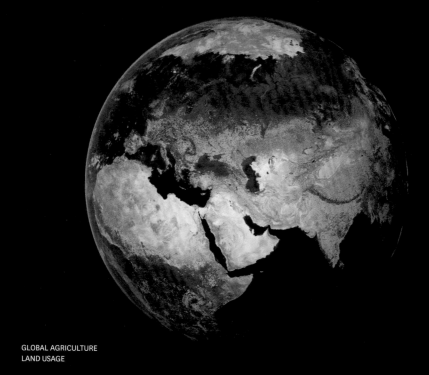

GLOBAL AGRICULTURE
LAND USAGE

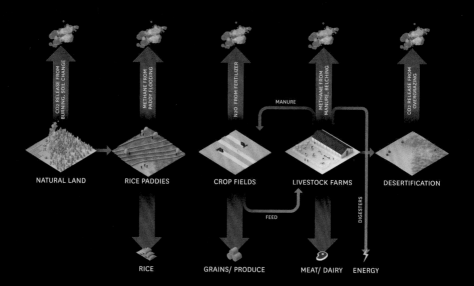

How can we feed 10 billion people without any greenhouse gas emissions?

Food production is a human necessity, with inherent emissive processes. Greenhouse gasses, such as methane from rice paddies or manure, come from a multitude of smaller actors. This makes solutions challenging to implement and monitor.

38%
LIVESTOCK

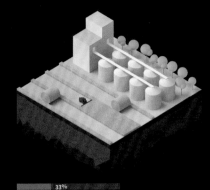

33%
CROP LAND

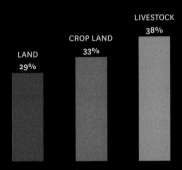

LIVESTOCK
38%

CROP LAND
33%

LAND
29%

TOTAL AGRICULTURE EMISSIONS

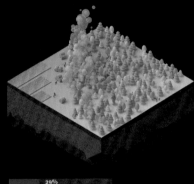

29%
LAND USE CHANGE

*For every square kilometer
of habitable land on Earth,
humanity uses half of it for
agriculture: 0.11KM² are used
for crop harvesting, and
0.38KM² are used for livestock
grazing pastures.*

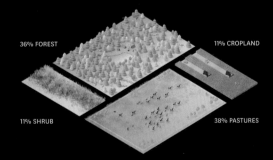

36% FOREST

11% CROPLAND

11% SHRUB

38% PASTURES

*In addition to production emissions, the ever-expanding land use necessary
for food poses a challenge in itself, as currently around half of the world's habitable
area, 51 million square kilometers, is occupied by agricultural crops and the grazing
livestock. This need for land usage and technological improvements will inevitably
push us to rethink the way we organize our food production and utilize the Earth.*

BIODIVERSITY

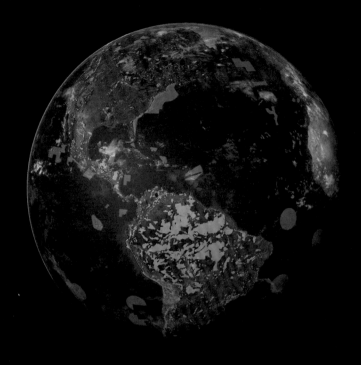

PROTECTED LAND AREA

PROTECTED MARINE AREA

TERRESTRIAL, MARINE, AND
COASTAL PROTECTED AREAS

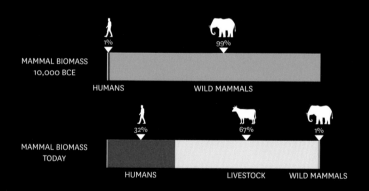

MAMMAL BIOMASS
10,000 BCE

1%

99%

HUMANS

WILD MAMMALS

MAMMAL BIOMASS
TODAY

32%

67%

1%

HUMANS

LIVESTOCK

WILD MAMMALS

How can we make biodiversity thrive in a world with more and more humans?

Humans are the cause of the current mass extinction, the Holocene, or Anthropocene extinction, driving the disappearance of species to be 100 to 1,000 times the normal background rate.

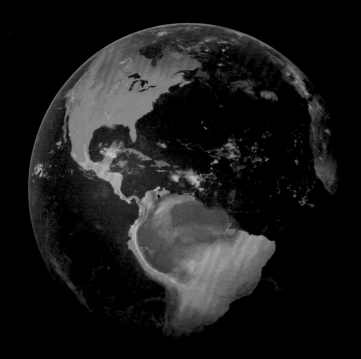

LESS ABUNDANT   MORE ABUNDANT

SPECIES RICHNESS: MAMMALS

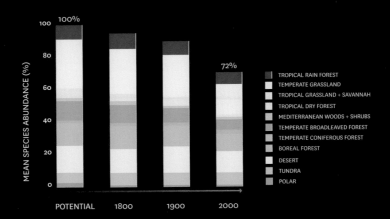

100%

MEAN SPECIES ABUNDANCE (%)

72%

TROPICAL RAIN FOREST
TEMPERATE GRASSLAND
TROPICAL GRASSLAND + SAVANNAH
TROPICAL DRY FOREST
MEDITERRANEAN WOODS + SHRUBS
TEMPERATE BROADLEAVED FOREST
TEMPERATE CONIFEROUS FOREST
BOREAL FOREST
DESERT
TUNDRA
POLAR

POTENTIAL   1800   1900   2000

As the human population continues to grow, the demand for land and water is expected to continue to isolate and impoverish natural habitats. This degradation is not just a loss in itself, but also has adverse effects on humankind, as natural ecosystems provide essential services, such as crop pollination, or the mitigation of floods and soil erosion.

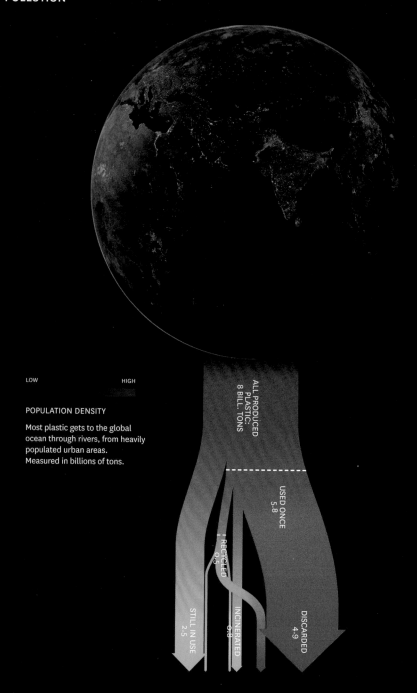

LOW   HIGH

POPULATION DENSITY

Most plastic gets to the global
ocean through rivers, from heavily
populated urban areas.
Measured in billions of tons.

ALL PRODUCED
PLASTIC:
8 BILL. TONS

USED ONCE
5.8

RECYCLED
0.5

STILL IN USE
2.5

INCINERATED
0.8

DISCARDED
4.9

How can we nullify our multiple forms of toxicity on the natural world?

*Our expanding presence has a toll, and harms both us and the natural world.
What solutions exist to mitigate the ever-increasing contamination of air, land,
and ocean?*

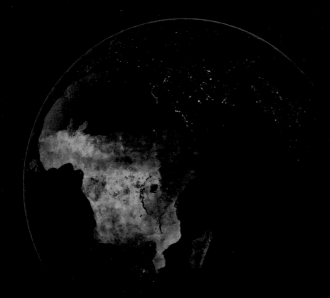

MALARIA DEATHS
/100,000 PEOPLE, 2017

<0.001   >100

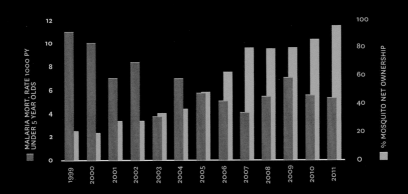

MOSQUITO BED NETS USAGE, RUFIJI, TANZANIA.
Simple mosquito bed nets are an effective shield from
malaria, and calculated as one of the cheapest ways
to save human life worldwide.

*What are the biggest threats to our health and well-being as a species,
and how succesfully are we currently mitigating them?*

*The crisis instituted by the COVID-19 pandemic, last in a long string of pandemic
events thoughout our history, lays bear our enduring fragility as a biological species.
Can design and planning truly make a difference in this struggle?*

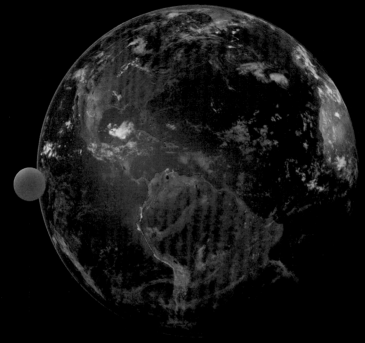

ALL WATER ON, IN,
AND ABOVE EARTH

1,386,000,000 KM^3

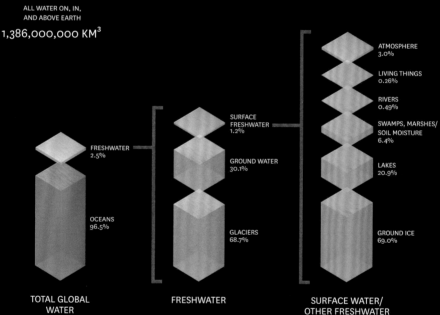

FRESHWATER
2.5%

OCEANS
96.5%

**TOTAL GLOBAL
WATER**

SURFACE
FRESHWATER
1.2%

GROUND WATER
30.1%

GLACIERS
68.7%

FRESHWATER

ATMOSPHERE
3.0%

LIVING THINGS
0.26%

RIVERS
0.49%

SWAMPS, MARSHES/
SOIL MOISTURE
6.4%

LAKES
20.9%

GROUND ICE
69.0%

**SURFACE WATER/
OTHER FRESHWATER**

How will we supply the world's growing water demand?

The world's total usage has increased six times this century, to four trillion cubic meters yearly. Severe water scarcity affects two-thirds of the global population for at least one month of the year. As the world's temperature rises, drought-affected areas of the world are only expected to expand.

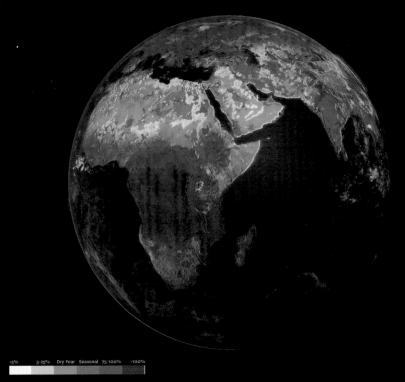

<5% 5-25% Dry Year Seasonal 75-100% >100%

ANNUAL WATER DEPLETION

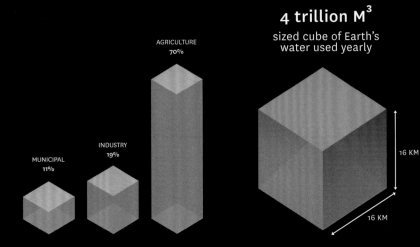

AGRICULTURE
70%

4 trillion M³

sized cube of Earth's
water used yearly

INDUSTRY
19%

MUNICIPAL
11%

16 KM

16 KM

TOTAL WATER USAGE

*Desalination, the current solution to increasing demand, is expected to
grow globally, despite the hurdles of salt pollution, geography, and high energy
expenditure. Yet, ample opportunity exists for both more effective technology and
an enhanced consideration of our existing water-management systems.*

RESOURCES

- **COPPER**
- **ALUMINUM**
- **LEAD-ZINC**
- **IRON**
- **HYDROTHERMAL**
- **SUPERFICIAL DEPOSITS**

METAL DEPOSITS

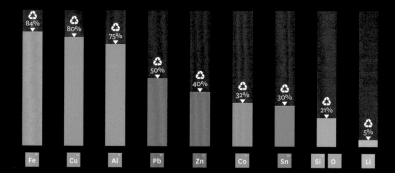

Fe	Cu	Al	Pb	Zn	Co	Sn	Si O	Li
84%	80%	75%	50%	40%	32%	30%	21%	5%

METAL REYCLING RATES

Where will the resources for the coming green technological revolution come from?

To fully replace the world's energy, transport, and industry infrastructure with zero-carbon technologies, a substantial amount of new mining is required. Yet this coming strain could potentially be eased by a global reexamination of how we recycle our resources, and produce more from less.

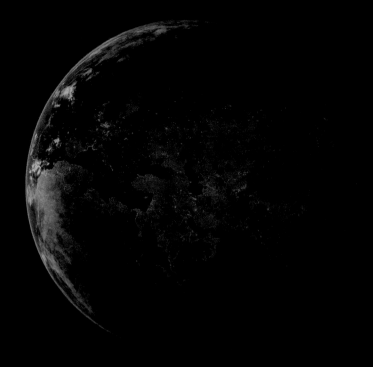

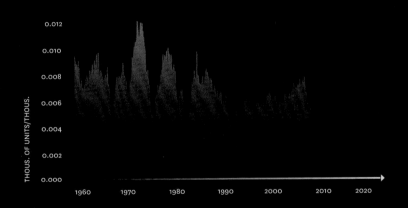

NEW HOUSING UNITS STARTED
PER TOTAL POPULATION. U.S. 1960–2020

How can we design our cities so that they withstand the challenges of the present and the future?

Most of our innovation and ingenuity happens within the context of our built environment. The challenge ahead is not only to build our cities so that they can prosper within the demands of a changing climate, but also to ensure that as many as possible can enjoy their prosperity.

THE EARTH'S POPULATION IN 2050

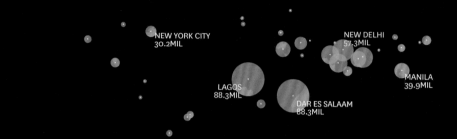

NEW YORK CITY
30.2MIL

NEW DELHI
57.3MIL

MANILA
39.9MIL

LAGOS
88.3MIL

DAR ES SALAAM
88.3MIL

75 MIL   50 MIL   25 MIL   10 MIL

ESTIMATED CITY GROWTH
OVER THE NEXT CENTURY

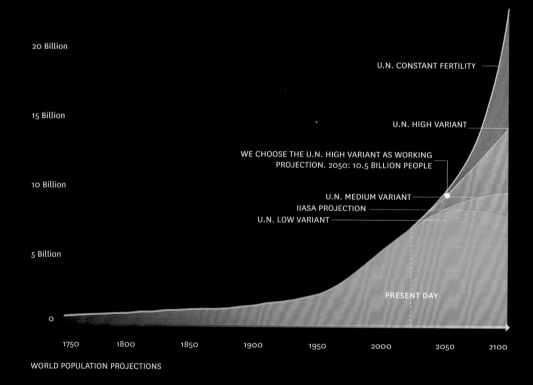

20 Billion

U.N. CONSTANT FERTILITY

15 Billion

U.N. HIGH VARIANT

WE CHOOSE THE U.N. HIGH VARIANT AS WORKING
PROJECTION. 2050: 10.5 BILLION PEOPLE

10 Billion

U.N. MEDIUM VARIANT
IIASA PROJECTION
U.N. LOW VARIANT

5 Billion

PRESENT DAY

0

1750   1800   1850   1900   1950   2000   2050   2100

WORLD POPULATION PROJECTIONS

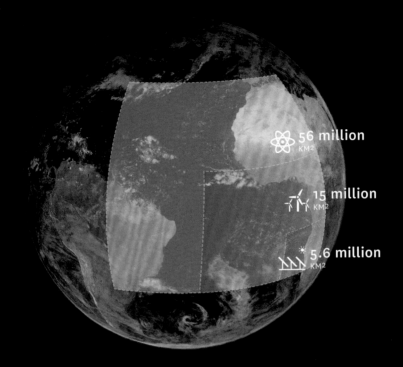

56 million KM2

15 million KM2

5.6 million KM2

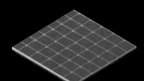

In a world where everyone had the level of energy use of developed nations (Singapore used here), powering the world, including transport and industry, with solar PV would demand 5.6 million km².

We take 1 KM² of solar PV to generate 100 GWh per year.

In the same scenario, offshore wind turbines (10MW) would need to cover 15 million KM².

We take 1KM² of offshore wind to generate 35,9 GWh per year.

Nuclear plants themselves would not occupy much space; however, their required "Plume Exposure Emergency Planning Zones" (10 mile radius each) would cover a whopping 56 million KM².

One 1,000 MW Nuclear Plant generates 7,880 GWh/year.

What world should we be planning for?

In asking what the world's ideal energy needs are, we can not assume that developing regions do not seek the same welfare that developed nations enjoy today. Here, we pick Singapore's current energy consumption, 56,371 Kilowatt hours/year per capita, as the average demand in a world of 10 billion. At this increased level, we can assume all of the world's people would benefit from mobility, climatization, basic commodities, and all other necessities that people of developed nations enjoy today.

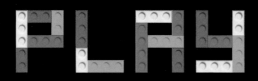

What we love about LEGO is that it is not a toy—it is a tool—a tool that empowers children to create their own world and to inhabit that world through play. And to invite friends to join in cocreating—and cohabiting that world. And that is exactly what formgiving is. As human beings we have the power—the tools—to give form to the future we want to live in. And we have the power to listen, and look, and to learn how life always goes beyond our intentions to discover and explore new ways to cohabit the world that we have created. If work is what makes the world go around, play is what makes it go beyond.

Architects make models to represent what they intend to build in the world. At the PLAY room in the Formgiving Exhibition the process has been the other way around. 25 LEGO models have been recreated from BIG designs and constructed in LEGO by master builders from all over the world. Each model was paired with the three-dimensional digital building information model that embodies all the technical aspects of the project—the functional layouts, the structure, the mechanical services, the circulation, and materials into a single digital twin of the built reality. With these two data points— the physical abstraction and the digital specification—the visitor could get an insight into the complex work behind the playful simplicity. Finally, at the heart of the room we provided the tools inviting each guest to play for themselves.

THE TWIST

Jevnaker, NORWAY
Bricks: 6,000
BIG Builder: Lars Barstad

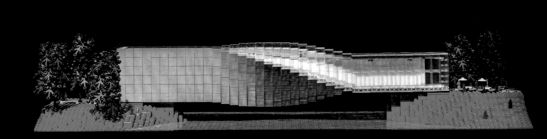

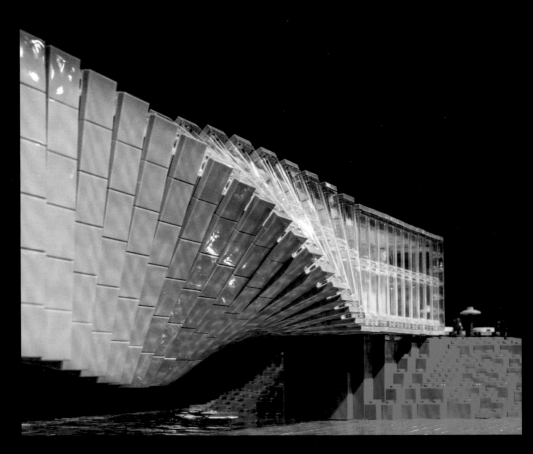

EXPO 2010 DANISH PAVILION

Shanghai, CHINA
Bricks: 11,500
BIG Builder: Helgi Toftegaard

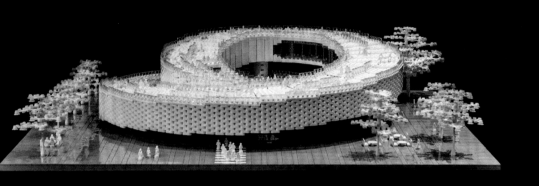

LEGO HOUSE

Billund, DENMARK
Bricks: 22,000
BIG Builder: Lasse Vestergård

TIMES SQUARE VALENTINE

New York, USA
Bricks: 8,000
BIG Builder: Are J. Heiseldal & Helgi Toftegaard

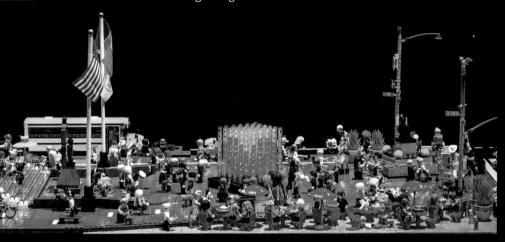

AUDEMARS PIGUET HOTEL

Le Brassus, SWITZERLAND
Bricks: 19,224
BIG Builder: Jessica Farrell

MARITIME YOUTH HOUSE

Copenhagen, DENMARK
Bricks: 25,000
BIG Builder: Anne Mette Vestergård

COPENHILL

Copenhagen, DENMARK
Bricks: 28,000
BIG Builder: Lasse Vestergård

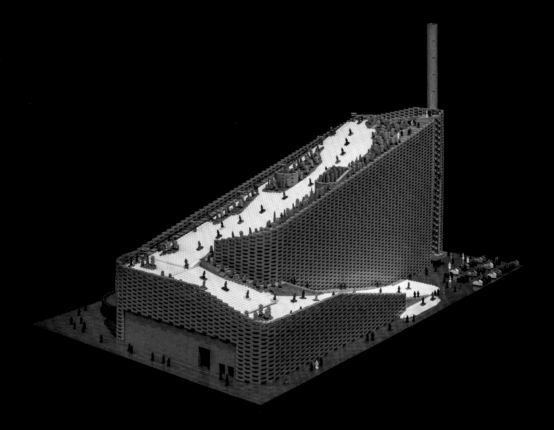

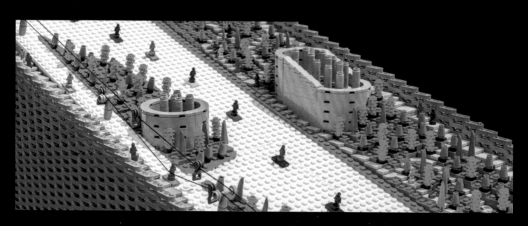

URBAN RIGGER

Copenhagen, DENMARK
Bricks: 16,000
BIG Builder: Anne Mette Vestergård

PANDA HOUSE

Copenhagen, DENMARK
Bricks: 10,000
BIG Builder: Emil Lidé

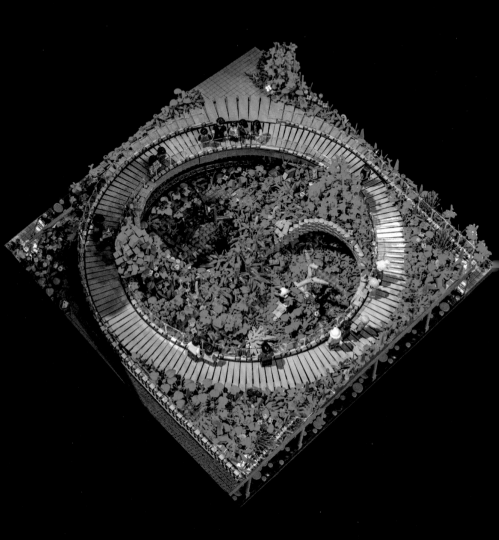

THE MOUNTAIN

Copenhagen, DENMARK
Bricks: 30,000
BIG Builder: Esben Kolind

THE HONEYCOMB

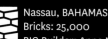

Nassau, BAHAMAS
Bricks: 25,000
BIG Builder: Anne Mette Vestergård

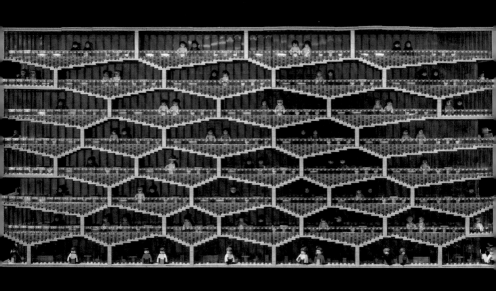

HUALIEN RESIDENCES

Hualien, TAIWAN
Bricks: 6,000
BIG Builder: Zio Chao, Hsinwei Chi & Kimura Hsieh

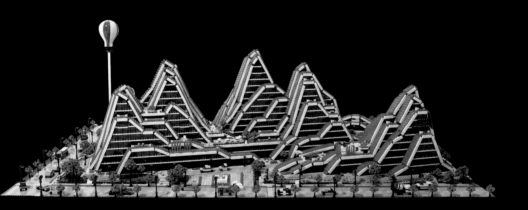

GLASIR

Tórshavn, FAROE ISLANDS
Bricks: 27,000
BIG Builder: Helgi Toftegaard

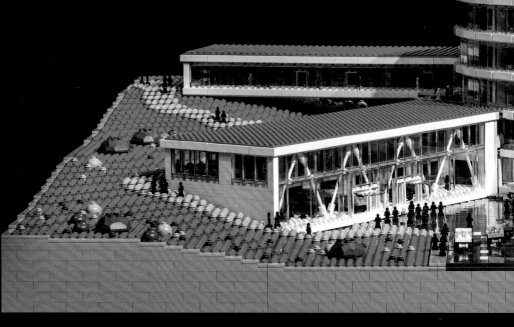

DORTHEAVEJ 2

Copenhagen, DENMARK
Bricks: 42,900
BIG Builder: Esben Kolind & Helgi Toftegaard

Autistic builders in the DONG project
Specialisterne has been a huge part of the building of the DONG model. Specialisterne is an organization that helps people
with autism find their right place in life and in the work field. Here they create value for the given company as well as for themselves.
Specialisterne Foundation is a not-for-profit foundation with the goal to create one million jobs globally for people with autism.
www.specialisterne.com

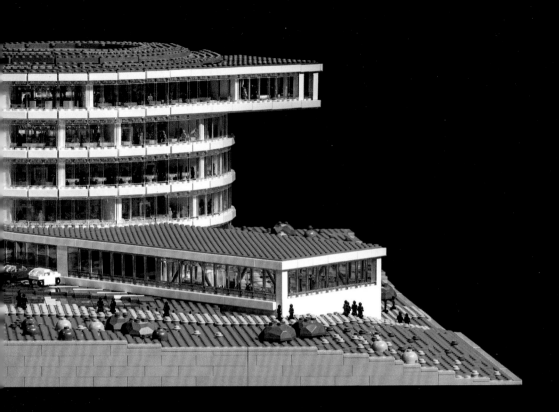

All LEGO Images by Rasmus Hjortshøj | COAST STUDIO

COPENHILL

Copenhagen, DENMARK
Bricks: 910
BIG Builder: Nicolas Carlier

PANDA HOUSE

Copenhagen, DENMARK
Bricks: 539
BIG Builder: Nicolas Carlier

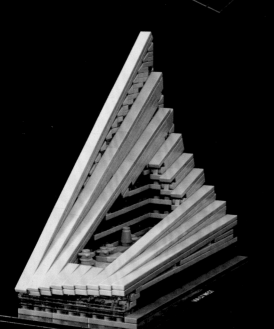

VIA WEST 57

New York City, USA
Bricks: 663
BIG Builder: Nicolas Carlier

LEGO

8 HOUSE

Copenhagen, DENMARK
Bricks: 711
BIG Builder: Nicolas Carlier

URBAN RIGGER

Copenhagen, DENMARK
Bricks: 360
BIG Builder: Nicolas Carlier

THE MOUNTAIN

Copenhagen, DENMARK
Bricks: 872
BIG Builder: Nicolas Carlier

FROM FACT
TO FICTION

Architecture is the art and science of turning fiction into fact. The world we inhabit is largely imagined and then realized by the people that came before us. A giant fantasy carved out in stone and poured in concrete. The most powerful creative output we have as a species is the world we create for each other. Due to our ingenuity and imagination, our perseverance and persistence, we keep expanding the repertoire of spaces in our cities: Industrial ports become swimming pools, powerplants become ski slopes, flood berms become public parks, museums become bridges, and bridges become plazas in the sky.

The way we contribute to this process at BIG is through a process best described as Narrative Design. But first, we must explain its opposite: The design narrative. The design narrative is a tool designers use to explain their ideas to the rest of the world. Often it is a retroactive justification of what has been done using metaphor and post-rationalization, invented once the design process is already over. Counter to the design narrative— Narrative Design is the process of using narrative as a curatorial tool to sharpen a design and the values, principles, and ideas that guide it. By initially identifying what the project is all about—what the problems and potentials are, which conflicts and controversies we will attempt to address—we create a kind of treatment or outline of the project. And then we start designing, with multiple designers giving form to various ideas. Any team member has license to give form—but once we meet and decide which aspects to pursue further, which ones to refine and combine, and which ones to leave on the editing room floor, the narrative takes shape by retelling the story behind the design to each other. The narrative shapes the proposals which in turn reshapes the narrative. In this process of coevolution, the narrative and the design gradually evolve. Once it becomes time to tell the story to a third party, we don't have to invent it from scratch—the story is already in the very DNA of the design, and vice versa.

Architecture is a creative art form that is bound by multiple parameters including gravity, function, program, accessibility, safety, zoning, law, climate, context, culture, material, and economy. It takes years to realize a project and costs millions or even billions to complete. And even if it often has a named individual behind it with the main creative responsibility, it is always the work of tens or hundreds or even thousands of individuals working in concert. Quite similar to the long-form fiction of film and series.

Consequently, I have always been fascinated by film—the discipline of screen writing, the aesthetics of production design, and the art of direction. When designers talk about spaces, one of the richest resources of cultural common reference is the world of cinema. And just like reality often imitates art—sometimes art needs to enlist reality. With Lars von Trier, we were challenged to explore the macabre tectonics of frozen human forms. With Lisa Joy and Jonah Nolan, we were invited to imagine what a plausible future might look and feel like.

MATT DILLON

BRUNO GANZ

THE HOUSE THAT JACK BUILT

LARS VON TRIER

Lars von Trier—the Danish film director who famously co-founded the Dogme movement and helped reignite Danish cinema's most recent renaissance, is nothing if not controversial. Titles such as "Antichrist," "Melancholia," and "Nymphomaniac" suggest why. His producer called me and said that Lars wanted to meet because he was directing a film about a mass murderer and needed an architect to help make the namesake scene of the film, The House that Jack Built, seem credible.

SPOILER ALERT!

To trigger a Dantean turn of events toward the end of the film, he needed the main character to construct a house out of frozen corps. It needed to resemble a child's idea of a house. Archaic and iconic. It had to be credible as something made in a hurry, but also terrifyingly compelling as an architectural vision of horror.

Louis Kahn famously reminded us: "It's important, you see, that you honor the material that you use... 'What do you want, Brick?' And Brick says to you, 'I like an Arch.' Now it was our turn to ask, 'What do you want, corpse?'"

The most fitting analogy we could think of was traditional timbered houses from the Danish countryside; a wooden framework forms a skeleton of forces to be filled with hay and clay. In this case, the force diagram is drawn by human silhouettes. We took 60 scale people (the number of victims) in scale 1:50 and started to build a house. The white monochrome models resembled tombs and temples with marble statues and carvings. Almost too beautiful to scare. But once we used real 3D scans of various BIG team members, the antics gave way to the gothic. Lars was happy. The only question left was how to procure the building blocks.

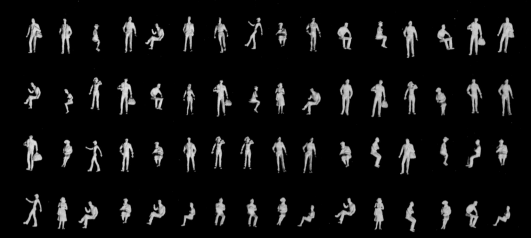

64 bodies

front elevation

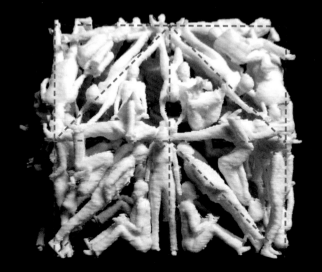

side elevation

0   0.25   0.5   1   2M

FREE WILL IS NOT FREE

WESTWORLD

HBO

I have followed the work and writing of Jonah Nolan since I watched Memento, which Jonah and his brother Christopher Nolan created, in 2000. A model of how the topological structure of a film can enable the audience to empathize with a protagonist who can not form short-term memories, by unfolding the narrative in reverse. Lately, his collaboration with his partner in life and film Lisa Joy has captivated me. I had watched Crichton's Westworld as a child and I was having a hard time imagining how to turn it into a relevant contemporary narrative. I couldn't have been more wrong. Rather than the original precursor for Jurassic Park with robots in the place of dinosaurs, the Nolans invited us to empathize with artificially intelligent and sentient robot protagonists. Over two seasons we witnessed the genesis of a new species— through its own eyes. A mutual friend introduced us and we became friends. The Nolans were thinking about season three, in which they had to show a future in the late 21st century. It was going to be shot in LA in 2019—the same year that the original Blade Runner takes place. It turned out LA 2019 did not end up looking like the world in Blade Runner. They enlisted us to help inform a new vision of the future. We shared all our work on urban mobility made with Audi, Toyota, Biomega, Google, and Virgin Hyperloop. Mobility as a service and multimodal forms of personal mobility would give way to more inhabitable and walkable public spaces. The elimination of car-dominated streets would give space for social life and green landscapes. We pointed to Singapore as a fascinating place where Piranesian three-dimensional urban environments by law would ensure parks and plants throughout the vertical section of the city. In Barcelona where I was living at the time we introduced them to our friend Ricardo Bofill, to his incredible home, a cement factory turned biophilic palace could become a villains lair. And finally, turning failed fact to fiction, we opened our 3D archives, allowing the Nolans to pick and choose from our conceptual cemetery of unrealized designs, to help populate the futuristic panoramas of LA. As a result, they created what I believe to be a blatantly credible vision of what the future might look like. Rather than the oversimplified and polarized world of today's political discourse, it offers a refreshingly complex ambivalent world where dystopia and utopia, hero and villain can be difficult to distinguish, aesthetically as well morally.

\W/

RASMUS HJORTSHØJ

RASMUS HJORTSHØJ

1900   ꝏꝏꝶ
1800   ꝏꝏꝶ
1700

RASMUS HJORTSHØJ

RASMUS HJORTSHØJ

RASMUS HJORTSHØJ

RASMUS HJORTSHØJ

COPENHILL

LOCATION:
COPENHAGEN, DENMARK

YEAR: 2010

**YEAR OF
COMPLETION:** 2019

SIZE: 41,000 M²
441,300 SF

CLIENT: AMAGER
RESOURCE CENTER,
FONDEN AMAGER BAKKE

PROGRAM: INDUSTRIAL,
BODY CULTURE

Partners in Charge: Bjarke Ingels, David
Zahle, Jakob Lange, Brian Yang
Project Manager: Jesper Boye
Andersen, Claus Hermansen
Project Architect: Nanna Gyldholm Møller

Team: Adam Mahfudh, Alberto Cumerlato, Aleksander
Wadas, Alexander Codda, Alexander Ejsing, Alexandra
Gustafsson, Alina Tamosiunaite, Armor Gutierrez, Anders
Hjortnæs, Andreas Klok Pedersen, Annette Jensen, Ariel
Wallner, Ask Andersen, Balaj Ilulian, Blake Smith, Borko
Nikolic, Brygida Zawadzka, Buster Christensen, Casey
Tucker, Chris Falla, Chris Zhongtian Yuan, Daniel Selensky,
Dennis Rasmussen, Espen Vik, Finn Nørkjær, Franck
Fdida, Gonzalo Castro, Gül Ertekin, George Abraham,
Helen Chen, Henrick Poulsen, Henrik Rømer Kania,
Horia Spirescu, Jakob Ohm Laursen, Jean Strandholt,
Jelena Vucic, Jeppe Ecklon, Ji-young Yoon, Jing Xu,
Joanna Jakubowska, Johanna Nenander, Kamilla
Heskje, Kasper Worsøe Pejtersen, Katarzyna Siedlecka,
Krzysztof Marciszewski, Laura Wätte, Liang Wang, Lise
Jessen, Long Zuo, Maciej Zawadzki, Mads Enggaard
Stidsen, Marcelina Kolasinska, Marcos Bano, Maren Allen,
Mathias Bank, Matthias Larsen, Matti Nørgaard, Michael
Andersen, Narisara Ladawal Schröder, Niklas A. Rasch,
Nynne Madsen, Øssur Nolsø, Pero Vukovic, Richard
Howis, Ryohei Koike, Sebastian Liszka, Se Hyeon Kim,
Simon Masson, Sunming Lee, Toni Mateu, Xing Xiong,
Zoltan David Kalaszi, Tore Banke, Yehezkiel Wiliardy

THE TWIST

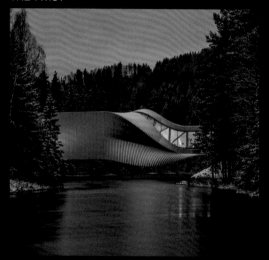

LOCATION: NORWAY

YEAR: 2011

**YEAR OF
COMPLETION:** 2019

SIZE: 1,000 M²
10,800 SF

CLIENT: KISTEFOS
MUSEUM

PROGRAM: CULTURE

Partners in Charge: Bjarke Ingels,
David Zahle, Brian Yang
Project Leader: Eva Seo-Andersen
Project Architect: Mikkel Marcker Stubgaard
Project Designer: Carlos Ramos Tenorio

Team: Aime Desert, Alberto Menegazzo, Aleksandra
Domian, Aleksandra Sobczyk, Alessandro
Zanini, Alina Tamosiunaite, Andre Zanolla, Balaj
Alin Ilulian, Brage Mæhle Hult, Carlos Ramos
Tenorio, Carlos Suriñach, Casey Tucker, Cat
Huang, Channam Lei, Christian Dahl, Christian Eugenius
Kuczynski, Claus Rytter Bruun de Neergaard, Dag
Præstegaard, David Tao, Edda Steingrimsdottir, Espen
Vik, Finn Nørkjær, Frederik Lyng, Jakob Lange, Joanna
M. Lesna, Kamilla Heskje, Katrine Juul, Kei Atsumi,
Kristoffer Negendahl, Lone Fenger Albrechtsen,
Mads Mathias Pedersen, Mael Barbe, Marcelina
Kolasinska, Martino Hutz, Matteo Dragone, Naysan
John Foroudi, Nick Huizenga, Nobert Nadudvari,
Ovidiu Munteanu, Rasmus Rosenblad, Richard Mui,
Rihards Dzelme, Roberto Fabbri, Ryohei Koike, Sofia
Rokmaniko, Sunwoong Choi, Tiina Liisa Juuti, Tomas
Ramstrand, Tore Banke, Tyrone Cobcroft, Xin Chen

THE HYPERLOOP

LOCATION: DUBAI, UAE

YEAR: 2016

SIZE: 140 KM
87 MILES

CLIENT: VIRGIN
HYPERLOOP ONE

PROGRAM: URBANISM

Partners in Charge: Bjarke Ingels, Jakob Lange
Project Leader: Sören Grünert

Team: Adi Krainer, Ashton Stare, Cheyenne
Vandevoorde, Cristian Lera, Daniele Pronesti, Derek
Wong, Domenic Schmid, Erik Berg Kreider, Evan Wiskup,
Francesca Portesine, Hugo Soo, Kristian Hindsberg, Lam
Le Nguyen, Lasse Kristensen, Linda Halim, Maureen
Rahman, Ovidiu Munteanu, Pei Pei Yang, Ryan Duval,
Stephen Steckel, Terrence Chew, Thomas Christoffersen,
Tore Banke, Veronica Moretti, Yehezkiel Wiliardy

THE ARTERY

LOCATION: ABU
DHABI, UAE

YEAR: 2017

SIZE: 29,000 M²
312,100 SF

CLIENT: ABU DHABI
CAPITAL GROUP, IMKAN

PROGRAM: CULTURE

Partners in Charge: Bjarke Ingels,
Jakob Lange, Finn Nørkjær
Project Leaders: Dimitrie Grigorescu,
Lucian Racovitan, Tomas Ramstrand
Project Manager: Anders Kofod
Project Architect: Alberto Menegazzo

Team: Dominic James Black, Allen Dennis Shakir, Steen
Kortbæk Svendsen, Damiano Mazzocchini, Roberto Fabbri,
Andrea Terceros, Stefan Plugaru, David Vega Y Rojo,
Matthew McCluskey, Kristoffer Negendahl, Tore Banke,
Yasmina Yehia, Shaojun Zheng, Pawel Bussold, Carmelo
Gagliano, Anna Odulinska, Vejlko Mladenovic, Anastasia
Voutsa, Paula Madrid, Miguel Rebelo, Teodor Fratila,
David Verbeek, Ulrik Montnemery, Ksymena Borczynska

THE BIG U

LOCATION: LOWER MANHATTAN, NEW YORK, USA

YEAR: 2013

YEAR OF COMPLETION: 2026

SIZE: 10 MILES

CLIENT: UNITED STATES DEPARTMENT OF HOUSING AND URBAN DEVELOPMENT

PROGRAM: URBANISM

Partners in Charge: Bjarke Ingels, Kai-Uwe Bergmann, Thomas Christofferson
Project Leader: Jeremy Alain Siegel, Daniel Kidd

Team: Kurt Nieminen, Dammy Lee, Yifu Sun, Jack Lipson, David Spittler, Blake Smith, David Dottelonde, Ken Amoah, Choonghyo Lee, Wesley Chiang, Daisy Zhong, Hector Garcia, Yaziel Juarbe, Taylor Hewett

TOYOTA WOVEN CITY

LOCATION: SUSONO, SHIZUOKA, JAPAN

YEAR: 2019

SIZE: 708,200 M² 7,623,000 SF

CLIENT: TOYOTA MOTOR CORPORATION + KALEIDOSCOPE CREATIVE

PROGRAM: MIXED-USE

Partners in Charge: Bjarke Ingels, Leon Rost
Project Manager: Yu Inamoto
Project Leader: Giulia Frittoli

Team: Agla Egilsdottir, Alvaro Velosa, Brian Zhang, Fernando Longhi, Jennifer Son, John Hein, Joseph Baisch, Mai Lee, Margherita Gistri, Minjung Ku, Nicolas Lapierre, Peter Sepassi, Raven Xu, Samantha Okolita, Shane Dalke, Thomas McMurtrie, Yi Lun Yang, Nasiq Kahn, Jeffrey Shumaker
Render Credits: Squint Opera

MUSÉE ATELIER AUDEMARS PIGUET

LOCATION: LE BRASSUS, SWITZERLAND

YEAR: 2013

YEAR OF COMPLETION: 2020

SIZE: 3,000 M² 33,000 SF

CLIENT: AUDEMARS PIGUET

PROGRAM: CULTURE

Partners in Charge: Bjarke Ingels, Thomas Christoffersen, Daniel Sundlin, Beat Schenk
Project Leaders: Rune Hansen (Project Manager), Simon Scheller (Project Manager), Matthew Oravec (Project Architect), Otilia Pupezeanu (Project Designer), Ji-Young Yoon (Concept)

Team: Adrien Mans, Alessandra Peracin, Ashton Stare, Blake Theodore Smith, Claire Thomas, Dammy Lee, Eva Maria Mikkelsen, Evan Wiskup, Høgni Laksafoss, Iva Ulam, Jan Casimir, Jason Wu, Julien Beauchamp-Roy, Kristian Hindsberg, Marcin Fejcak, Marie Lancon, Maureen Rahman, Maxime Le Droupeet, Natalie Kwee, Pascal Loschetter, Pierre Goete Teodor Javanaud Emden, Tore Bank, Ute Rinnebach, Veronica Lalli, Vivien Cheng, Yaziel Juarbe

HÔTEL DES HORLOGERS

LOCATION: LE BRASSUS, SWITZERLAND

YEAR: 2018

SIZE: 7,000 M² 75,300 SF

CLIENT: AUDEMARS PIGUET

PROGRAM: HOTEL

Partners in Charge: Bjarke Ingels, Thomas Christoffersen, Daniel Sundlin, Beat Schenk
Project Manager: Simon Scheller
Project Architect: Matthew Oravec, Stephanie Choi, Lou Arencibia and Manon Otto (Landscape)
Project Designer: Otilia Pupezeanu, Pantea Tehrani (Interiors)

Team: Aaron Mark, Amro Abdelsalam, Aurelie Frolet, Casey Tucker, Catalina Rivera, Claire Thomas, Claire Wadey, Deborah Campbell, Ethan Duffey, Eva Maria Mikkelsen, Evan Wiskup, Francesca Portesine, Gaurav Janey, Haochen Yu, Ibrahim Salman, Il Hwan Kim, Jan Leenknegt, Jason Wu, Ji-Young Yoon, Josiah Poland, Ku Hun Chung, Lu Zhang, Malcolm Rondell Galang, Martynas Norvila, Melissa Jones, Morgan Mangelsen, Nicolas Gustin, Nicolas Lapierre, Pascal Loschetter, Pierre Goete Teodor Javanaud Emden, Rasmus Streboel, Rune Hansen, Seth Byrum, Shidi Fu, Sijia Zhou, Supakrit Wongviboonsin, Terrence Chew, Tracy Sodder, Xinyu Wang

TELUS SKY

LOCATION: CALGARY, CANADA

YEAR: 2013

YEAR OF COMPLETION: 2020

SIZE: 70,725 M² 761,000 SF

CLIENT: WESTBANK PROJECTS CORP., TELUS, ALLIED DEVELOPMENT CORP.

PROGRAM: COMMERCIAL

Partners in Charge: Bjarke Ingels, Thomas Christoffersen
Project Manager: Christopher White, Carl MacDonald
Project Architect: Stephanie Choi, Michael Zhang
Project Designer: Iannis Kandyliaris

Team: Alex Wu, Barbora Srpkova, Beat Schenk, Benjamin Caldwell, Benjamin Johnson, Brian Rome, Bryan Hardin, Carolien Schippers, Choonghyo Lee, Chris Gotfredsen, Daisy Zhong, David Spittler, Davide Maggio, Deborah Campbell, Dennis Harvey, Douglas Alligood, Elena Bresciani, Florencia Kratsman, Gaurav Janey, Haoyue Wang, Ho Kyung Lee, Iris van der Heide, Isshin Morimoto, Ivy Hume, Jakob Lange, Jan Leenknegt, Jennifer Phan, Julie Kaufman, Justyna Mydlak, Ku Hun Chung, Manon Gicquel, Mateusz Rek, Maya Shopova, Megan van Artsdalen, Michael Zhang, Mike Evola, Peter Lee, Quentin Stanton, Sun Yifu, Tara Hagan, Terry Lallak, Tianqi Zhang, Yaziel Juarbe, Yoanna Shivarova
Project Leader, Interiors: Francesca Portesine
Team, Interiors: Agne Rapkeviciute, Christopher White, Cristian Lera, Jack Lipson, John Kim, Lina Bondarenko, Nicholas Coffee

OMNITURM

LOCATION: FRANKFURT, GERMANY

YEAR: 2015

YEAR OF COMPLETION: 2020

SIZE: 70,000 M²
754,000 SF

CLIENT: COMMERZ REAL AG

PROGRAM: COMMERCIAL

Partners in Charge: Bjarke Ingels, Andreas Klok Pedersen, Finn Nørkjær
Project Manager: Jörn Hendrik Fischer
Project Architect: Dominic James Black
Project Leader: Lorenzo Boddi

Team: David Verbeek, Günther Weber, Helen Chen, Joanna Gajda, Joseph James Haberl, Lukas Kerner, Maria Teresa Fernandez Rojo, Natalie Isabel Stachnik, Nicolas Millot, Sabine Kokina, Thomas Sebastian Krall, Viktoria Millentrup, Yan Ma, Emily King, Enea Michelesio, Gabrielė Ubarevičiūtė, Giedrius Mamavicius, Jesper Boye Andersen, Jakob Lange, Joanna Jakubowska, Katarzyna Joanna Piekarczyk, Julieta Muzillo, Lorenzo Boddi, Lucas Carriere, Lucian Tofan, Max Aldunate Reitour, Raphael Ciriani, Sabine Kokina, Tore Banke, Yannick Macken, Vinish Sethi

MARBLE COLLEGIATE CHURCH TOWER

LOCATION: NEW YORK CITY, USA

YEAR: 2016

SIZE: 72,557 M²
781,000 SF

CLIENT: HFZ CAPITAL

PROGRAM: COMMERCIAL

Partners in Charge: Bjarke Ingels, Thomas Christoffersen
Project Architect: Youngjin Yoon
Project Designer: Doug Stechschulte
Project Manager: Elizabeth McDonald

Team: Agne Rapkeviciute, Alan Tansey, Amir Mikhaeil, Anton Bashkaev, Armen Menendian, Ashton Stare, Barbara Stallone, Beat Schenk, Bell Cai, Benjamin Caldwell, Benjamin Novacinski, Casey Tucker, Christopher White, Christopher Tron, Cristian Lera, Deborah Campbell, Douglass Alligood, Elizaveta Sudravskaya, Emily Mohr, Filippo Cioffi, Francesca Portesine, Gaurav Sardana, Giulia Chagas, Isela Liu, James Babin, Jan Leenknegt, Jeff Bourke, Jeremy Babel, Juan David Ramirez, Julie Kaufman, Kam Chi Cheng, Kelly Neill, Ku Hun Chung, Lam Le Nguyen, Linda Halim, Ma Ning, Mackenzie Keith, Manon Otto, Margaret Tyrpa, Margherita Gistri, Michael Zhang, Neha Sadruddin, Nicholas Potts, Oliver Thomas, Pabi Lee, Pantea Tehrani, Rasmus Streboel, Rita Sio, Seo Young Shin, Seth Byrum, Sidonie Muller, Simon Lee, Stephanie Hui, Terrence Chew, Tianqi Zhang, Tracy Sodder, Yerin Won, Yiwei Li, Zhonghan, Sean O'Brien, Joanne Chen, Kayeon Lee Huang
Model: Margherita Gistri, Yerin Won

UNION CENTER

LOCATION: TORONTO, CANADA

YEAR: 2017

SIZE: 118,707 M²
1,280,000 SF

CLIENT: WESTBANK, ALLIED DEVELOPMENT

PROGRAM: MIXED-USE

Partners in Charge: Bjarke Ingels, Thomas Christoffersen, Martin Voelkle, Agustin Perez-Torres
Project Leaders: Fabian Lorenz, Andreas Buettner

Team: Kurt Nieminen, Ace Nguyen, Andreas Bak, Ashton Stare, Chiayu Liu, Doug Stechschulte, Elias Brulin, Emmett Walker, Fabian Lorenz, Filippo Cioffi, Florencia Kratsman, Gabriel Jewell-Vitale, Gary Polk, Jonathan Steffen Hein, Julian Andres Ocampo Salazar, Kam Chi Cheng, Kristoffer Negendahl, Maxwell Moriyama, Oliver Thomas, Phawin Siripong, Sijia Zhou, Terrence Chew, Tingting Lyu, Tracy Sodder, Valerie Derome-Masse, Veronica Acosta, Veronica Watson; Model: Izabella Banas, Mai Lee, James Caruso, Walid Bhatt, Carlos Castillo

THE XI

LOCATION: NEW YORK CITY, USA

YEAR: 2016

YEAR OF COMPLETION: 2020

SIZE: 83,000 M²
900,000 SF

CLIENT: 76 ELEVENTH PROPERTY OWNER, LLC

PROGRAM: MIXED-USE

Partners in Charge: Bjarke Ingels, Thomas Christoffersen, Beat Schenk
Project Architect: Andreas Buettner
Project Designer: Doug Stechschulte

Team: Agne Rapkeviciute, Alana Goldweit, Ali Chen, Amir Mikhaeil, Benjamin Caldwell, Christopher David White, Christopher Farmer, Daniella Eskildsen, Deborah Campbell, Douglass Alligood, Francis Fontaine, Hector Romero, Hung Kai Liao, Jan Leenknegt, Ji-Young Yoon, Juan David Ramirez, Justyna Mydlak, Lasse Kristensen, Marcus Kujala, Margaret Tyrpa, Mateusz Wieckowski-Gawron, Maureen Rahman, Nicolas Gustin, Pauline Lavie, Rune Wriedt, Veronica Moretti, Youngjin Yoon
Render Credits: DBOX

SHENZHEN ENERGY HQ

LOCATION:
SHENZHEN, CHINA

YEAR: 2010

**YEAR OF
COMPLETION:** 2018

SIZE: 96,000 M²
1,030,000 SF

CLIENT: SHENZHEN
ENERGY COMPANY

PROGRAM: COMMERCIAL

Partners in Charge: Bjarke Ingels,
Andreas Klok Pedersen
Project Leaders: Catherine Huang,
Song He, Andre Schmidt
Project Manager: Martin Voelkle

Team: Alessio Zenaro, Alina Tamosiunaite, Alysen
Hiller, Ana Merino, Andreas Geisler Johansen,
Annette Jensen, Armor Rivas, Balaj Ilulian, Brian
Yang, Baptiste Blot, Buster Christiansen, Cecília Ho,
Christian Alvarez, Christin Svensson, Claudia Hertrich,
Claudio Moretti, Cory Mattheis, Dave Brown, Dennis
Rasmussen, Doug Stechschulte, Eskild Nordbud,
Felicia Guldberg, Fred Zhou, Gaetan Brunet, Gül
Ertekin, Henrik Kania, James Schrader, Jan Magasanik,
Jan Borgstrøm, Jeppe Ecklon, Jelena Vucic, João
Albuquerque, Jonas Mønster, Karsten Hansen, Malte
Kloe, Mikkel Marcker Stubgaard, Michael Andersen,
Michal Kristof, Min Ter Lim, Oana Simionescu, Nicklas
A. Rasch, Philip Sima, Rasmus Pedersen, Rune
Hansen, Rui Huang, Sofia Gaspar, Stanley Lung, Sun
Ming Lee, Takuya Hosokai, Todd Bennett, Xi Chen,
Xing Xiong, Xiao Lu, Xu Li, Yijie Dan, Zoltan Kalaszi,
Alex Cozma, Kuba Snopek, Fan Zhang, Flavien Menu

THE HONEYCOMB & THE SANCTUARY

LOCATION: NASSAU,
BAHAMAS

YEAR: 2013

**YEAR OF
COMPLETION:** 2018

SIZE: 21,000 M²
226,000 SF

CLIENT: TAVISTOCK
GROUP

PROGRAM: MIXED-USE

Partners in Charge: Bjarke Ingels,
Thomas Christoffersen, Beat Schenk
Project Manager: Sören Grünert
Project Architect: Brian Foster, Yu Inamoto,
Daniel Jackson Kidd, Tran Le

Team: Amina Blacksher, Benzi Rodman, Brandon
Cook, David Spittler, Hsiao Rou Huang, Jakob Lange,
Jan Leenknegt, Jennifer Phan, Jennifer Shen, Karen
Shiue, Ku Hun Chung, Lujac Desautel, Raphael
Ciriani, Romea Muryn, Seth Byrum, Terry Lallak,
Tianqi Zhang, Tran Le, Aran Coakley, Brian Foster,
Hung Kai Liao, Jan Casimir, Jennifer Phan, Lam Le
Nguyen, Maki Matsubayashi, Nicholas Coffee, Santtu
Hyvarinen, Wojciech Swarowski, Zhonghan Huang

LYCIUM

LOCATION: FANØ
BAD, DENMARK

YEAR: 2016

SIZE: 1,100 M²
12,000 SF

CLIENT: STEEN LASSEN

PROGRAM: CULTURE

Partners in Charge: Bjarke Ingels, David Zahle

Team: Gabriele Ubareviciute, Lina Bondarenko, Lucian
Racovitan, Michael Kepke, Nina Vuga, Ole Elkjær-Larsen,
Alessandro Zanini, Andreas Klok Pedersen, Annette
Birthe Jensen, Geet Gawri, Giedrius Mamavicius,
Kristoffer Negendahl, Lina Bondarenko, Tore Banke

VANCOUVER HOUSE

LOCATION: VANCOUVER,
CANADA

YEAR: 2011

**YEAR OF
COMPLETION:** 2020

SIZE: 60,600 M2
650,000 SF

CLIENT: WESTBANK

PROGRAM: HOUSING

Partners in Charge: Bjarke Ingels, Thomas
Christoffersen, Beat Schenk
Project Leader: Agustín Pérez-Torres
Project Manager: Carl MacDonald, Melissa Bauld

Team: Aaron Mark, Alan Tansey, Alex Wu, Alexandra Gustafsson,
Alina Tamosiunaite, Amina Blacksher, Aran Coakley, Arash Adel
Ahmadian, Armen Menendian, Barbora Srpkova, Ben Zunkeler,
Benjamin Caldwell, Benjamín Novacinski, Bennett Gale, Birk
Daugaard, Blake Theodore Smith, Brian Foster, Brian Rome,
Carolien Schippers, Christopher James Malcolm Jr., Christopher
Junkin, Christopher Tron, David Brown, David Dottelonde,
Deborah Campbell, Doug Stechschulte, Douglass Alligood,
Edward Yung, Elena Bresciani, Filip Milovanovic, Francesca
Portesine, Gabriel Hernandez Solano, Gabriel Jewell-Vitale,
Hector Garcia, Ivy Hume, Jan Leenknegt, Janice Rim, John
Kim, Josiah Poland, Julian Liang, Julianne Gola, Julie Kaufman,
Karol Bogdan Borkowski, Kurt Nieminen, Lauren Turner, Lorenz
Krisai, Lucio Santos, Marcella Martinez, Martin Voelkle, Matthew
Dlugosz, Megan Ng, Michael Robert Taylor, Otilia Pupezeanu,
Paula Domka, Phillip MacDougall, Ryan Yang, Sean Franklin,
Sebastian Grogaard, Simon Scheller, Spencer Hayden, Taylor
Fulton, Terrence Chew, Terry Lallak, Thomas Smith, Tianqi
Zhang, Tobias Hjortdal, Tran Le, Valentina Mele, Xinyu Wang,
Yaziel Juarbe, Yoanna Shivarova, Zach Walters, Zhifei Xu,
Fabian Lorenz, Shu Zhao, Ryan Duval, Alejandra Cortes, Bryan
Hardin Corliss Ng, Cristina Medina-Gonzalez, Erik Berg Kreider,
Florencia Kratsman, Joshua Woo, Kelly Neill, Elnaz Rafati, Michael
Evola, Ema Bakalova, Jonas Swienty Andresen, Melissa Jones

BIG

LOCATION: NUUK, GREENLAND

YEAR: 2016

SIZE: 34,600 M²
373,000 SF

CLIENT: BENDIX CONSULT

PROGRAM: CULTURE

Partners in Charge: Bjarke Ingels, David Zahle, Andreas Klok Pedersen
Project Leaders: Allen Shakir, Jakob Henke

Team: Åsmund Skeie, Ivan Genov, Yannick Macken, Daniel Selensky, Ji Young-Yoon, Gul Ertekin, Aleksander Tokarz, Alessio Zenaro, Johan Cool, Nicklas Antoni Rasch; **Model:** Robert Bichlmaier

LOCATION: AMHERST, MASSACHUSETTS, USA

YEAR: 2016

YEAR OF COMPLETION: 2019

SIZE: 6,500 M²
70,000 SF

CLIENT: UNIVERSITY OF MASSACHUSETTS BUILDING AUTHORITY

PROGRAM: EDUCATION

Partners in Charge: Bjarke Ingels, Thomas Christoffersen, Beat Schenk, Daniel Sundlin
Project Leaders: Yu Inamoto, Pauline Lavie-Luong, Hung Kai Liao

Team: Alice Cladet, Amina Blacksher, Barbara Stallone, Cheyenne Vandevoorde, Daniel Kidd, Davide Maggio, Deborah Campbell, Denys Kozak, Derek Wong, Domenic Schmid, Douglass Alligood, Elena Bresciani, Emily Mohr, Fabian Lorenz, Francesca Portesine, Ibrahim Salman, Jan Leenknegt, Justyna Mydlak, Kai-Uwe Bergmann, Ku Hun Chung, Linda Halim, Lucas Hong, Manon Otto, Maria Eugenia Dominguez, Mustafa Khan, Nicolas Gustin, Pei Pei Yang, Peter Lee, Seoyoung Shin, Simon Lee, Terrence Chew, Tianqi Zhang, Yixin Li
BIG Ideas: Tore Banke, Yehezkiel Wiliardy, Kristoffer Negendahl

TIRPITZ MUSEUM

LOCATION: BLÅVAND, DENMARK

YEAR: 2012

YEAR OF COMPLETION: 2017

SIZE: 2,850 M²
30,700 SF

CLIENT: VARDEMUSEERNE

PROGRAM: CULTURE

Partners in Charge: Bjarke Ingels, Finn Norkjaer
Project Leader, Concept: Brian Yang
Project Leader, Detailed Design: Frederik Lyng
Project Manager: Ole Elkjær-Larsen

Team: David Zahle, Andreas K. Pedersen, Snorre Emanuel Nash Jørgensen, Michael Andersen, Hugo Soo, Marcella Martinez, Geoffrey Eberle, Adam Busko, Hanna Johansson, Jakob Andreassen, Charlotte Cocco, Mikkel Marcker Stubgaard, Michael Schønemann Jensen, Alejandro Mata Gonzales, Kyle Thomas David Tousant, Jesper Boye Andersen, Alberte Danvig, Jan Magasanik, Enea Michelesio, Alina Tamosiunaite, Ryohei Koike, Brigitta Gulyás, Katarzyna Krystyna Siedlecka, Andrea Scalco, Tobias Hjortdal, Maria Teresa Fernandez Rojo
BIG Ideas: Jakob Lange, Tore Banke, Yehezkiel Wiliardy, Kristoffer Negendahl

GALERIES LAFAYETTE CHAMPS-ÉLYSÉES

LOCATION: PARIS, FRANCE

YEAR: 2015

YEAR OF COMPLETION: 2019

SIZE: 6,800 M²
74,000 SF

CLIENT: GROUPE GALERIES LAFAYETTE

PROGRAM: COMMERCIAL

Partners in Charge: Bjarke Ingels, Jakob Sand
Project Managers: Karim Muallem, Gabrielle Nadeau
Project Leaders: Karim Muallem, Gabrielle Nadeau, Xavier Delanoue, Francesca Portesine, Pauline Lavie-Luong

Team: Agla Sigridur Egilsdottir, Alvaro Maestro García, Amro Abdelsalam, Anis Souissi, Anna Juzak, Aurelie Frolet, Catalina Rivera, Christian Lopez, Clementine Huck, Dimitrie Grigorescu, Emily Pickett, Emine Halefoglu, Enea Michelesio, Ethan Duffey, Étienne Duval, Filip Milovanovic, Francisco Javier Sarria Salazar, Gerhard Pfeiler, Hugo Yun Tong Soo, Hye-Min Cha, Jakob Lange, Janie Green, Joanna M. Lesna, José Carlos de Silva, Katarzyna Swiderska, Laurent de Carnière, Lucas Stein, Lucian Racovitan, Malgorzata Mutkowska, Marie Lancon, Miguel Rebelo, Monika Dauksaite, Paula Domka, Philip Rufus Knauf, Quentin Blasing, Rahul Girish, Ramona Montecillo, Raphael Ciriani, Sergi Sauras i Collado, Stefano Zugno, Taylor Fulton, Terrence Chew, Thomas Sebastian Krall, Thomas Smith, Tomas Karl Ramstrand, Tracy Sodder,

THE SMILE

LOCATION: NEW YORK CITY, USA

YEAR: 2013

YEAR OF COMPLETION: 2020

SIZE: 25,600 M²
275,000 SF

CLIENT: BLUMENFELD DEVELOPMENT GROUP

PROGRAM: HOUSING

Partners in Charge: Bjarke Ingels, Thomas Christoffersen, Beat Schenk, Kai-Uwe Bergmann
Project Leader: Michelle Stromsta, Lucio Santos
Project Leader, Interiors: Francesca Portesine, Rita Sio

Team: Adrien Mans, Agne Rapkeviciute, Annette Miller, Ava Nourbaran, Ben Caldwell, Benjamin DiNapoli, Chi Chi Lin, Daniele Pronesti, Deborah Campbell, Dennis Harvey, Douglass Alligood, Elena Bresciani, Eva Maria Mikkelsen, Everald Colas, Gabriel Hernandez Solano, Iannis Kandyliaris, Jan Leenknegt, Jennifer Ng, Jennifer Phan, Jennifer Wood, Jeremy Babel, John Kim, Jose Jimenez, Julie Kaufman, Julien Beauchamp-Roy, Kurt Nieminen, Lina Bondarenko, Mark Rakhmanov, Quentin Stanton, Sarah Habib, Taylor Fulton, Terrence Chew, Terry Lallak, Valentina Mele, Wells Barber, Wojciech Swarowski, Yaziel Juarbe, Yoanna Shivarova

TRANSITLAGER

LOCATION: BASEL/ MÜNCHENSTEIN, SWITZERLAND

YEAR: 2011

YEAR OF COMPLETION: 2017

SIZE: 30,000 M²
323,000 SF

CLIENT: NÜESCH DEVELOPMENT AG, UBS FUND MANAGEMENT, CHRISTOPH MERIAN STIFTUNG

PROGRAM: HOUSING

Partners in Charge: Bjarke Ingels, Andreas Klok Pedersen, Finn Nørkjær
Project Leader: Jakob Henke

Team: Agnete Jukneviciute, Alexandra Gustaffson, Andreas Johansen, Annette Jensen, Barbara Srpkova, Buster Christensen, Camila Stadler, Dennis Rasmussen, Dominic Black, Enea Michelesio, Erik de Haan, Gül Ertekin, Franck Fdida, Helen Chen, Ioannis Gio, Jan Magasanik, Jesper Andersen, Lorenzo Boddi, Marcelina Kolasinska, Teresa Fernandez, Martin Voelkle, Miao Zhang, Michael Schønemann, Mikkel Marcker Stubgaard, Ole Elkjær-Larsen, Ricardo Palma, Ryohei Koike, Sergiu Calacean, Tobias Hjortdal

3 XEMENEIES

LOCATION: BARCELONA, SPAIN

YEAR: 2018

SIZE: 60,000 M²
646,000 SF

CLIENT: METROVACESA, ENDESA

PROGRAM: MIXED-USE

Partners in Charge: Bjarke Ingels, Catherine Huang
Project Leader: Lucas Carriere

Team: Maria Sole Bravo, Carlos Suriñach, Marcos Anton Banon, Wei Lesley Yang, Tomás Rosselló Barros, Edda Steingrimsdottir, Florencia Kratsman, Adrianna Karnaszewska

S. PELLEGRINO FLAGSHIP FACTORY

LOCATION: SAN PELLEGRINO TERME, BERGAMO, ITALY

YEAR: 2016

YEAR OF COMPLETION: 2021

SIZE: 16,300 M²
175,450 SF

CLIENT: SANPELLEGRINO S.P.A.

PROGRAM: COMMERCIAL

Partners in Charge: Bjarke Ingels, Thomas Christoffersen
Project Leader: Jelena Vucic
Project Manager: Simon Scheller, Vincenzo Polsinelli
Project Architect: Giulio Rigoni

Team: Christopher Tron, Benson Chien, Ma Ning, Nicole Passarella, Kurt Nieminen, Nicholas Reddon, Lorenz Krisai, Hsiao Rou Huang, Santtu Hyvarinen, Stephanie Hui, Armen Menendian, Yang Yang Chen, Stephen Steckel, Derek Wong, Terrence Chew, Edda Steingrimsdottir, Fabian Lorenz, Christian Salkeld, Wells Barber, Jan Leenknegt, Josiah Poland, Veronica Moretti, Julie Kaufman, Fernando Longhi Pereira da Silva, Ava Nourbaran, Aslan Taheri, Gabriella Den Elzen, Benjamin Caldwell, Danna Lei, Megan Van Artsdalen, Veronica Acosta, Lawrence Olivier Mahadoo, Melissa Jones, Maria Eugenia Dominguez, Tracy Sodder, Amro Abdelsalam, Tianqi Zhang, Jennifer Wood, Sharon Kwan, Kelly Neill, Adi Krainer, Ji-Young Yoon, Gaurav Janey, Francesca Portesine, Ethan Duffey, Deborah Campbell, Maki Matsubayashi, Denys Kozak, Megan Ng, Kevin Pham, Stephen Kwok, Margaret Tyrpa
BIG Ideas: Tore Banke, Yehezkiel Wiliardy, Kristoffer Negendahl

BIG

670 MESQUIT

LOCATION: LOS ANGELES, CALIFORNIA, USA

YEAR: 2016

SIZE: 241,500 M²
2,600,000 SF

CLIENT: RCS-VE LLC

PROGRAM: CULTURE

Partners in Charge: Bjarke Ingels, Thomas Christoffersen
Project Leaders: Jakob Henke, Sanam Salek

Team: Juan David Ramirez, Wells Barber, Sijia Zhou, Derek Landon Wong, Mateusz Wieckowski-Gawron, Ella den Elzen, Yixin Li, Lasse Kristensen, Ovidiu Munteanu, Terry Chew

GARE DU PONT DE BONDY

LOCATION: PARIS, FRANCE

YEAR: 2016

YEAR OF COMPLETION: 2030

SIZE: 10,000 M²
107,600 SF

CLIENT: SGP - SOCIÉTÉ DU GRAND PARIS

PROGRAM: URBANISM (METRO STATION)

Partners in Charge: Bjarke Ingels, Jakob Sand
Project Manager: Robert Grimm
Project Architect: Michael Leef

Team: Andrea Angelo Suardi, Ewa Szajda, Gabrielè Ubareviciutè, Floriane Fol, Giedrius Mamavicius, Jakob Lange, Kristoffer Negendahl, Laurent de Carnière, Malgorzata Mutkowska, Mariana de Soares e Barbieri Cardoso, Matteo Baggiarini, Marie Lancon, Orges Guga, Pascale Julien, Patrice Gruner, Rahul Girish, Santiago Muros Cortes, Tiago Sa, Tore Banke, Vilius Linge, Sara Najar, Francisco Castellanos, Claudia Bertolotti, Filip Rozkowski, Alex Ritivoi

THE HEIGHTS

LOCATION: ARLINGTON, VIRGINIA, USA

YEAR: 2014

YEAR OF COMPLETION: 2019

SIZE: 16,700 M²
180,000 SF

CLIENT: ARLINGTON PUBLIC SCHOOLS

PROGRAM: EDUCATION

Partners in Charge: Bjarke Ingels, Daniel Sundlin, Beat Schenk, Thomas Christoffersen
Project Managers: Aran Coakley, Sean Franklin
Project Leaders: Tony-Saba Shiber, Ji-Young Yoon, Adam Sheraden

Team: Amina Blacksher, Anton Bashkaev, Benjamin Caldwell, Bennett Gale, Benson Chien, Cadence Bayley, Cristian Lera, Daisy Zhong, Deborah Campbell, Douglass Alligood, Elena Bresciani, Elnaz Rafati, Evan Rawn, Francesca Portesine, Ibrahim Salman, Jack Gamboa, Jan Leenknegt, Janice Rim, Jin Xin, Josiah Poland, Julie Kaufman, Kam Chi Cheng, Ku Hun Chung, Margherita Gistri, Maria Sole Bravo, Mark Rakhmanov, Mateusz Rek, Maureen Rahman, Nicholas Potts, Pablo Costa, Ricardo Palma, Robyne Some, Romea Muryn, Saecheol Oh, Seo Young Shin, Seth Byrum Shu Zhao, Sidonie Muller, Simon David, Tammy Teng, Terrence Chew, Valentina Mele, Vincenzo Polsinelli, Zach Walters, Ziad Shehab

AARHUS Ø

LOCATION: AARHUS, DENMARK

YEAR: 2013

YEAR OF COMPLETION: 2019

SIZE: 26,500 M²
285,250 SF

CLIENT: KILDEN & MORTENSEN APS

PROGRAM: MIXED-USE

Partners in Charge: Bjarke Ingels, Finn Nørkjær, Andreas Klok Pedersen
Project Leader: Søren Martinussen
Project Manager: Ali Arvanaghi, Jesper Bo Jensen

Team: Agne Rapkeviciute, Aaron Hales, Agne Tamasauskaite, Alberte Danvig, Aleksander Wadas, Ana Vindfeldt, Anna Wisborg, Annette Jensen, Ariel Joy Norback Wallner, Brigitta Gulyás, Claes Robert Janson, Enea Michelesio, Frederike Werner, Hsiao Rou Huang, Ioana Fartadi Scurtu, Jacob Lykkefold Aaen, Jakob Lange, Jakob Andreassen, Jakob Ohm Laursen, Jan Magasanik, Jesáfa Templo, Jesper Boye Andersen, Kamilla Heskje, Katarina Mácková, Katerina Joannides, Katrine Juul, Kekoa Charlot, Kristoffer Negendahl, Lise Jessen, Lucian Racovitan, Lucian Tofan, Roberto Outumuro, Sergiu Calacean, Sofie Maj Sørensen, Spencer Hayden, Teodor Javanaud Emden, Tobias Hjortdal, Tore Banke, Xuefei Yan, Yehezkiel Wiliardy; **Model:** Ella Murphy, Ricardo Oliveira, Dominiq Oti

CAPITASPRING

LOCATION: SINGAPORE

YEAR: 2015

**YEAR OF
COMPLETION:** 2021

SIZE: 93,000 M²
1,000,000 SF

CLIENT: CAPITALAND

PROGRAM: COMMERCIAL

Partners in Charge: Bjarke Ingels, Brian Yang
Project Manager: Eric Li, Günther Weber
Project Leader: Gorka Calzada Medina, Martino Hutz, Song He

Team: Aime Desert, Aleksander Wadas, Aleksandra Domian, Alessandro Zanini, Andrew Lo, Anke Kristina Schramm, Antonio Sollo, Augusto Lavieri Zamperlini, Bartosz Kobylakiewicz, Dalma Ujvari, David Schwarzman, David Vega y Rojo, Dimitrie Grigorescu, Dina Brændstrup, Dominika Trybe, Elise Cauchard, Eriko Maekawa, Espen Vik, Ewa Szajda, Federica Locati, Filippo Lorenzi, Francisco Castellanos, Frederik Skou Jensen, Gabrielé Ubareviciute, Helen Chen, Hongduo Zhuo, Jacek Baczkowski, Jakob Lange, Jakub Wlodarczyk, Jonas Käckenmester, Julieta Muzzillo, Kirsty Badenoch, Kristoffer Negendahl, Luca Pileri, Luis Torsten Wagenführer, Lukas Kerner, Malgorzata Mutkowska, Maria Teresa Fernandez Rojo, Matilde Tavanti, Moa Carlsson, Nataly Timotheou, Niu Jing, Orges Guga, Patrycja Lyszczyk, Pedro Savio jobim Pinheiro, Philip Rufus Knauf, Praewa Samachai, Qamelliah Nassir, Rahul Girish, Ramon Julio Muros Cortes, Rebecca Carrai, Roberto Fabbri, Ryohei Koike, Samuel Rubio Sanchez, Shuhei Kamiya, Sorcha Burke, Steen Kortbæk Svendsen, Szymon Kolecki, Talia Fatte, Teodor Fratila Cristian, Ulla Hornsyld, Viktoria Millentrup, Vilius Linge, Vinish Sethi, Weijia Lu, Xin Su, Xinying Zhang, Zari van de Merwe, Zhen Tong
BIG Ideas: Tore Banke, Anders Holden Deleuran

GOWANUS ZIGGURAT

LOCATION: NEW
YORK, USA

YEAR: 2018

SIZE: 78,000 M²
840,000 SF

CLIENT: RFR HOLDING LLC

PROGRAM: MIXED-USE

Partners in Charge: Bjarke Ingels, Martin Voelkle
Project Leader: Shane Dalke

Team: Andreas Buettner, Andreea Gulerez, Andrew Hong, Ania Podlaszewska, Bernardo Schuhmacher, Ema Bakalova, Jakob Henke, Jeremy Alain Siegel, Jin Park, Melissa Jones, Nasiq Khan, Ruicong Tang

VERTICAL OASES

LOCATION: DUBAI, UAE

YEAR: 2015

SIZE: 80,000 M²
861,000 SF

CLIENT: EMAAR
PROPERTIES

PROGRAM:
OBSERVATION TOWER

Partners in Charge: Bjarke Ingels,
Andreas Klok Pedersen
Project Leader: Kristian Hindsberg

Team: Santtu Johannes Hyvärinen, Bartosz Kobylakiewicz, Thomas Sebastian Krall, Tomas Karl Ramstrand, Helen Chen, Giedrius Mamavicius, Lorenzo Boddi

MIAMI PRODUCE

LOCATION: MIAMI,
FLORIDA

YEAR: 2018

SIZE: 125,000 M²
1,345,500 SF

CLIENT: UIA
MANAGEMENT LLC

PROGRAM: HOUSING

Partners in Charge: Bjarke Ingels, Agustin Perez Torres, Thomas Christoffersen
Project Leader: Sanam Salek, Shane Dalke

Team: Agne Rapkeviciute, Chris Tron, Emily Chen, Emine Halefoglu, Karolina Bourou, Kevin Pham, Kig Veerasunthorn, Manon Otto, Matthijs Engele, Phillip MacDougall, Siva Sepehry Nejad, Terrence Chew, Tracy Sodder, Veronica Acosta, Xander Shambaugh, Sanam Salek, Julie Kaufman, Ryan Duval, Thomas Smith, Josiah Poland, Jacob Karasik, Paulina Panus, Taylor Hewett, Ziyu Guo, Alejandra Cortes , Raymond Castro Haochen Yu
BIG Ideas: Tore Banke, Anders Holden Deleuran, Bart Ramakers, Kristoffer Negendahl

LA PORTE

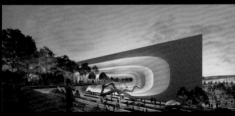

LOCATION: GONESSE,
FRANCE

YEAR: 2017

SIZE: 34,000 M²
366,000 SF

CLIENT: EUROPA CITY,
ALLIAGES & TERRITOIRES

PROGRAM: CULTURE

Partners in Charge: Bjarke Ingels, Jakob Sand
Project Leader: Gabrielle Nadeau

Team: Raphaël Ciriani, Mattia di Carlo, Lucas Stein, Semiha Toptas, Sarkis Sarkisyan, Marie Lançon, Bernhard Touzet; Model: Francisca Hamilton, Amanda Cunha
Render Credits: BRICKS

BIG

LEGO HOUSE

LOCATION: BILLUND, DENMARK

YEAR: 2012

YEAR OF COMPLETION: 2017

SIZE: 12,000 M² 1,042,000 SF

CLIENT: LEGO

PROGRAM: CULTURE

Partners in Charge: Bjarke Ingels, Finn Nørkjær, Brian Yang
Project Architect: Snorre Nash

Team: Andreas Klok Pedersen, Agne Tamasauskaite, Annette Birthe Jensen, Ariel Joy Norback Wallner, Ask Hvas, Birgitte Villadsen, Chris Falla, Christoffer Gotfredsen, Daruisz Duong Vu Hong, David Zahle, Esben Christoffersen, Franck Fdida, Ioana Fartadi Scurtu, Jakob Andreassen, Jakob Ohm Laursen, Jakob Sand, Jakub Matheus Wlodarczyk, Jesper Bo Jensen, Jesper Boye Andersen, Julia Boromissza, Kasper Reimer Hansen, Katarzyna Krystyna Siedlecka, Katarzyna Stachura, Kekoa Charlot, Leszek Czaja, Lone Fenger Albrechtsen, Louise Bøgeskov Hou, Mads Enggaard Stidsen, Magnus Algreen Suhr, Manon Otto, Marta Christensen, Mathias Bank Stigsen, Michael Kepke, Ole Dau Mortensen, Ryohei Koike, Sergiu Calacean, Søren Askehave, Stefan Plugaru, Stefan Wolf, Thomas Jakobsen Randbøll, Tobias Hjortdal, Tommy Bjørnstrup

MÉCA

LOCATION: BORDEAUX, FRANCE

YEAR: 2011

YEAR OF COMPLETION: 2019

SIZE: 18,000 M² 194,000 SF

CLIENT: RÉGION NOUVELLE-AQUITAINE

PROGRAM: CULTURE

Partners in Charge: Bjarke Ingels, Jakob Sand, Finn Nørkjær, Andreas Klok Pedersen
Project Manager: Laurent de Carnière, Marie Lancon, Gabrielle Nadeau

Team: Alexander Codda, Alicia Marie Sarah Borhardt, Annette Birthe Jensen, Åsmund Skeie, Aya Fibert, Bartosz Kobylakiewicz, Bernhard Touzet, Brigitta Gulyás, David Tao, Edouard Champelle, Espen Vik, Greta Krenciute, Greta Tafel, Hyojin Lee, Ivan Genov, Jan Magasanik, Jeffrey Mark Mikolajewski, Karol Bogdan Borkowski, Katarzyna Swiderska, Kekoa Charlot, Lorenzo Boddi, Maria Teresa Fernandez Rojo, Melissa Andres, Michael Schønemann Jensen, Nicolas Millot, Ola Hariri, Ole Dau Mortensen, Pascale Julien, Paul-Antoine Lucas, Raphael Ciriani, Santiago Palacio Villa, Se Hyeon Kim, Sebastian Liszka, Seunghan Yeum, Snorre Emanuel Nash Jørgensen, Teresa Fernández, Thiago De Almeida, Thomas Jakobsen Randbøll, Yang Du, Zoltan David Kalaszi, Tore Banke, Yehezkiel Wiliardy

ALBANIAN NATIONAL THEATER

LOCATION: TIRANA, ALBANIA

YEAR: 2017

SIZE: 9,300 M² 100,000 SF

CLIENT: FUSHA LLC

PROGRAM: CULTURE

Partners in Charge: Bjarke Ingels, David Zahle, Cat Huang
Project Leaders: Lucas Carriere

Team: Adrianna Karnaszewska, Alexander Niemantsverdriet, Anton Malthe Ling, Carlos Suriñach, Christopher Taylor, Izabella Banas, Jakub Klimes, Jinho Lee, Edda Steingrimsdottir, Dimitrie Grigorescu, Juhye Kim, Ka Yiu Karry Li, Kei Atsumi, Kekoa Charlot, Kristoffer Negendahl, Liliana Cruz-Grimm, Matteo Dragone, Matteo Pavanello, Milyausha Garaeva, Nataly Timotheou, Ovidiu Munteanu, Sunwoong Choi, Tomas Barros, Tore Banke, Wei Yang, Yehezkiel Wiliardy, Yunzi Wang

PARIS PARC

LOCATION: PARIS, FRANCE

YEAR: 2011

YEAR OF COMPLETION: 2021

SIZE: 15,000 M² 162,000 SF

CLIENT: SORBONNE UNIVERSITÉ

PROGRAM: EDUCATION

Partners in Charge: Bjarke Ingels, Jakob Sand, Andreas Klok Pedersen, Finn Nørkjær, Daniel Sundlin
Project Leaders: Francisco Castellanos, Gabrielle Nadeau
Project Manager: Robert Grimm;
Project Architect: Alex Rivito

Team: Alexandre Carpentier, Camille Crepin, Edouard Boisse, Jakob Sand, Nanna Gyldholm Møller, Ole Elkjær-Larsen, Robinson Neuville, Tiina Juuti, Tobias Hjortdal, Yang Du, Quentin Blaising, Michael Leef, Gabrielle Nadeau, Filip Rozkowski, Matteo Baggiarini, Francois Ducatez, Gerhard Pfeiler, Andrea Angelo Suardi, Gul Ertekin, Boris Kadiyski, Fabio Garau, Andy Coward, Cecilie Søs Brandt-Olsen, Bjakre Koch-Ørvad, Andreas Bak, Roberto Fabbri, Aimee Desert
Render Credits: OFF Architecture

SLUISHUIS

LOCATION:
AMSTERDAM,
THE NETHERLANDS

YEAR: 2016

**YEAR OF
COMPLETION:** 2022

SIZE: 46,000 M²
495,000 SF

CLIENT: VORM / BESIX

PROGRAM: HOUSING

Partners in Charge: Bjarke Ingels, Andreas
Klok Pedersen, Finn Nørkjær
Design Lead: Jan Magasanik, Dimitrie Grigorescu
Project Manager: Jeppe Langer, Birgitte Villadsen

Team: Dimitrie Grigorescu, Alberto Menegazzo, Alex
Ritivoi, Andrea Angela Suardi, Anna Bertolazzi, Anna
Odulinska, Borko Nikolic, Brage Mæhle Hult, David
Vega, Dina Brændstrup, Dominika Trybe, Duncan
Horswill, Filip Radu, Frederik Skou Jensen, Helen Chen,
Hessam Dadkhah, Hongduo Zhou, Jean Valentiner
Strandholt, Jakob Lange, Jeppe Langer, Jonas Aarsø
Larsen, Justyna Mydlak, Keuni Park, Kim Christensen,
Kirsty Badenoch, Liliana Cruz-Grimm, Lone Fenger
Albrechtsen, Luca Pileri, Mads Enggaard Stidsen,
Mads Mathias Pedersen, Martino Hutz, Nina Vuga,
Olly Veugelers, Santtu Johannes Hyvärinen, Sascha
Leth Rasmussen, Sebastian Liszka, Sze Ki Wong, Ulla
Hornsyld, Victoria Ross-Thompson, Vinish Sethi, William
Pattison, Yannick Macken, Yu Xun Zhang, Yulong Li
BIG Ideas: Tore Banke, Bart Ramakers,
Kristoffer Negendahl, Mark Pitman

KING TORONTO

LOCATION: TORONTO,
ONTARIO, CANADA

YEAR: 2016

**YEAR OF
COMPLETION:** 2023

SIZE: 57,000 M²
613,500 SF

CLIENT: WESTBANK
PROJECTS CORP.

PROGRAM: MIXED-USE

Partners in Charge: Bjarke Ingels,
Thomas Christoffersen
Project Manager: Ryan Harvey
Project Designer: Lorenz Krisai
Project Architect: Andrea Zalewski

Team: Francesca Portesine, Samantha Okolita, Thomas
Smith, Janie Green, Joseph Kuhn, Jenna Dezinski,
Giulia Chagas, James Babin, Jan Leenknegt, Aaron
Mark, Agustin Perez-Torres, Alan Tansey, Alvaro Velosa,
Amina Blacksher, Andreas Buettner, Ava Kim, Beat
Schenk, Benjamin Caldwell, Bryan Maddock, Breno
Felisbino da Silveira, Bryan Hardin, Casey Tucker,
Casimir Esbach, Chengjie Li, Chris Tron, Corliss
Ng, Deborah Campbell, Douglass Alligood, Edda
Steingrimsdottir, Elnaz Rafati, Evan Saarinen, Fabian
Lorenz, Gabriel Jewell-Vitale, Ian Gu, Jae Min Seo,
Jin Park, Joshua Burns, Juan David Ramirez, Karolina
Bourou, Kayeon Lee, Lucio Santos, Iris Van der Heide,
Luke Lu, Margaret Tyrpa, Mateusz Wieckowski Gawron,
Josiah Poland, Margaret Kim, Megan Ng, Norain Chang,
Oliver Thomas, Ovidiu Munteanu, Phawin Siripong, Rita
Sio, Shu Zhao, Simon Scheller, Siva Sepehry Nejad, Agla
Sigridur Egilsdottir, Cristina Medina-Gonzalez, Florencia
Kratsman, Julian Ocampo Salazar, Pabi Lee, Yuanxun
Xia, Tore Banke, Bart Ramakers, Kristoffer Negendahl
Concept: Daniel Kidd, Tiago Sá, Alvaro Velosa, Brian
Rome, Chris Tron, Christian Lera, Ibrahim Salman,
John Hilmes, Jakob Lange, Terrence Chew, Ziyu
Guo, Linqi Dong **Render Credits:** Hayes Davidson

LE MARAIS À L'INVERSE

LOCATION: LE MARAIS,
PARIS, FRANCE

YEAR: 2018

SIZE: 6,500 M² NEW +
6,500 M² RENOVATION
140,000 SF (TOTAL)

CLIENT: CITY NOVE

PROGRAM: MIXED-USE

Partners in Charge: Bjarke Ingels, Jakob Sand
Project Leader: Marie Lancon, Gul Ertekin
Project Architect: Joanna Jakubowska

Team: Laurent de Carniere, Ka Yiu Karry Li, Danyu
Zeng, Luca Pileri, Francisco Castellanos, Hulda
Jonsdottir, Seungham Yeum, Masashi Hirai, Davide
Pelligrini, Fabianna Cortolezzis, Monika Dauksaite,
Jakub Klimes, Andrea Angelo Suardi, Sarkis Sarkisyan

IL PORTICO

LOCATION: MILAN, ITALY

YEAR: 2019

**YEAR OF
COMPLETION:** 2023

SIZE: 53,500 M²
576,000 SF

CLIENT: GENERALI
REAL ESTATE

PROGRAM: COMMERCIAL

Partners in Charge: Bjarke Ingels,
Andreas Klok Pedersen
Project Leader: Lorenzo Boddi

Team: Filip Radu, Gualtiero Mario Rulli, Sabina Blasiotti,
Siqi Chen, Jonathan Russell, Andy Coward, Chis Falla,
Lauren Connell, Andy Young, Claire Thomas, Ryohei
Koike, Nefeli Stamatari, Ioannis Gio, Youngjin Jun
Render Credits: Beauty and the Bit

PARQUE DE LA INNOVACIÓN

LOCATION: BUENOS AIRES, ARGENTINA

YEAR: 2019

SIZE: 220,000 M²
236,800 SF

CLIENT: GRUPO INVERSOR PETROQUÍMICA

PROGRAM: MIXED-USE

Partners in Charge: Bjarke Ingels, Agustin Perez-Torres
Project Leader: Kristian Hindsberg

Team: Andres Romero, Autumn Visconti, Haochen Yu, James Hartman, Josiah Poland, Julian Ocampo Salazar, Julie Kaufman, Kelly Neil, Mike Munoz, Siqi Zhang, Yi Lang, Mo Li, Doug Breuer, Won Ryu

WEGROW

LOCATION: NEW YORK, USA

YEAR: 2017

YEAR OF COMPLETION: 2019

SIZE: 1,830 M²
19,700 SF

CLIENT: WEGROW, THE WE COMPANY

PROGRAM: EDUCATION

Partners in Charge: Bjarke Ingels, Daniel Sundlin, Beat Schenk
Project Designer: Otilia Pupezeanu
Project Architect: Jeremy Babel, Rita Sio

Team: Bart Ramakers, Douglass Alligood, Erik Berg Kreider, Evan Saarinen, Filip Milovanovic, Florencia Kratsman, Francesca Portesine, Il Hwan Kim, Jakob Lange, Ji Young Yoon, Kristoffer Negendahl, Josiah Poland, Mengzhu Jiang, Ryan Yang, Stephen Kwok, Terrence Chew, Tore Banke, Tracy Sodder, Bernard Peng, Zakir Hamza, Thea Wiradinata
BIG Ideas: Tore Banke, Kristoffer Negendahl

URBAN RIGGER

LOCATION: COPENHAGEN, DENMARK

YEAR: 2014

YEAR OF COMPLETION: 2016

SIZE: 680 M²
7,300 SF

CLIENT: UDVIKLING DANMARK A/S

PROGRAM: HOUSING

Partners in Charge: Bjarke Ingels, Jakob Sand, Jakob Lange, Finn Nørkjær
Project Leader: Joos Jerne, Jesper Boye Andersen, Lise Jessen, Christian Bom

Team: Jonas Aarsø Larsen, Duncan Horswill, Brage Mæhle Hult, Birgitte Villadsen, David Zahle, Magdalene Maria Mroz, Jesper Bo Jensen, Dimitrie Grigorescu, Tore Banke, Annette Birthe Jensen, Perle van de Wyngert, Viktoria Millentrup, Dag Præstegaard, Toni Ma teu, Aleksandra Sliwinska, Brigitta Gulyás, Adam Busko, Nicolas Millot, Carlos Soria, Stefan Wolf, Mads Odgaard Johansen, Stefan Plugaru, Kamila Rawicka, Elina Skujina, Jacob Lykkefold Aaen, Raphael Ciriani, Agne Tamasauskaite, Aaron Hales, Ioana Fartadi Scurtu, Christian Bom, Lise Jessen

KLEIN HOUSE

LOCATION: NEW YORK, USA

YEAR: 2016

YEAR OF COMPLETION: 2018

SIZE: 17 M²
183 SF

CLIENT: KLEIN HOUSE

PROGRAM: HOUSING

Partners in Charge: Bjarke Ingels, Thomas Christoffersen
Project Leader: Max Moriyama
Project Architect: Rune Hansen

Team: Jian Yong Khoo, Kalina Piłat, Tianqi Zhang, Anton Bak

DORTHEAVEJ 2

LOCATION: COPENHAGEN, DENMARK

YEAR: 2011

YEAR OF COMPLETION: 2018

SIZE: 6,800 M²
73,200 SF

CLIENT: BO-VITA

PROGRAM: HOUSING

Partners in Charge: Bjarke Ingels, Finn Nørkjær
Project Managers: Ole Elkjær-Larsen, Per Bo Madsen

Team: Alberte Danvig, Alejandro Mata Gonzales, Alina Tamosiunaite, Birgitte Villadsen, Cat Huang, Claudio Moretti, Dag Præstegaard, Daruisz Duong Vu Hong, David Zahle, Enea Michelesio, Esben Christoffersen, Ewelina Moszczynska, Frederik Lyng, Henrik Kania, Høgni Laksáfoss, Jakob Andreassen, Jonas Aarsø Larsen, Karl Aarso Larsen, Katerina Joannides, Krista Meskanen, Laura Wätte, Lucas Torres Aguero, Maciej Jakub Zawaszki, Maria Teresa Fernandez Rojo, Michael Schønemann Jensen, Mikkel Marcker Stubgaard, Nigel Jooren, Rasmus Pedersen, Robinson Neuville, Sergiu Calacean, Taylor McNally-Anderson, Terrence Chew, Tobias Hjortdal, Tobias Vallø Sørensen
Model: Edward Burnett, Ricardo Oliveira

KAKTUS TOWERS

LOCATION:
COPENHAGEN, DENMARK

YEAR: 2017

**YEAR OF
COMPLETION:** 2021

SIZE: 26,100 M²
281,000 SF

CLIENT: CATELLA

PROGRAM: HOUSING

Partners in Charge: Bjarke Ingels, David Zahle
Project Leader: Jesper Bo Jensen
Project Architects: Katrine Juul, Carlos Ramos Tenorio

Team: Alex Ritivoi, Alexander Codda, Andreas Mullertz, Bart Ramakers, Birgitte Villadsen, Borko Nikolic, Brage Mæhle Hult, Christian Vang Madsen, Dominika Trybe, Eskild Schack Pedersen, Espen Vik, Francois Ducatez, Gül Ertekin, Hanne Halvorsen, Helen Chen, Henrik Jacobsen, Ivana Stancic, Jean Valentiner Strandholt, Jesper Boye Andersen, Jiajie Wang, Johan Bergström, Joos Jerne, Kristoffer Negendahl, Liia Vesa, Mads Mathias Pedersen, Marcos Anton Banon, Maria Stolarikova, Mark Korosi, Nina Vuga, Pawel Bussold, Richard Howis, Richard Mui, Sascha Leth Rasmussen, Sergiu Calacean, Sze Ki Wong, Teodor Fratila Cristian, Yehezkiel Wiliardy, Fabiana Cortolezzis, Beatrise Šteina, Friso van Dijk, Christian Eugenius Kuczynski Tore Banke, Kristoffer Negendahl, Bart Ramakers, Mark Pitman

PANDA HOUSE

LOCATION:
COPENHAGEN, DENMARK

YEAR: 2015

**YEAR OF
COMPLETION:** 2019

SIZE: 2,450 M²
26,000 SF

CLIENT:
COPENHAGEN ZOO

PROGRAM: CULTURE

Partners in Charge: Bjarke Ingels, David Zahle
Project Manager: Ole Elkjær-Larsen
Project Leaders: Nanna Gyldholm Møller, Kamilla Heskje, Tommy Bjørnstrup

Team: Alberto Menegazzo, Alex Ritivoi, Carlos Soria, Christian Lopez, Claus Rytter Bruun de Neergaard, Dina Brændstrup, Eskild Schack Pedersen, Fabiana Cortolezzis, Federica Longoini, Frederik Skou Jensen, Gabrielé Ubareviciute, Gökce Günbulut, Hanne Halvorsen, Høgni Laksáfoss, Jiajie Wang, Jinseok Jang, Joanna Plizga, Lone Fenger Albrechtsen, Luca Senise, Maja Czesnik, Margarita Nutfulina, Maria Stolarikova, Martino Hutz, Matthieu Brasebi, Pawel Bussold, Richard Howis, Seongil Choo, Sofia Sofianou, Stefan Plugaru, Tobias Hjortdal, Tore Banke, Víctor Bejenaru, Xiaoyi Gao

OCEANIX CITY

YEAR: 2019

SIZE: 75 HECTARES

CLIENT: OCEANIX

PROGRAM: URBANISM

Partners in Charge: Bjarke Ingels, Daniel Sundlin
Project Leaders: Alana Goldweit, Jeremy Alain Siegel

Team: Andy Coward, Ashton Stare, Autumn Visconti, Bernardo Schuhmacher, Carlos Castillo, Cristina Medina-Gonzalez, Florencia Kratsman, Jacob Karasik, Kristoffer Negendahl, Mai Lee, Manon Otto, Terrence Chew, Thomas McMurtrie, Tore Banke, Tracy Sodder, Walid Bhatt, Will Campion, Yushan Huang, Ziyu Guo

NOMA 2.0

LOCATION:
COPENHAGEN, DENMARK

YEAR: 2015

**YEAR OF
COMPLETION:** 2018

SIZE: 1,290 M²
13,880 SF

CLIENT: NOMA

PROGRAM: CULTURE

Partners in Charge: Bjarke Ingels, Finn Nørkjær
Project Managers: Ole Elkjær-Larsen, Tobias Hjortdal
Project Leader: Frederik Lyng

Team: Olga Litwa, Lasse-Lyhne-Hansen, Athena Morella, Enea Michelesio, Jonas Aarsø Larsen, Eskild Schack Pedersen, Claus Rytter Bruun de Neergaard, Hessam Dadkhah, Allen Dennis Shakir, Gökce Günbulut, Michael Kepke, Stefan Plugaru, Borko Nikolic, Dag Præstegaard, Timo Harboe Nielsen, Margarita Nutfulina, Nanna Gyldholm Møller, Joos Jerne, Kim Christensen, Tore Banke, Kristoffer Negendahl, Jakob Lange, Hugo Yun Tong Soo, Morten Roar Berg, Yan Ma, Tiago Sá, Ryohei Koike, Yoko Gotoh, Kyle Thomas David Tousant, Geoffrey Eberle, Jonseok Hang, Ren Yang Tan, Nina Vuga, Giedrius Mamavicius, Yehezkiel Wiliardy, Simona Reiciunaite, Yunyoung Choi, Vilius Linge, Tomas Karl Ramstrand, Aleksander Wadas, Andreas Mullertz, Angelos Siampakoulis, Manon Otto, Carlos Soria

BIG

THE ORB

LOCATION: NEVADA, USA

YEAR OF COMPLETION: 2019

SIZE: 25.5 M (84 F) IN DIAMETER SPHERE

PROGRAM: CULTURE

Partners in Charge: Bjarke Ingels, Jakob Lange, Kai-Uwe Bergmann
Project Leader: Laurent de Carniere

Team: Andy Coward, Autumn Visconti, Cecilie Søs Brandt Olsen, Chelsea Chiu, Emine Halefoglu, Ewa Zapiek, Garret Farmer, Hilda Heller, Hugo Soo, Jarrod Caranto, Karsten Vang, Lars Simesen, Lawrence Olivier Mahadoo, Mariana De Soares E Barbieri Cardoso, Natalia Serra, Quim Rabassa, Samantha Okolita, Silas Drewchin, Timo Harboe Nielsen, Sarkis Sarkisyan, Sebastian Grogaard; **Model:** Seunghan Yeum

DUBAI EXPO PLAZA

LOCATION: DUBAI, UAE

YEAR: 2016

SIZE: 20.000 M² 215.300 SF

CLIENT: DUBAI EXPO 2020

PROGRAM: CULTURE

Partners in Charge: Bjarke Ingels, Brian Yang
Project Leader: Lucian Racovitan
Project Manager: Andrew Lo

Team: Alejandro Hildago, Anders Kofoed, Anne Katrine Sandstrøm, Duncan Horswill, Joanna M. Lesna, Joseph James Haberl, Philip Rufus Knauf, Rahul Girish, Talia Fatte, Ulla Hornsyld, Xin Chen, Yang Huang

79 & PARK

LOCATION: STOCKHOLM, SWEDEN

YEAR: 2011

YEAR OF COMPLETION: 2018

SIZE: 25,000 M² 270,000 SF

CLIENT: OSCAR PROPERTIES

PROGRAM: HOUSING

Partners in Charge: Bjarke Ingels, Jakob Lange, Finn Nørkjær
Project Manager: Per Bo Madsen
Project Leaders: Enea Michelesio, Catherine Huang
Project Architects: Høgni Laksáfoss

Team: Agata Wozniczka, Agne Tamasauskaite, Alberto Herzog, Borko Nikolic, Christin Svensson, Claudio Moretti, Dominic Black, Eva Seo-Andersen, Frederik Wegener, Gabrielle Nadeau, Jacob Lykkefold Aaen, Jaime Peiro Suso, Jan Magasanik, Jesper Boye Andersen, Jonas Aarsø Larsen, Julian Andres Ocampo Salazar, Karl Johan Nyqvist, Karol Bogdan Borkowski, Katarina Mácková, Katrine Juul, Kristoffer Negendahl, Lucian Racovitan, Maria Teresa Fernandez Rojo, Max Gabriel Pinto, Min Ter Lim, Narisara Ladawal Schröder, Romea Muryn, Ryohei Koike, Sergiu Calacean, Song He, Taylor McNally-Anderson, Terrence Chew, Thomas Sebastian Krall, Tiago Sá, Tobias Vallø Sørensen, Tore Banke, Jakob Andreassen, Tobias Hjortdal, Henrik Kania

OAKLAND A'S BALLPARK

LOCATION: CALIFORNIA, USA

YEAR: 2018

SIZE: 36,000 M² 387,500 SF

CLIENT: ATHLETICS INVESTMENT GROUP LLC

PROGRAM: BODY CULTURE

Partners in Charge: Bjarke Ingels, Agustin Perez Torres
Project Leader: Simon Scheller, Otilia Pupezeanu, Frankie Sharpe

Team: Alejandra Cortes, Ashton Stare, Bennett Oh, Benson Chien, Breno Felisbino da Silveira, Catalina Rivera, Douglass Alligood, Francesca Portesine, James Caruso, Kam Chi Cheng, Kig Veerasunthorn, Margaret Kim, Maxwell Moriyama, Mengzhu Jiang, Norain Chang, Olga Khuraskina, Patrick Hyland, Stephanie Mauer, Stephen Kwok, Tara Abedinitafreshi, Terrence Chew, Tracy Sodder, Yeling Guo, Yerin Won, Yiyao Tang, Nojan Adami, Ziyu Guo, Haochen Yu

GOOGLE CARIBBEAN

LOCATION: SUNNYVALE, CALIFORNIA, USA

YEAR: 2017

SIZE: 96,800 M² 1,04M SF

CLIENT: GOOGLE

PROGRAM: COMMERCIAL

Partner in Charge: Bjarke Ingels, Leon Rost
Project Leaders: Kristian Hindsberg;
Technical: Sebastian Claussnitzer
Project Manager: Linus Saavedra

Team: Daniel Sundlin, Thomas Christoffersen, Amro Abdelsalam, Andriani Atmadja, Beat Schenk, Benjamin Caldwell, Bernard Peng, Deb Campbell, Dong-Joo Kim, Douglass Alligood, Dylan Hames, Ema Baklova, Emily Chen, Florencia Kratsman, Ghita Bennis, Isabella Marcotulli, Isela Liu, Jan Leenknegt, Jason Wu, Jeff Bourke, Jian Yong Khoo, Jiashi Yu, Kayeon Lee, Kevin Yoon, Maki Matsubayashi, Manon Otto, Margaret Tyrpa, Matthew Dlugosz, Megan Ng, Nick Flutter, Patrick Hyland, Peter Sepassi, Sanam Salek, Sanghoon Park, Shane Dalke, Shidi Fu, Thea Wiradinata, Wenjing Zhang, Zhonghan Huang

GLASIR

LOCATION: TÓRSHAVN, FAROE ISLANDS

YEAR: 2009

YEAR OF COMPLETION: 2018

SIZE: 19.200 M²
207.000 SF

CLIENT: MENTAMALARADID (MINISTRY OF CULTURE) / LANDSVERK

PROGRAM: EDUCATION

Partners in Charge: Bjarke Ingels, Finn Nørkjær, Ole Elkjær Larsen
Project Architect: Høgni Laksáfoss

Team: Alberte Danvig, Alejandro Mata Gonzales, Alessio Valmori, Alexandre Carpentier, Annette Birthe Jensen, Armen Menendian, Athena Morella, Baptiste Blot, Boris Peianov, Camille Crepin, Claudio Moretti, Dag Præstegaard, Daniel Pihl, David Zahle, Edouard Boisse, Elisha Nathoo, Enea Michelesio, Eskild Nordbud, Ewelina Moszczynska, Frederik Lyng, Goda Luksaite, Henrik Kania, Jakob Lange, Jakob Teglgård Hansen, Jan Besikov, Jan Kudlicka, Jan Magasanik, Jeppe Ecklon, Jesper Boye Andersen, Ji-Young Yoon, Johan Cool, Kari-Ann Petersen, Kim Christensen, Long Zuo, Martin Cajade, Michael Schønemann Jensen, Mikkel Marcker Stubgaard, Niklas Rausch, Norbert Nadudvari, Oana Simionescu, Richard Howis, Sabine Kokina, Simonas Petrakas, Sofia Sofianou, Takumi Iwasawam, Tobias Hjortdal, Tommy Bjørnstrup, Victor Bejenaru, Xiao Xuan Lu
BIG Ideas: Tore Banke, Kristoffer Negendahl

GOOGLE BAYVIEW

LOCATION: MOUNTAIN VIEW, CALIFORNIA, USA

YEAR: 2015

YEAR OF COMPLETION: 2020

SIZE (GBV+GCE):
600,000 M²
6,456,000 SF

CLIENT: GOOGLE

PROGRAM: COMMERCIAL

Partners in Charge: Bjarke Ingels, Thomas Christoffersen, Daniel Sundlin, Leon Rost
Project Leaders: Blake Smith, Ryan Harvey, David Iseri, Florencia Kratsman (interiors)
Project Managers: Linus Saavedra, Ziad Shehab

Team: Agla Egilsdottir, Alan Tansey, Alessandra Peracin, Ali Chen, Andriani Atmadja, Ania Podlaszewska, Armen Menendian, Beat Schenk, Benjamin Caldwell, Bernard Peng, Brian Zhang, Camilo Aspeny, Cheyne Owens, Christopher Wilson, Claire Thomas, Cristian Lera Silva, Cristina Medina Gonzalez, Danielle Kemble, Deborah Campbell, Derek Wong, Diandian Li, Douglass Alligood, Dylan Hames, Erik Berg Kreider, Eva Maria Mikkelsen, Guarav Sardana, Guillaume Evain, Hacken Li, Helen Chen, Isabella Marcotulli, Isela Liu, Jan Leenknegt, Jason Wu, Jennifer Dudgeon, Jennifer Wood, Ji-young Yoon, Jia Chengzhen, Jian Yong Khoo, Joshua Plourde, Kalina Pilat, Kurt Nieminen, Manon Otto, Marcus Kujala, Michelle Stromsta, Nandi Lu, Nicole Passarella, Olga Khuraskina, Oliver Colman, Patrick Hyland, Peter Kwak, Ramona Montecillo, Rita Sio, Sebastian Grogaard, Seo Young Shin, Siva Sepehry Nejad, Terrence Chew, Thomas McMurtrie, Tiago Sa, Timothy Cheng, Tingting Lyu, Tracy Sodder, Valentino Vitacca, Vincenzo Polsinelli, Walid Bhatt, Yesul Cho, Yina Moore, Zhonghan Huang

GOOGLE CHARLESTON EAST

LOCATION: MOUNTAIN VIEW, CALIFORNIA, USA

YEAR: 2015

YEAR OF COMPLETION: 2020

SIZE (GBV+GCE):
600,000 M²
6,456,000 SF

CLIENT: GOOGLE

PROGRAM: COMMERCIAL

Partners in Charge: Bjarke Ingels, Thomas Christoffersen, Daniel Sundlin, Leon Rost
Project Leaders: Sebastian Claussnitzer, Jason Wu, Joshua Plourde, Jennifer Dudgeon, Jonathan Fournier, Pantea Tehrani (Interiors)
Project Managers: Linus Saavedra, Ziad Shehab

Team: Aaron Ly, Agla Sigridur Egilsdottir, Alan Tansey, Alessandra Peracin, Ali Chen, Andriani Atmadja, Ania Podlaszewska, Armen Menendian, Beat Schenk, Benjamin Caldwell, Benjamin Novacinski, Bernard Peng, Blake Theodore Smith, Brian Zhang, Camilo Aspeny, Cheyne Owens, Christopher Wilson, Claire Thomas, Cristian Lera, Cristina Medina-Gonzalez, Danielle Kemble, David Iseri, Deborah Campbell, Derek Wong, Diandian Li, Douglass Alligood, Dylan Hames, Erik Berg Kreider, Eva Maria Mikkelsen, Florencia Kratsman, Francesca Portesine, Francis Fontaine, Gaurav Sardana, Guillaume Evain, Hacken Li, Helen Chen, Isabella Marcotulli, Isela Liu, Jan Leenknegt, Jennifer Dudgeon, Jennifer Wood, Ji-Young Yoon, Jia Chengzhen, Jian Yong Khoo, Jonathan Pan, Joshua Burn, Kalina Pilat, Kiley Feickert, Ku Hun Chung, Kurt Nieminen, Mads Kjaer, Manon Otto, Marcus Kujala, Meghan Bean, Michelle Stromsta, Nandi Lu, Nicole Passarella, Olga Khuraskina, Oliver Colman, Patrick Hyland, Peter Kwak, Ramona Montecillo, Rita Sio, Ryan Harvey, Sebastian Grogaard, Seo Young Shin, Siva Sepehry Nejad, Terrence Chew, Thomas Mcmurtrie, Tiago Sa, Timothy Cheng, Tingting Lyu, Valentino Vitacca, Vincenzo Polsinelli, Walid Bhatt, Yesul Cho, Yina Moore

THE SPIRAL

LOCATION: NEW YORK, USA

YEAR: 2015

YEAR OF COMPLETION: 2023

SIZE: 265,000 M²
2,853,000 SF

CLIENT: TISHMAN SPEYER

PROGRAM: COMMERCIAL

Partners in Charge: Bjarke Ingels, Daniel Sundlin, Thomas Christoffersen
Technical Director: Douglass Alligood
Project Manager: Nicholas Potts, Carolien Schippers
Project Designer: Dominyka Voelkle, Jennifer Wood
Project Architect: Armen Menendian

Team: Benjamin Johnson, Ute Rinnebach, Beat Schenk, Daniele Pronesti, Stephen Kwok, Dylan Hames, Brian Rome, Peter Lee, Sarkis Sarkisyan, Lawrence Olivier Mahadoo, Adam Sheraden, Alvaro Velosa, Gabriella Den Elzen, Joshua Burns, Veronica Acosta, Francesca Portesine, Christopher Tron, Tracy Sodder, Adrien Mans, Kurt Nieminen, Cheyenne Vandevoorde, Ali Chen, Simon Lee, Thea Gasseholm, Ibrahim Salman, Davide Maggio, Deborah Campbell, Christopher David White, Janice Rim, Otilia Pupezeanu, Seoyoung Shin, Wells Barber, David Brown, Cadence Bayley, Benjamin Caldwell, Hung Kai Liao, Terrence Chew, Yaziel Juarbe, Julie Kaufman, Maureen Rahman, Dong-Joo Kim, Jack Lipson, Jan Casimir, Zoltan David Kalaszi, Rachel Coulomb, Erin Yook, Jan Leenknegt, Lucio Santos, Yenhsi Tung, Martynas Norvila, Phawin Siripong, Mateusz Rek, Lisbet Christensen, Josiah Poland, Denys Kozak, Maria Eugenia Dominguez, Veronica Moretti, Juan David Ramirez, Andrew Lee, Will Fu, Michael Zhang, Ryan Duval, Haochen Yu, Luke Lu, Megan Van Artsdalen, Gabriel Jewell-Vitale, Anton Bashkaev, Gaurav Sardana, Margaret Tyrpa, Mackenzie Keith, Margaret Andreas Büttner, Agla Egilsdottir, Janie Green, Terry Chew, Tracy Sobert and Bernardo Schuhmacher
BIG Landscape: Manon Otto, Kelly Neill, Simon David, Emily Chen, Giulia Frittoli, Varat Limwibul, Kate Cella, Morgan Mangelsen
BIG Ideas: Tore Banke, Kristoffer Negendahl
Render Credits: Neoscape

BIG HQ

LOCATION: COPENHAGEN, DENMARK

YEAR: 2017

SIZE: 4,710 M²
50,700 SF

CLIENT: BIG – BJARKE INGELS GROUP

PROGRAM: OFFICE

Partners in Charge: Bjarke Ingels, Finn Nørkjær, David Zahle
Project Leader: Frederik Lyng
Project Manager: Ole Elkjær-Larsen

Team: Alda Sol, Amro Abdelsalam, Andrea Angela Suardi, Andrea Hektor, Andreas Klok Pedersen, Andy Coward, Anna Bertolazzi, Anna Wozniak, Aya Fibert, Bart Ramakers, Cecile Søs Brandt-Olsen, Dina Brændstrup, Duncan Horswill, Ewa Zapiec, Fabiana Cortolezzis, Felicia Olofsson, Gül Ertekin, Hanne Halvorsen, Helen Chen, Henrik Jacobsen, Hilda Heller, Høgni Laksáfoss, Ines Zunic, Jakob Lange, Jesper Kanstrup Pedersen, Jonathan Russell, Juhye Kim, Kanetnat Puttimettipanan, Katrine Juul, Kim Christensen, Kristoffer Negendahl, Ksenia Zhitomirskaya, Lars Thonke, Lenya Schneehage, Lisbet Fritze Christensen, Luca Pileri, Mads Enggaard Stidsen, Margarita Nutfulina, Mariana de Soares e Barbieri Cardoso, Mathieu Jaumain, Mikki Seidenschnur, Nandi Lu, Sherief Al Rifal, Tobias Hjortdal, Tore Banke, Ulla Hornsyld, Xinying Zhang, Yehezkiel Wiliardy, Yunyoung Choi, Mads Primdahl Rokkjær, Marius Tromholt-Richter, Lenya Nikola Schneehage, Francisca Hamilton

CITY OF NEW HOPE

LOCATION: THE MOON

YEAR: 2019

SIZE: CONFIDENTIAL

CLIENT: STEALTH CLIENT

PROGRAM: CONFIDENTIAL

Partners in Charge: Bjarke Ingels, Martin Voelkle
Project Leader: Jason Wu

Team: Melissa Jones, Florencia Kratsman, Christian Salkeld

MARS SCIENCE CITY

LOCATION: DUBAI, UAE

YEAR: 2017

SIZE: 56,810 M²
611,500 SF

CLIENT: GOVERNMENT OF UNITED ARAB EMIRATES

PROGRAM: CULTURE

Partners-in-Charge: Bjarke Ingels, Jakob Lange, Andreas Klok Pedersen
Project Leader: Dimitrie Grigorescu

Team: Ovidiu Munteanu, Tyrone Cobcroft, Teodor Fratila Cristian, Joao Albuquerque, Yasmin Asan, Viktoria Millentrup, Joanna M. Lesna, Diana Daod, Mattia Di Carlo, Andrea Terceros, Paula Madrid, Luca Pileri
Engineering: Cecilie Søs Brandt-Olsen, Duncan Horswill
BIG Ideas: Kristoffer Negendahl, Tore Banke, Yehezkiel Wiliardy, Hugo Soo
Landscape: Christian Eugenius Kuczynski, Ulla Hornsyld, Joanna Anna Jakubowska, Sze Ki Wong

MASTERPLANET

LOCATION: THE PLANET EARTH

YEAR: 2019

SIZE: 510.1 MILLION KM^2
196,940,000 SQ MI

PROGRAM: RESEARCH PROJECT

Partners in Charge: Bjarke Ingels, Andreas Klok Pedersen
Project Leader: Lucian Tofan

Team: Sophie Peterson, Parinaz Kadkhodayi – Kholghi, Filip Radu, Carmen Wientjes, William Campion, Christina Ødegaard Grytten, Paula Madrid, Naysan Foroudi

LOCATION: COPENHAGEN, DENMARK

YEAR: 2018

SIZE: 10 M^2
108 SF

CLIENT: KUNSTHAL CHARLOTTENBORG

PROGRAM: EXHIBITION

Partners in Charge: Bjarke Ingels, David Zahle
Project Leader: Joanna Jakubowska

Team: Adrianna Karnaszewska, Amro Abdelsalam, Anton Malthe Ling, Antonio Pessoa, Beatrise Steina, Dave von Toor, Felicia Olofsson, Filip Radu, Joanna Wirkus, Jonas Søgaard, Matteo Pavanello, Miaomiao Chu, Monika Dauksaite, Rihards Dzelme, Seunghan Yeum, Tomas Rosello Barros, Xinying Zhang

FORMGIVING EXHIBITION AT THE DANISH ARCHITECTURE CENTER

LOCATION: COPENHAGEN, DENMARK

YEAR: 2019

SIZE: 1,350 M^2
1,4530 SF

CLIENT: DAC – DANISH ARCHITECTURE CENTER

PROGRAM: EXHIBITION

Partners in Charge: Bjarke Ingels, Kai-Uwe Bergmann, Andreas Klok Pedersen
Project Manager: Gabrielle Nadeau

Team: Jakob Sand, Brian Yang, Cat Huang, Jakob Lange, Mattia di Carlo, Matteo Pavanello, Dimitrie Grigorescu, Scott Moon, Paula Madrid, Andre Zanolla, Amanda Cunha, Dominiq Oti, Edvard Connor Burnett, Irie Meree, Palita Tungjaroen, Ella Murphy, Francisca Hamilton, Marija Lukoseviciute, Pernille Kinch Andersen, Ricardo Oliveira, Robert Bichlmaier, Victor Moegreen, Daria Pahhota, Jesslyn Guntur, James Caruso, Jiyoon Lee, Carmelo Gagliano, Bernardo Schuhmacher, Izabella Banas, Mads Primdahl Rokkjær, Norain Chang, Davide Pellegrini, Peter Sepassi, Ada Gulyamdzhis, Qamelliah Nassir, Tiffany Wong, Elnaz Rafati, Mai Lee, Ana Maria Vindfeldt, Walid Bhatt, January Chen, Søren Dam Mortensen, Cecilie Søs Brandt-Olsen, Mantas Povilaika, Giovanni Simioni, Jae Min Seo, Ombretta Colangelo, Agnieszka Majkowska, Nick Flutter, Adam Poole, Jan Leenknegt, Tobias Hjortdal, Monika Dauksaite, Artemis Antonopoulou, Marius Tromholt-Richter, Lenya Nikola Schneehage, Tomas Barros, Cheng-Huang Lin, Alexander Jacobson, Tore Banke, Jens Majdal Kaarsholm, Kristoffer Negendahl, Anders Holden Deleuran, Duncan Horswill, Andy Coward, John Harding, Leah Peschel, Sarah Amick

BACK TO THE FUTURE

LOCATION: NEW YORK CITY, USA

YEAR: 2020

SIZE: 16.2 HECTARES

CLIENT: VAN ALEN INSTITUTE & NEW YORK CITY COUNCIL

PROGRAM: PUBLIC SPACE

Partners in Charge: Bjarke Ingels, Kai-Uwe Bergmann, Martin Voelkle
Associate-in-Charge: Jeremy Alain Siegel
Project Leader: Brandon Cappellari, Veronica Acosta

Team: Jeffrey Shumaker, Jamie Maslyn Larson, Christian Salkeld, Alan Fan, Lorenz Krisai, Adam Poole

EDITOR-IN-CHIEF	Bjarke Ingels
PROJECT LEADER	Paula Madrid
CORE TEAM	Geetika Bhutani, Ipek Akin, Jesslyn Guntur
FORMGIVING TEAM	Gabrielle Nadeau, Kai-Uwe Bergmann, Andreas Klok Pedersen, Jakob Sand, Brian Yang, Cat Huang, Jakob Lange, Mattia di Carlo, Matteo Pavanello, Dimitrie Grigorescu, Scott Moon, Andre Zanolla, Amanda Cunha, Dominiq Oti, Edvard Connor Burnett, Irie Meree, Palita Tungjaroen, Ella Murphy, Francisca Hamilton, Marija Lukoseviciute, Pernille Kinch Andersen, Ricardo Oliveira, Robert Bichlmaier, Victor Moegreen, Daria Pahhota, James Caruso, Jiyoon Lee, Carmelo Gagliano, Bernardo Schuhmacher, Izabella Banas, Mads Primdahl Rokkjær, Norain Chang, Davide Pellegrini, Peter Sepassi, Ada Gulyamdzhis, Qamelliah Nassir, Tiffany Wong, Elnaz Rafati, Mai Lee, Ana Maria Vindfeldt, Walid Bhatt, January Chen, Søren Dam Mortensen, Cecilie Søs Brandt-Olsen, Mantas Povilaika, Giovanni Simioni, Jae Min Seo, Ombretta Colangelo, Agnieszka Majkowska, Nick Flutter, Adam Poole, Jan Leenknegt, Tobias Hjortdal, Monika DauksWaite, Artemis Antonopoulou, Marius Tromholt-Richter, Lenya Nikola Schneehage, Tomas Barros, Cheng-Huang Lin, Alexander Jacobson, Tore Banke, Jens Majdal Kaarsholm, Kristoffer Negendahl, Anders Holden Deleuran, Duncan Horswill, Andy Coward, John Harding, Leah Peschel, Sarah Amick, Mackenzie Keith
TEXT	Bjarke Ingels
TEXT EDITING	Morgan Day, Danielle Carter, Jeffrey Inaba
TASCHEN	Julius Wiedemann (Editor), Daniel Siciliano Brêtas (Editorial coordination), Thomas Grell, Frank Goerhardt (Production)
PHOTOGRAPHERS	Aldo Amoretti, Alex Filz, Alex Medina, Alexander Piruli, Andreas Nuntun, ArchExist Photography, Benjamin Ward, Cat Huang, Chao Zhang, Cheryl Flemming & James Lane, Chris Coe, Christopher Mcanneny, Dave Burk, David Rasmussen, Dominic James Black, Ehrhorn Hummerston, Ema Peter, Eric Lefvander, Eva Seo-Andersen, Field Condition, Florent Michel, Glenn Santiago, Golden Dusk Photography, Gonçalo Pacheco, Habib Karimov, Hufton + Crow, Iwan Baan, Jakob Lange, Jamen Percy, Katelyn Perry, Kim Erlandsen, Laurent De Carniere, Laurian Ghinitoiu, Ma Ning, DSL Studio – Marco Cappelletti & Delfino Sisto Legnani, Marcus Wagner, Maris Mezulis, Matthew Carbone, Max Touhey, Nils Koenning, Olaf Rohl, Rasmus Hjortshøj, Ron Friesen, Salem Mostefaoui, Shawn Orton, Signe Don, Søren Aagaard, Søren Martinussen, Søren Rose Studio, Tomasz Majewski, Tony Oursler, Urban Rigger APS, Warren Dowson, WestBank. Render Credits: Squint Opera, DBOX, Bloomimages, OFF Architecture, Hayes Davidson, Beauty and the Bit, Neoscape
LEGO BUILDERS	Helgi Toftegaard, Lasse Vestergård, Anne Mette Vestergård, René Askham, Lars Barstad, Rocco Buttliere, Zio Chao, Hsinwei Chi, Trine Dalsgaard Jensen, Jessica Farrell, Are Heiseldal, Elisabeth Horte, Kimura Hsieh, Shenghui Jiang, Glenn Knøsgaard, Esben Kolind, Emil Lidé, Jan Smed, Anders Thuesen, Zio Chao, Hsinwei Chi, Kimura Hsieh, Nicolas Carlier
DAC	Kent Martinussen, Martin Bang, Beate Bernhoft, Maibritt Borgen, Roger Brodzki, Jacob Bruun Hansen, Kennie Buchmann, Christine Clemmesen, Anthony Del Campo, Ricky Hansen, Yasmin Kokseby, Gökhan Kuvvetli, Maya Lahmy, Lykke Ley, Tanya Lindkvist, Mette Mousten, Andreas Rasmussen, Kenneth Skovby, Arthur van der Zaag, Kim Vedsted, Jesper Værn
TRIENNALE	Stefano Boeri, Lorenza Baroncelli, Violante Spinelli, Valentina Barzaghi, Alessandra Montecchi, Dario Zampiron, Eugenia Fassati, Roberto Giusti, Damiano Gulli, Gabriele Rosmino
CREATIVE REVIEW	Andrew Zuckermann, Spencer Bailey, Omar Sosa, Scott Dadich, Patrick Godfrey, Dev Finley, Kirsten Golden

THANKS TO BIG PARTNERS

Andreas Klok Pedersen, Finn Nørkjær, Sheela Maini Søgaard, Kai-Uwe Bergmann, David Zahle, Jakob Lange, Thomas Christoffersen, Jakob Sand, Brian Yang, Daniel Sundlin, Cat Huang, Agustín Pérez-Torres, Beat Schenk, Leon Rost, Martin Voelkle, Ole Elkjær-Larsen and to all BIGsters in Copenhagen, New York, London and Barcelona

THANKS TO our clients and collaborators

Jeffrey Inaba, Didier Lootens, Solène Wolff, Jan Bunge, Che Pearlman, Helgi Toftegaard, Lasse Vestergård, Anne Mette Vestergård, René Askham, Lars Barstad, Rocco Buttliere, Zio Chao, Hsinwei Chi, Trine Dalsgaard Jensen, Jessica Farrell, Are Heiseldal, Elisabeth Horte, Anders Horvath, Kimura Hsieh, Shenghui Jiang, Glenn Knøsgaard, Esben Kolind , Emil Lidé, Jan Smed, Anders Thuesen, AFOL, Adam and Rebekah Neumann, Jonah Nolan and Lisa Joy, Aaron Koblin, Chris Milk, Douglas Coupland, David Eagleman, Jeppe Hein, Scott Dadich, Andrew Zuckermann, Michel Rojkind, Vardemuseerne, University Of Massachussets, Blumenfeld Development Group, Ubs Fund Management, Nüesch Development, Christoph Merian Stiftung, Metrovacesa, Endesa, Groupe Galeries Lafayette, Vella Group, Audemars Piguet, S. Pellegrino, Nestlé, Commerz Real, Hfz Capital Group, Lassen Ricard, Kommuneqarfik Sermersooq, Nexus, Tavistock Group, Shenzhen Energy Company, Stoneweg Spain, Axa, The City Of New York, Mayor's Office Of Resiliency, Rockefeller Foundation/Rebuild By Design, Amager Ressource Center, Fonden Amager Bakke, Københavns Kommune, Tårnby Kommune, Hvidovre Kommune, Frederiksberg Kommune, Dragør Kommune, Copenhill, Virgin Hyperloop One, Imkan, Mads Peter Veiby, Westbank, Kistefos, Région Nouvelle-Aquitaine, Frac, Alca, Oara, Europacity, Fusha, Municipality Of Tirana, Lego, Besix, Vorm, Sorbonne Université, Citynove, Glasir, Société Du Grand Paris, Taller Multidisciplinar, Arlington Public Schools, Rune Kilden, Rfr Holding, Capitaland, Tishman Speyer, Silverstein Properties, Emaar Properties, Uia Management, Expo 2020, Austin Sports & Entertainment, Oscar Properties, Durst Organization, Oakland A's, WeWork, WeGrow, Klein House, Serpentine Galleries, Bo-Vita, Catella, Høpfner Projects, Urban Rigger, Noma, Copenhagen Zoo, Philadephia Zoo, Oceanix, Google, By & Havn, Taiwan Land Development Corporation, Mohammed Bin Rashid Space Centre, Dubai Municipality, Government Of United Arab Emirates, Dubai Future Foundation, Ruth Otero and Darwin Otero Ingels

SPECIAL THANKS TO DANISH ARCHITECTURE CENTER AND TRIENNALE MILANO

AGC *INTERPANE*

Artemide

B
BECKETT·FONDEN

BrandFactory
TURNING CONCEPTS INTO REALITY

Transport-, Bygnings-
og Boligministeriet

DOW

ERHVERVSSTYRELSEN

Fogs Fond

FRITZ HANSEN

GAGGENAU

GROHE — *Pure Freude an Wasser*

HAY

HOLMRIS B8

**INDUSTRIENS
FOND** FREMMER DANSK
KONKURRENCEEVNE
The Danish Industry Foundation

JANSEN
Steel Systems

JUNG

Kultur
MINISTERIET

kvadrat

LAUFEN

LEGO

SPECIAL THANKS TO HBO AND ZENTROPA PRODUCTIONS

2020

I am writing this epilogue from Miralles and Tagliabue's Santa Catarina Market in Barcelona. I am wearing a facemask. And so is everybody else. In the city, in the country, in the world. The photos in my iPhone look like stills from HBO's dystopian resurrection of Watchmen. I finished the prologue for this book right before The Great Lockdown of 2020. Half a year later, the world looks a lot different.

As of today, the global death toll is 677,684 and rising. According to the IMF, the global cost of The Great Lockdown is projected to be 12 trillion dollars by the end of 2022, not to mention the number of casualties we have already seen. The United States has exploded in frustration over racial and social inequalities exacerbated by the absence of a welfare state with free public healthcare, free education, and social security, which, with catastrophic events like COVID-19 impact different people very differently. The force of the movement and the global solidarity it has sparked could generate hope that change will follow.

During the first weeks of the lockdown, we saw the potential power of distributed production as architects, designers, and makers across the world returned to their workshops and production plants to fabricate emergency medical equipment. Our 3D print farms managed to crank out more than 20,000 face shields as well as parts to amplify the capacity of ventilators to resupply the hospitals in the United States, United Kingdom, Spain, and Denmark. There is a certain comfort in this novel idea of a distributed dormant production power nested in the fabric of society, free and flexible to adapt and respond to unforeseen demands as they arise.

We saw the social impact of the framework we create for our cities. I was moved to see that the triangular balconies of the V-house transformed the façade into a vertical plaza where all 125 families would unite in celebration of birthdays and holidays in safe social distance but nonetheless together. Or how the inhabitants of the 8-House would meet every evening before sunset and sing together; 500 families rediscovering the power of community. Communities that we have helped facilitate by giving form to their physical framework and the social and visual connections they create.

We saw the global community deploy 12 trillion dollars in a mixture of opportunity costs and public subsidies in the face of an immediate threat. This sparks optimism that we might be able to do the same in the face of the climate crisis: The immense threat that we have known was on the way, but we have somehow been unable to respond to it. We have been galvanized into global solidarity because our interconnectedness was so clearly demonstrated when an outbreak in a remote Chinese province could paralyze the entire planet in a matter of weeks. It makes me optimistic that, if presented eligible solutions, both public and private funds might be willing to deploy the required resources and make the necessary legislation to avoid climate collapse. Perhaps the collective crowdsourced master plan for the planet that we have initiated in the form of the MASTERPLANET might become a useful tool for a global population that has felt the consequences when we ignore the scientists warnings and recommendations for too long.

We discovered that remote collaboration isn't as bad as we thought. In fact by not having to be physically present everywhere all the time, we have been afforded the luxury of being mentally present instead. Suddenly local talent became global talent. If the best woman for the job was located in the other office, nothing would stop us from assembling the ideal team, regardless of geography. And in some way, the added friction of Zoom and Teams makes it even more paramount that we articulate our values and principles with greater clarity and awareness than ever before. Rather than being seduced by the material or coerced by the power of consensus, remote collaboration may afford us a new clarity in how we turn principles into design principles—how we turn values into volumes. I sense an enhanced clarity and rigor in the work we have been doing the last several months while entirely isolated from each other, which feels like a renaissance for the power of principle.

Finally, as congestion and claustrophobia became threats to our physical and mental health, it became clear that our cities—the productive and creative hubs that they are—are lacking the one resource that happens to be the raw material of architects: space. Outdoor, open air, free and flexible, public space. Full of space for organic life that with its biophilia not only purifies the air and converts CO_2 into oxygen but also enhances human health and well-being, productivity, and creativity. Abundant with space for social life for all—free of charge and with no limits to access and no VIP enclosures or bouncers.

At the beginning of the year, we had already embarked on the journey of suggesting how advances in urban mobility, connectedness, autonomy, and mobility as a service could transform a Japanese urban neighborhood of car streets into a Woven City of parks, promenades, and streets interwoven in a meshwork of interconnected social and environmental spaces. During the lockdown, we imagined applying these prototypical ideas to the Brooklyn Bridge—the New York landmark outside the windows of our DUMBO office. We discovered that at its peak the Brooklyn Bridge had moved more than three times as many people across the river as it does today. Today we are basically moving cars instead of people. And we are cramming the people—pedestrians and cyclists—onto congested and dangerous walkways in the cloud of diesel fumes from the cars below. We proposed to convert car lanes into People Streets—starting with the Brooklyn Bridge—by dedicating the bridge's southern half to a new plaza or promenade in the sky and its northern half to a high capacity mixture of smart and autonomous mobility, including space for bicycles. We suggested that this idea might spread to infiltrate the rest of the five boroughs to become a network of People Streets offering free space, personal mobility, and spaces for culture and recreation; to include the social and environmental dimensions of the city; to take the pressure off the relentlessly congested city. Perhaps the urgent and exacerbated needs of The Great Lockdown will end up having a permanent impact on our cities—for the better. And perhaps it won't take a pandemic next time to create the opportunity to make the world more friendly and fair, more generous and gracious, more social and sustainable. Because the better we are at viewing what we have with critical eyes and curious minds, the more we are able to question the status quo, and feed our fantasy to imagine a future we would rather live in. And then all we have to do is remember that we have the power to give it form.

BACK TO THE FUTURE

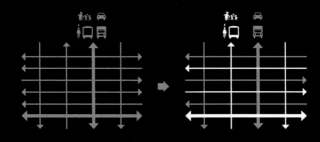

The Reimagining Brooklyn Bridge competition brought together over 250 professionals and young students to share ideas and solutions for responsive short-term interventions and longer-term, large-scale reconfigurations of one of the most memorable and iconic structures in New York City, and the world. Back to the Future envisions a radical, yet incremental rethinking of the bridge by returning the 19th-century structure to its original iconic state, both architecturally and functionally, while piloting innovations in autonomous mobility and public space design. At the bridge anchorages, as the bridge transitions away from vehicular use, legacy car infrastructure can be removed, and life can be brought back to the historic vaults and surroundings. 32 acres of public space, more than five times the area of the High Line, will be created—reconnecting neighborhoods and offering natural and recreational spaces for adjacent communities and a growing city. Looking beyond the bridge, as New York City's aging subway system strains to keep up with demand, and the city continues to search for new and safe ways to commute in the coming years, the creation of safe, dedicated, and shaded corridors for biking and collective transit is the most high-impact, low-cost urban investment in recovery. The corridors can be interwoven seamlessly with the existing network of vehicular streets, creating twin streetscapes with room for both people and logistical demands. This network of People Streets can branch out across the city, strategically linking to the neighborhoods that need them most, and as the Brooklyn Bridge did one-and-a-half centuries ago, bring New York back to the forefront of urban innovation.

New York City, USA
16.2 Hectare / Public Space

Each and every TASCHEN book plants a seed!
TASCHEN is a carbon neutral publisher. Each year, we offset our annual carbon
emissions with carbon credits at the Instituto Terra, a reforestation program
in Minas Gerais, Brazil, founded by Lélia and Sebastião Salgado. To find out more
about this ecological partnership, please check: www.taschen.com/zerocarbon
Inspiration: unlimited. Carbon footprint: zero.

To stay informed about TASCHEN and our upcoming titles, please subscribe
to our free magazine at www.taschen.com/magazine, follow us on Instagram
and Facebook, or e-mail your questions to contact@taschen.com.

© 2020 TASCHEN GmbH

Hohenzollernring 53
D–50672 Köln
www.taschen.com

Copyright © 2020 BIG, Bjarke Ingels Group

Drawings, renderings and illustrations © BIG, Bjarke Ingels Group

Printed in Slovenia
978-3-8365-7704-5